SMALL EXPECTATIONS

Society's Betrayal of Older Women

LEAH COHEN

McClelland and Stewart

The Canadian Publishers
McClelland and Stewart Limited
25 Hollinger Road
Toronto M4B 3G2

Canadian Cataloguing in Publication Data

Cohen, Leah, 1945-
  Small expectations : society's betrayal of older women

ISBN 0-7710-2167-4 (bound). — ISBN 0-7710-2168-2 (pbk.).

1. Aged women – Social conditions.   2. Aged women – Canada – Social conditions.   I. Title.

HQ1061.C58 1984   362.6'088042   C84-098109-0

Every reasonable attempt has been made to attribute copyright material used in this publication. Information regarding inadvertent errors or omissions of copyright information
would be welcomed, and efforts will be made to correct same
in future editions.

The publication of this work has been generously supported
by grants from the Canada Council and the Ontario Arts
Council.

Printed and bound in Canada

Contents

Introduction

I did not start out fearing old age. I did not see myself becoming one of society's rejects, poverty-stricken, abandoned, stripped of my dignity. My image of old age was that of my grandmother: wise, humorous, warm, and timeless. Until she was well over ninety, she had her own home, her health, and her dignity.

What happened to her in the last two years of her life has led me to write this book on women and aging. I remember her pain, shock, and horror at finding herself in a nursing home. She lingered for four months in great pain, and went to her death frustrated and humiliated by the insensitive treatment she received in the home. It was her anger that was so compelling.

That blazing impotence is my sad and final memory of my grandmother. But I have other memories, important memories. She lived a life that spanned the end of the nineteenth century and the first seventy-six years of the twentieth. When I was very little, she would rock me in her arms and tell me that the world was mine – there was nothing I could not do. I was a golden child. When I was six, I proudly announced that I was going to be an archeologist, unearthing other civilizations in hot steaming deserts. Quite solemnly she replied, "Yes, I can imagine you a scholar, a traveler, an explorer in far off places." I did not become an archeologist, but my grandmother genuinely and respectfully listened to all my enthusiasms, encouraging me to become anything and everything; nothing was too farfetched.

I remember when I was a very young teenager, perhaps thirteen or fourteen, staying at her home, lying in bed together, holding hands as she talked into the night explaining why it was hard to grow up, why I argued with my father, why the world was so violent and insane.

My grandmother always attempted to answer complex questions. She had great curiosity and was strong-willed. At times, she was cheated, lied to, and made fun of, but she remained dignified and self-contained. Perhaps what was best about her was her fiery anger. She was far from the stereotype of the passive, sweet, old grandmother, self-sacrificing and a martyr to her family's needs. That may be why she lived so long and, for the most part, so well.

My grandmother worked until her mid seventies. At various times, she ran a boarding house, owned a chicken store, and sold charcoal. When she became a widow, at eighty, she continued to live in her own home, spending most of her days sitting on an old wooden trunk by the living-room window, watching people in the street outside. She saw successive waves of immigration come to her neighborhood and always managed to learn enough of their respective languages to hold a conversation. I often sat with her on that old wooden trunk, entranced by her knowledge of people's lives, her concern for their welfare, her involvement in the small and large events in their lives. Over the years, she developed a reputation among her neighbors as a wise, old woman. Out of respect, they would bring presents of food and flowers.

My grandmother was eccentric. She hated to cook and hated housework even more; yet she believed in hospitality. Whenever I brought a friend along to visit, she would bring out a bottle of home-made raisin wine and sagely advise us that a drink in the afternoon was good for the digestion, cleared the brain, and stimulated the heart.

For years I was convinced that my grandmother could not speak a word of English, until the day she began chatting to my best friend in almost flawless English. When she noticed my surprise, she said that she could speak English when she felt like it, but preferred to talk Yiddish to me, so I would retain my fluency.

I was very proud of my grandmother and wanted to share her with my friends, especially as I grew older and met women who ached for some warmth in their lives. If I

10

met an alienated woman, I would drag her off to my grand-mother's, assuring her of instant love. My friend would always come away entranced, feeling less lonely, having been touched by my grandmother's charm.

As I grew older, I realized that my grandmother would not be with me forever. I developed vague anxieties when-ever I was traveling, fearing that she would die while I was gone. Yet I always pictured that her death would be dig-nified, surrounded by her daughters and grandchildren.

But I was wrong. Even my very special grandmother was diminished by society's cruel treatment of the old. When she became weak and in need of care, the hospitals, doc-tors, and care-givers treated her like a slightly demented child, incapable of making decisions. Yet, in some ways she was luckier than most. She had a modest income, she lived near caring children, and she maintained her independ-ence far longer than most older women can. I cannot change the sad circumstances of my grandmother's death, but I can examine how older women are treated in our society and attempt to expose the grave injustices they suffer.

Life as an Older Woman

The elderly in our society are generally rejected, but we are particularly disdainful of older women. The discrimination begins in infancy and escalates as we become mature women. But it doubles as we grow older, for then are we not only women, but old women, perceived as unattractive, un-needed, and parasitical.

In our forties, when we can expect another forty years of life, the double rejection begins. Yet, a man in his forties is perceived to be at the height of his attractiveness and desirability; he can anticipate another twenty-five years of active, productive life.

The majority of women over sixty-five live below the pov-erty line. Most live alone, in poor housing, having outlived or been abandoned by their spouses. They are the victims of indifferent, fragmented medical care and have a great fear of rape, mugging, street harassment, robberies, and swindles.

Older women are often lumped together by social-service

agencies, charitable foundations, and religious organizations, who generally make the condescending assumption that crafts, bingo, and concerts are the only activities that older women enjoy and find satisfying. They pay little attention to the fact that we become most individual and unique as we age.

It is stressful to become an older woman. We can expect a loss of status and a sense of being useless. We are in danger of being pronounced senile, although 15 per cent of women termed senile suffer from over-medication, under-stimulation, and rejection.

At the present time women can expect to live to 83.6 years. By the year 2020, approximately 20 per cent of our number will be sixty-five or older. Women constitute the bulk of the older population, since we, on average, outlive men by at least seven years.

Our numbers and our presence receive only limited attention from researchers and policy makers. Most of the geriatric literature focuses on men. Research on women is primarily done in institutional settings such as nursing homes or chronic-care hospitals, yet only 8 per cent of older women are institutionalized. It is not surprising that the "evidence" depicts us as frail, unbalanced, and objects of sympathy. What of the other 92 per cent of older women, the poorest people in our society? Our lifetime as either low-status wage earners and/or as homemakers and child rearers, does not appear to merit concern or attention, let alone reward. In face of this indifference and neglect, older women experience a sense of futility and despair in attempting to live with dignity.

Very early in my research I spoke to a woman in her mid eighties. She lived in a tiny room, far from transportation, on a subsistence income. Her only pleasure in life was attending adult education classes at a local community college. She told me that she was aggressively confronted by a male student of about thirty years old. "I don't want my tax dollars paying for your education," he said. "You're an older woman. Why are you taking a place away from a younger student who could take this education and do something productive with it?" "I guess," she mused, "society wishes we would disappear, maybe drop dead at widowhood or retirement. If they could, they would line us up and shoot us."

I traveled extensively in the United States, Canada, and Europe, focusing at first on women in their sixties, seventies, eighties, and nineties. But I soon discovered that the fear of aging begins much earlier. Women in their twenties confront the aging process when they see their first gray hair or wrinkle. This concern about the imminent loss of youthfulness becomes anxiety when a woman reaches her forties. For most women find that, just as they reach a rich maturity and are often endowed with new energy and vitality, society perceives them as declining and almost obsolete.

However upsetting it is to be a middle-aged woman, the real indignities are reserved for older women. I found that most women over sixty are far from content. I interviewed them about their feelings, perceptions, and personal experiences in a society that is youth-oriented and youth-obsessed. They expressed bewilderment and dismay at the prejudice, indifference, and alienation they suffer. Many are frightened that if they openly state their anger, they will suffer grave consequences. They are repeatedly told by politicians, by the media, by academics, by gerontologists that they are far better off than their foresisters. "Far better off" usually translates into surviving considerably below the poverty line. The quality of their lives is generally abysmal, for they are alienated, and abandoned, cut off from the mainstream of life. As a society, we do not respect or admire our older women. We force them to live financially, emotionally, and intellectually impoverished lives and expect them to be grateful to us.

My purpose in writing this book is to encourage older women to speak openly of their lives, their deprivation, and their outrage. Older women are conditioned to be pleasant, "grandmotherly," passive, and compliant. Many of the women whom I interviewed feared that there would be serious reprisals by social agencies and institutions if they candidly related the grim details of their discontent. For this reason, I have changed names, locations, and certain details to protect their identities.

A very small group of older women have managed, by

super-human efforts, to live relatively happy lives. It was primarily from them that I have evolved a series of "utopian" solutions. It is their insights, experiences, and collective wisdom that I have tried to convey. They have a vision of a meaningful, dignified old age and how it can be achieved. If we do not heed their wisdom, very soon we will be old women ourselves, living on the edge of life, suffering the same humiliations and degradation as they are struggling against.

1

Self-Image and the
Cult of Sexuality

Introduction

There is a point in every woman's life at which the physical
reality of aging makes its first appearance. One morning,
while glancing in the mirror, I noticed my first gray hair.
On closer inspection, I had to admit that there were the
beginnings of a fine network of lines around my eyes, that
the dark circles under my eyes were permanent features,
that the laugh lines around my mouth had deepened, and
that I was indeed an adult, mature, and aging woman. Part
of me responded by thinking that these signs of aging are
my badges of honor, an expression of my maturity and
coming of age. But another part of me felt angry and frustrated because I am aware that I will be punished for growing older.

My punishment will take many different forms, beginning insidiously with advertising and social pressures to
wage a serious, concentrated battle against my physical
aging. I am told that if I wish to be considered attractive
and still desirable, I must hide, cover, or in some way min-
imize the visible signs of my aging. I am exhorted to dye
my hair, wear heavy makeup and trendy clothes, and struggle to become fashion-model thin.

I am also aware that my own sexual ineligibility is not
far off. Our culture dictates that we fiercely deny and fight
our physical aging if we wish to be perceived as sexually
attractive women. When aging can no longer be masked
behind a cosmetic or surgical illusion, we are relegated to
the sidelines of life.

Our aging is both a biological and emotional phenomenon, but, more importantly, it is a very individual process. There are no two women or men who age in an identical way. At best, chronological age is only a rough indicator of biological age. What statistics show is that women live longer than men and that the life expectancy for both sexes is growing.

There is a staggering number of myths about what we can expect once we reach forty. A recent article in *Chatelaine* magazine, "How Growing Older Affects Your Body," epitomizes our society's obsession with physical appearance. Although the article purported to be a positive analysis of biological aging, the drawings of a typical aging woman (if there is such a thing) were replete with negative images and depressing jargon such as "crows' feet, belly bulge, spare tire, sagging breasts, jowls, baggy eyes, and crepey skin."[1] Rather than instill confidence about the physical changes we can expect as part of a normal process, the tone of and the drawings in the article play on our fears and, indeed, can lead one to the conclusion that physical aging is pathological.

The endless harping on the decline of our bodies cannot help but affect our feelings about our value as human beings. Many women I interviewed, especially those older than sixty, claimed that their perceived declining physical appearance made them feel invisible. As one woman said, "You don't exist any more; you're seen as a gray-haired, dried up, not-too-bright old lady."

But women are characterized as having diminished intelligence, vigor, sexual attractiveness, and usefulness well before the age of sixty. Despite all the changes in self-image the feminist movement has achieved, the majority of women find the prospect of growing older terrifying and too frequently come to believe the myths of inevitable decline and uselessness. Even feminist women with positive self-esteem struggle with the myths of women's aging and also find them insidious and all-pervasive. Many powerful and successful women admitted in interviews that they expend an enormous amount of energy, time, and money to appear younger, softer, and more feminine. One woman who, at forty-two, is a senior executive said, "There are two devastating myths about women over forty: they are either

16

menopausal, weepy, and therefore incompetent, or tough, aging bitches. I try to straddle the line so that men will still find me sexy and approachable."

Another strong and successful woman, Christine Craft, who was demoted from her job as a TV newswoman in Kansas City, was told by her boss, "When the people of Kansas City see your face, they turn the dial."[2] She was also told that an audience survey showed that viewers thought she was "too old and unattractive and not deferential to men."[3]

She summed up her feelings: "I'm a very strong person, but I'm vulnerable like anyone else. It's hard to be told these things. For about six months, I was very self-conscious. I felt sometimes like putting a bag over my head."[4] Christine Craft is only thirty-eight years old, at the midpoint in what she had hoped would be a long and productive career.

These destructive stereotypes, which permeate our society, severely limit our options and opportunities for more than half our lives. Our general tendency to deny aging forces us to live in fear, masking and ignoring genuine problems and anxieties. It is incumbent on all women to work toward ridding society of these negative and damaging stereotypes, which have the power to destroy our self-esteem and our sense of worth. If we are active, stimulated, and happy, there is no evidence to suggest that our physical and mental decline is inevitable.

This chapter first addresses the billion-dollar beauty industry, which preys upon women's vulnerability and poor self-image. This is the most visible manifestation of women's sense of rapid physical deterioration and their feelings of sexual ineligibility. Indeed, the industry uses this dual image as a weapon, relentlessly reinforcing the myths and stereotypes of female aging. Our worth is defined only in terms of our youth and attractiveness. Fear of physical aging is instilled in us in our twenties, and even earlier. The beauty industry inundates us with the message that we must wage war against what are described as the "ravages" of age. What is particularly disturbing is that we are the recipients of this culturally promoted self-hatred, and also we are often actively involved in disseminating the message as authors. The goal of all this lavish attention to our appearance is to retain our sexual appeal to men, who are not punished for their aging and indeed are seen as improving as they grow older.

This chapter, then, explores the issues associated with stereotyping older women as sexless. This sexual disqualification affects women from their forties on, especially if they are single, widowed, separated, or abandoned. They are forced to compete for a dwindling supply of men their own age or older. Yet being manless is defined as being a social failure. All women experience this from their teens on, but in middle age, as our opportunities narrow, our sense of failure is felt more keenly. Many older women who live in institutions are presumed to neither need nor have the desire for sexual expression. Should an older woman develop a relationship with a younger man, she can expect to be denounced as pathetic and pitiable. Any woman older than seventy, however independent, is not perceived to be a candidate for sexually active relationships.

Although all women suffer from this endless barrage of negative images, a distinct and vocal minority of women is insisting, as men do, that their worth is tied up in their achievements, their character, and their maturity. It is with this hopeful minority that the chapter will conclude.

The Media and Self-Image: Downhill from Twenty-five

It is confusing and difficult for women of all ages to negotiate satisfying relationships with emotional depth. The message we receive is that our only bargaining power is our youth and our fertility. Our culture tells us that if we are young, fertile, and, preferably, attractive, we may have some choice in determining our relationships; if we are not attractive, by prevailing societal standards, we will be forced to accept less.

For most women, the wish is still to marry and have babies. There are a few variations on this theme, such as marrying later, having fewer children, and combining a career with the roles of wife, mother, and homemaker. A small number of women find one or both of these goals neither viable nor desirable. They reject the notion that youth and fertility essentially define their worth. They have been profoundly affected and politicized by the women's movement, which has struggled for the past twenty years to expand women's options and possibilities.

The battle to undo the systematic brainwashing we experience from childhood on is a massive task. It is not surprising that most young women, and especially those who meet society's ideal of attractiveness, conclude that their bodies are powerful tools to be used in securing the most advantageous relationships possible.

Most of us are acutely aware that we are living with a time bomb, set to go off at the first sign of aging. The women I interviewed who were in their twenties had great difficulty coping with the prospect of turning thirty. They tended to derive their self-esteem and much of their happiness from the amount of attention they received from men. Their anxieties and fears revolved around their perception that they would soon be unable to compete for men with younger women. The years beyond age thirty were a social wasteland. Since their self-image was inexorably bound up in male approval, their own identities as individuals were often blurred and poorly understood concepts.

At twenty-seven, Corrine believes that her youthfulness and sexual attractiveness will terminate at thirty.

I particularly feel sorry for women between the ages of fifty and eighty because no one finds them attractive enough to touch. Let's face it, men only want bed partners who are trim and unwrinkled, even though I understand that women flourish sexually from thirty-five on.

I think men prefer young girls because they are so malleable, so undeveloped, so passive. They are easily impressed because they lack self-confidence. An older man with a young woman is able to act as a teacher, a controller, dominating and directing the relationship.

It is easy for me to understand why women lie about their age after thirty—I probably will too. You get caught in a web of lies because all women fear the rejection that stems from growing old. I think most women see growing old as the end of everything they exist for.

I am not married and don't have a steady boyfriend. I'm twenty-seven; time is running out for me. I worry that I won't be able to compete for men with younger women once I am older than thirty. We were all raised to think that Lolita is the feminine ideal. How can I, at thirty or even twenty-seven, hope to look like a Lolita, who was all of thirteen?

The whole thing is so grossly unfair, when you consider that things get better for men as they age – they are seen as suave, handsome, even stylish, while women are seen as wrinkled, witchlike, and sexually unattractive. I have no illusions about what happens to women as they age. After all, our youth and our attractiveness are our ticket to security and love. We don't mellow like men as we age: we fade away and become invisible.

I want you to understand that this is what I see around me, not what I believe. In my opinion, women are sexy until they die, but no one seems to acknowledge that fact. I feel so much pressure to find a boyfriend, to marry. My family, particularly my father, is always advising me that if I am not careful I will have missed the boat. My aunts have taken me aside and told me I am breaking my parents' hearts by remaining single. The message is that I lack credibility as a person unless I become part of a couple. As much as I try not to concentrate on my approaching thirtieth birthday, I admit that I feel that I am in a race to find a man before I am considered to be too old and somehow suspect for having remained single.

I don't want people to feel sorry for me, but I feel it happening already.

Corrine feels enormous pressure to find a man who will take care of her. Her family – in particular her father – has defined women as property, as somehow helpless until they are married and producing children. The family, no doubt, believes that the pressures it is applying are necessary to mobilize Corrine in the hunt to find a good husband. The life the family envisages for their daughter is one that is the least stressful and, above all, one that conforms to the societal "norm." Without a man, Corrine sees her life as a failure and essentially valueless.

Sheila is twenty-eight.

I am aware that I no longer look like a fresh eighteen-year-old. When I look in the mirror and see the beginnings of wrinkles around my eyes, I have this sense of horror. I don't like looking older, and I am scared at the prospect of turning thirty and then moving on to forty.

The men I go out with are always reassuring me that they like me as I am, looking natural. What they don't realize is that I work very hard at looking "natural"; I wear very subtle makeup and I spend a lot of time working on my hair. One of the guys I go out with gets very impatient when we are going out and complains that I spend too much time fussing with myself. But I don't think he would find me attractive if I let myself go and went out with messy hair and a face without makeup. He just thinks he likes the natural look because he has never really seen me looking bad.

Sometimes I get tired of trying to look attractive, but at this point I have created an image of myself that is very pulled together, very well groomed, and I don't think I could handle the "natural" me. This image, not my unmadeup self, has become my "natural" state.

My involvement with looks started very young. When I was a teenager I thought my girlfriends were far better looking than I was. The boys were very attracted to my girlfriends and I was always ignored and left out of things. It became clear to me that if I ever wanted to attract a man I would have to look good. I dieted until I was reed thin, I tried out all kinds of makeup, I spent hours on my hair, and I pored over fashion magazines.

One of my girlfriends was an idiot around men: she simpered, she batted her eyelashes, she laughed at everything they said, no matter how stupid, but she was the most popular girl at school. I knew that I was as nice as she was, if not nicer, and I was sure I had a better personality, but none of the boys was remotely interested. They just responded to looks.

I have spent so much time and money on myself and I now feel that I have achieved "The Look." It's ironic that just as I feel pretty and on top of things, I find myself worrying about being too old to be really considered attractive.

I don't think I'm unusual. Most of my friends and the women I work with feel the same way. We all feel that we are running against the clock. Twenty-eight is old. I am starting to wonder if I can compete with younger women.

Somewhere between the ages of twenty and twenty-five, women in our culture are presumed to peak in terms of attractiveness. Many of the women I interviewed felt something akin to panic as they approached thirty. It was their perception that, after the thirtieth year, a woman's age became her dirty little secret, that a woman's value as a sexual being plummeted.

In our twenties we experience the first indication that our youthfulness and attractiveness cannot be taken for granted. We are bombarded, by the advertising industry, to begin the endless and the slavish process of preserving the illusion of youth.

A woman who has not established a stable relationship with a man receives the message that she is in danger of being left behind in the desperate race to snag a man; that she will be nothing, no matter what she accomplishes.

The superficial symptoms of age — the first fine line around the eyes, the first gray hair — are somehow more significant in women than in men. Sheila is almost obsessed with looking thin, well-groomed, and sexually attractive. She is terrified that she has gone as far as she can and that once she is older than thirty her physical and sexual decline is inevitable. The overriding fear is that an insidious process of rejection begins at thirty and escalates in middle age and beyond, until women become both undesirable and untouchable. The visible signs of aging in women are culturally defined as an affront to nature.

The Billion-Dollar Illusion

The beauty industry is a vast conglomerate generating profits of approximately seven billion dollars per year.[5] No part of the female anatomy escapes the industry's rapacious attention. Products proliferate, promising an impeccable body from hair to toes. The body, according to the dictates of the industry, can never look more than twenty-five.

We are badgered to buy an astounding number of products to maintain each and every part of the body. Hair can be shampooed, conditioned, dyed, rinsed, tinted, bleached, permanently waved, straightened, sprayed, misted, set with gel, lotion or beer, blown dry, placed under heating lamps or dryers, and so on.

In addition, the beauty industry responds to changing fads, converting them into expensive and ever-expanding products. In the 1950s, the ideal female image was fleshy, curvy, and milk-white. To achieve this voluptuous look women went to extraordinary lengths with heavy makeup, teased, dyed hair, padded bras, and panty girdles.

Today's stereotype of beauty is strong and sinuous with a taut, toned, and tanned body. The beauty industry has capitalized brilliantly on the emphasis on health and fitness. Products are now called "natural" and the advertisements ring with words like *glisten*, *gleam*, and *deep-clean*.

Jane Fonda best epitomizes this current trend. In her forties, she is lean, tanned, and "well-preserved." Her career since the 1950s accurately reflects changing standards of beauty. She moved from being a cover girl for *Vogue* magazine in the 1950s to a sex object in Roger Vadim's film *Barbarella* in 1968. Today she sports a new, sinewy body and runs a chain of exercise studios. Her famous workout book, video, and record album have all been bestsellers.[6]

How many of us can realistically expect to conform to this new ideal? Under the clever guise of health and fitness, women who come in all sizes and shapes are bombarded with yet another impossible standard of eternal beauty.

Becoming older and mature is tantamount to committing a sin.

Hellie is twenty-eight and married to a man seventeen years her senior.

Women are like flowers — they look wonderful when they are fresh and young, but they look wilted and faded once they begin to age. For men the situation is the exact opposite — they start to look mature and handsome when they age, just as a tree does.

It has taken me a long time to face this fact, but I am trying to be realistic about what it means to be an older woman. When a woman shows the outward signs of aging — wrinkles, gray hair, sagging breasts, and so on — she is much less attractive than a man of the same age. Of course, this has nothing to do with what the woman is like inside — this is strictly my visual perception.

I am particularly aware of what beauty is about because I am considered to be exceptionally attractive. This isn't conceit on my part, just something I have always been told. When I was a teenager, everyone made quite a fuss over me. It used to upset me because I knew my looks were a freak thing and I was afraid that I would be rejected when I was no longer pretty.

The men in my life have always made quite a thing of my looks. In some ways I feel like Eliza in *My Fair Lady*. One boyfriend insisted that I look very natural. He became angry when I wore makeup or low-cut dresses. His image of me was in faded jeans, with my hair in a ponytail. It was almost as if he was afraid that if I looked too good, other men would notice and flirt with me. This was too threatening to him, so he made all these demands.

The next boyfriend I had expected me to be dressed to the nines at all times, wearing full face makeup. He became upset whenever I hadn't time to wash my hair or my nails weren't manicured. He noticed almost every detail of my appearance. I was a showpiece that he had on display. I was a pricey, classy item to be shown off and admired. Actually, when I think back on my relationships with men, it's always been one extreme or the other — I am asked to look like the girl next door or a high-fashion model.

I worry a lot about what will happen when I reach forty. I know I won't get the attention and interest from men that I now experience.

My husband will most likely die long before I do, so I am expecting to be a widow when I am in early middle age. It is not something I like to think about, but I don't think that I will fare any better than what I see happening to the widows in my family.

My favorite aunt was widowed in her late fifties; her husband died in a terrible car accident. This aunt was stunning as a young woman and extremely popular with men. The last five years have been very difficult for her. I don't mean financially; she is extremely well-off, but she has few opportunities to meet suitable men. She often tells me that she is looking for someone to pay attention to her, to make her feel important again. She desperately needs to be reassured that she is a desirable woman. What she finds is that the men of her age are interested only in younger women. My aunt is bitterly disappointed that men don't appreciate women for something other than looks. She still keeps herself very trim, dyes her hair, and is always carefully made up. I hope I don't end up feeling as she does: very lonely and unappreciated. I like to think that I will be valued for my maturity, but I'm not sure that is possible for women. Men only enjoy us when we are young and pretty — that's the way it is.

Hellie is a woman whose exceptional beauty has colored most of her life. Her marriage to an older man was not a random act. She was selling her looks and youth in exchange for money, power, and security. Her life experience is such that she does not believe anything other than her beauty — neither her personality nor her accomplishments — is appreciated and valued by either men or women.

She has the beauty that is society's ideal, but it only serves to exacerbate her anxiety and fear of aging. Most of her energy is consumed by maintaining her attractiveness and with worrying about what she perceives to be her inevitable decline.

Natalie has owned her own beauty salon for more than thirty years.

I was brought up in the world of cosmetics and makeup, and I know the media images of women are false. In my business you see the way women really look and the lengths they go to in order to look good.

I'm fifty-nine, but I still dye my hair and make my face up every day of my life. I've been doing it since I was fourteen years old. It's more habit than anything else, because I know that I don't look prettier or even younger with my dyed hair and made up face. No one doubts for a moment that I am an older woman.

I know better than most people how frightened women are of aging and that is why I can understand that plastic surgery is very important to a lot of women at some point in their lives. I've known women whose self-image is badly damaged as they age; they are the ones, if they can afford it, who should pursue plastic surgery. I don't think it will change their lives, but it may help their mental health. All plastic surgery can do is sustain you a bit longer.

The worst period is the years between fifty and sixty-five when your face rapidly deteriorates: your neck sags, your eyes become hooded, and wrinkles form around your mouth. When you look in the mirror, it's hard not to feel depressed.

I know that time is short both for looking reasonably attractive and for being included in life. I feel I must seize the moment while there is still time; that I must enjoy the time I have left. At fifty-nine, I still have a sense of youth, a certain vibrancy and bounce. People still see me as middle aged, not old and used up.

I think all women know that there is a double standard of aging, but I like to think that my daughters will do better than the women of my generation. We thought it was natural and normal to involve ourselves in our children and our husbands' needs and interests and not worry too much about our own. I was luckier than most of the women I know; I had my own business and as a result I am financially secure. When my husband died three years ago, I was able to manage on my own.

It bothers me, though, that I am stuck in this routine of working so hard on my looks. I would like to have the courage to stop dyeing my hair and to look as natural as I can, but I admit that I am afraid I would be considered terribly unattractive. I just can't chance it.

The premise upon which the beauty industry and its advertising is based is that a woman, even a very young woman, should never show her naked face. At the same time, we must appear dewy, fresh, natural-looking, and makeup free. This grand deceit requires astounding effort and an amazing amount of time. The message is that it is antisocial to age. A woman, according to advertising's dictates, can only exist on the level of physical attraction in the image presented so spectacularly by *Playboy* and *Cosmopolitan* magazines. The *Playboy* and *Cosmopolitan* "girls" exist only externally, behind an artfully conceived facade of flawless skin, a slender, polished, and oiled body, bulging, firm breasts, glistening, straight, white teeth, and a luminous, dreamy expression.[7]

Physical attractiveness and youthfulness combine to create the illusion of sexiness with just a hint of seduction. Nearly all the advertisements directed at women for products, from perfume to panty hose, show sleek, immaculate models wearing designer clothing and huge vacant smiles, suggesting passivity and, possibly, lust.

What the advertising emphatically stresses is that a woman's major goal is and should always be winning the approval of men. The message is that women are not important in their own right and can only gain a sense of worth in the eyes of men. For older women, the message is almost a command. Ads for products like Second Debut, to erase wrinkles, Geritol, to give energy, and dyes to wash away the gray make it clear that women are only creditable and can only hope to win male approval if they fight the visible signs of their aging.

Advertisements directed at an older woman do not limit their emphasis to a woman's physical deterioration as she ages; they also blatantly suggest that there is a psychological deterioration as well. Middle-aged women, these ads imply, are particularly prone to suffer depression, anxiety, stress, and withdrawal. Furthermore, we are told, we cannot cope with life and we run the risk of getting out of control. To alleviate these symptoms and to avoid becoming nonfunctioning, we are offered a bewildering number of drugs ranging from vitamins, hormones, and tonics to highly controversial tranquilizers and antidepressants. What is so insidious is the implicit warning that once we reach middle age we cannot return to the mythical bounce and self-assurance of our youth. Moreover, we can only hope to remain functioning at our present reduced level by ingesting a greater number and higher dosage of these same drugs as time passes.

Men, particularly "mature" men, are nearly always depicted in ads as being in control. They are generally allowed to show their age in a realistic and positive manner. Fine lines and a sprinkling of gray hair are sexy in a man and suggest power and involvement in exciting things. Male models are engaged in athletics, drive sporty cars, and make decisions. It is not necessary for a man to be vacuous or especially good looking to be a successful advertising model.[8]

Underlying the cloying images of women as young and beautiful is their dependency and need for a male protector who will provide security. Fundamentally, the advertising and beauty industries tell us that women cannot seriously achieve status in their own right, so they must rely on their beauty and youth. Very rarely are women shown as maturing and achieving intellectually, socially, or spiritually as they age. The focus in advertising is on how others react to us, not on the development of our own pleasure and our own self-image. The message is that we must market ourselves and compete with other women – we are products for the available male consumers. It is not surprising that, collectively, women do not believe that they can pursue their individual goals if they wish to succeed in this market-place. Ultimately, women are molded and managed by advertising, which ascribes to them a secondary, passive, nondirective role.

Unquestionably, this is not an inevitable process. These assumptions are constantly being questioned and challenged by a small but vocal minority. But at present, too many women feel trapped by this narrow, uncompromising stereotype.

Culturally Promoted Self-hatred

Many of the women I interviewed saw aging as a relentless enemy, which they felt compelled to fight in any way possible — up to and including potentially dangerous cosmetic surgery.

Lana is twenty-nine. She candidly admits that she is saving for her first face-lift.

> My mother, who is in her mid fifties, has already had two face-lifts and two eye-lifts. I think people should look as good as they can and if that means having cosmetic surgery, I'm all for it.
>
> My mother considered having her first cosmetic surgery when she was my age. She was very unhappy with the bags under her eyes and the lines around her mouth. But the doctor advised her to wait until she was forty, when the elasticity in her face would be gone. I was about thirteen when she went to California to a private hospital that specialized in cosmetic surgery. She told me there was a floor for nose jobs, one for eye-lifts, and that the penthouse was reserved for people having total face-lifts.
>
> My mother advised me to start thinking seriously about planning for early surgery. I realize that cosmetic surgery is only for middle-class and rich women. Most of the women I know are quite comfortable and can afford the luxury of taking very good care of themselves, including cosmetic surgery when it becomes necessary.

In a way, I envy poor women. I see them downtown, dressed in old housedresses with curlers in their hair. The company I work for employs a lot of women to work on the assembly line. Most of them are married, have children, and are around my age. I don't think they are particularly worried about their looks because they are surrounded by women who look exactly like themselves. They don't seem threatened by younger women, like my friends and I are. They are so busy making a living, taking care of their children and their homes, that they just let themselves go. By forty, most of them look worn out and very unattractive.

My friends are madly dieting, and nearly everyone has taken up some form of exercise. Who's to say who is happier? I break out in a cold sweat when I think about turning forty, even though I know I have all the advantages of modern medicine, excellent cosmetics, and the discipline to keep myself thin and fit.

When I was eighteen, I was considered quite a beauty. Inside, though, I was a silly, vacuous teenager. But I was enormously popular with men, particularly older men. I was seen as the epitome of sexiness, but in reality I knew next to nothing about my own or anyone else's sexuality. Men are really absurd when you think about it. They make it clear that youth is everything. Once a woman reaches thirty, she doesn't attract men in the same way. It bothers me and all I can do is try to look as good as I can. When you look at it that way, cosmetic surgery seems to be a logical conclusion. We really don't have much choice. We either look as young and sexy as we can or we are just ignored.

One of the most devastating influences on women, I found, was the proliferation of female-authored books advising women how to remain eternally young and sexually attractive. This advice represents an extreme form of self-hatred.

Most bookstores and drugstores have a whole section devoted to telling women how to fight aging. I deal with two of these books, not because they are unique, but because they epitomize the message contained in these books. The first of these is *Winning the Age Game*, by Gloria Heidi,[9] whose thesis is that a mature woman who disparages using all the means available to her to restore at least a semblance of youth is to be pitied. To be natural, apparently, is not a virtue to be cherished or applauded; it is laziness and self-deception. The natural face, Heidi claims, needs "the works." If we are to remain ageless and therefore desirable, she advises, we must reduce the threat of a wrinkled, grooved face by using a minimum of facial expression and by avoiding "old" gestures such as patting our hair and smoothing the creases out of our skirts. She also tells us how not to sit, walk, stand, and talk old.

How Women Can Achieve Fulfillment After 40,[10] at first glance, looks more hopeful and positive. But the coauthors, Sandra Gorney and Claire Cox, undercut their incisive analysis of the abhorrent and pervasive discrimination against older women by advising women that fulfillment can primarily be achieved by finding a man. They suggest that, to attract and keep a man, an older woman should become emotionally indispensable to him. They devote most of their book to detailing how women can improve and retain their looks with the aid of plastic surgery, weight loss, makeup, flattering hairdos, and youthful clothing. Their advice is endless, expensive, and condescending. After forty, a woman is frumpy, saggy, and ugly, unless she religiously devotes herself to a strict beauty regime. Older women cannot become beautiful by virtue of their maturity, character, or depth. The only distinction the authors make among older women is the classic one, between married and unmarried women. It is their perception that single older women frequently encounter more problems with aging than do married women since they worry more about money, illness, and lack of family ties. The authors suggest that the older "spinster" is an embittered woman who tends to feel cheated because she does not belong to anybody and therefore has difficulties achieving emotional stability.

But they save their strongest scorn and derision for the unmarried executive woman between forty-five and fifty-five, whom they consider the unhappiest women of all. Gorney's and Cox's obsession with youth and marriage is very discomforting and sad, and ultimately reinforces and legitimizes the double standard of aging. They treat women as an undistinguished herd, not as individuals. Their thesis is that we are grossly undesirable as our natural selves once we are older than forty; we are physically and emotionally dead unless we can create an illusion of youth and either hang on to our husbands or find new men.

What these and countless other books document is that women should feel shame about the aging process. There is a sad vulnerability about these advocates of restoring and preserving youth. They are merely a reflection of the pressures on women to maintain their appearance at a certain high standard by taking pains to keep their faces and bodies from showing the signs of growing older. A woman, it appears, can only be considered beautiful if she does not look old, because an older woman is, by definition, physically and sexually repulsive. To achieve the illusion, a woman must become the caretaker of her body and face by pursuing an essentially defensive strategy, which can only be described as a holding operation. Biologically normal aging must be masked because it is seen as disgusting.[11]

Men Mature, Women Age

So far, my focus has been on the pressure on younger women to conform to societal norms, to the standards set by the beauty industry and advertisers, and to parents' expectations. As a result of this indoctrination, many younger women are feverishly self-absorbed, lavishing enormous attention on their appearance with the hope that they can attract a "good catch." Whatever else they may be striving for – an education, a job, a career, a promotion – too frequently they are less than satisfied until they find a suitable male partner.

It is assumed, however, that middle-aged women still want marriage, just as they did when they were younger. Many women in their forties feel healthy, vital, and sexy, yet they are being forced to confront more directly society's sense of our diminishing worth. More than ever, these societal attitudes begin to impinge on the scope of our lives. We start to feel intensely the repercussions of a culture that denies possibilities of growth and maturation to women in mid life.

All around us are astonishingly false assumptions about the pattern of our lives. It is frequently suggested, particularly by advertisers, that after about forty-five women are interesting neither to themselves nor to anyone else. All we can do is to try to look as youthful as possible and then perhaps our husbands will not desert us, or we might be lucky enough to find new men.

Norma is forty-five and does not feel particularly old.

But everything in our culture makes me feel like a used up has-been. For a long time I thought I had an almost idyllic life – a handsome, successful husband, two bright and attractive daughters, and a full and satisfying social life. It's almost a year now since my husband left me for a twenty-five-year-old. For several months I kept hoping that it was all a bad dream and that I would wake up and everything would be as it always was.

I don't really totally understand what happened. It began very gradually, when my husband started to criticize my looks: he told me to do something with myself, that I looked drab. I was a bit bewildered, because I thought I looked quite nice – I have my hair done every week, I belong to a jogging club, I keep myself at my pre-marriage weight, and I wear very fashionable clothes. In fact, I think I look better than my husband does. He has always struggled with his weight and doesn't have time to exercise. Both of us are getting older and it shows. We both have gray hair and a few lines on our faces. I have scars from my Caesarean section and I guess my breasts aren't as full and firm as they once were.

I have agonized over and over again about what I did wrong. My husband, I think, just couldn't cope with growing older, with having two teenage daughters and a middle-aged wife. When we were first married, he made a point of telling me how attractive I was

33

and how proud he was of my sense of style. The woman he lives with now, and I suspect will eventually marry, looks a lot like I used to look – the same color of hair, the same height and build, and even the same color of eyes. It is very disturbing. It is almost as if he is looking for a younger version of me, so that he can recapture his early years.

I'm told by well-meaning friends that he will eventually return. But I'm not so sure I want him back any more. He has attacked my sense of worth and has condemned me for growing older. All the things we shared – a home, children, and a marriage – don't seem to count; just his childish need to feel young. I am starting to feel disgusted with him and angry that he has so carelessly hurt me and our daughters. It's hard to accept that someone you once loved and respected is nothing more than a spoiled child who thinks nothing of destroying a whole family for his own selfish ends.

This deep-seated self-hatred that many women feel about their aging is also fostered, on a more immediate and personal level, by their spouses and boyfriends. Men tend to think they age at a slower rate than do their women. Many middle-aged husbands have an image of themselves as vital, young, sexual, and virile men married to aging women. Men in their forties experience an enhanced self-image, often until retirement, which is fed by their accomplishments and their accumulated possessions.

A recent Canadian study found that men have great difficulty in relating positively to their wives as they age. For many men, particularly between the ages of thirty and fifty, their wives' physical aging reminds them of their mothers. They remember their mothers as old women with wrinkles and gray hair. The study showed that men who had been relatively happily married until mid life began to express vague dissatisfaction with their wives and a need to escape from their mothers. These men were, in fact, searching for younger, more attractive women than their wives, women who represented the fantasized mother of their earlier childhood.[12]

The Social Options for Older Women

Women who today find themselves single, deserted, widowed, or divorced in their mid fifties grew up in a generation in which a sexual relationship was only possible with a committed, loving, stable partner. Women outlive men, on average, by seven years and generally marry men at least three years older than themselves. These two factors dramatically limit available male partners, particularly since the majority of older women chooses from among men their own age or older.

Because of the way they were conditioned most women, particularly those fifty and older, cannot initiate relationships with men. They must wait patiently for men to choose them.

The prevailing idea of single women older than fifty is that their only all-consuming life goal is marriage. Of the many women I interviewed between the ages of fifty and ninety, not one presented marriage as a priority. The majority felt oppressed by the sense that society was organized solely to serve the interests and needs of couples.

The pressure to become part of a couple is a lifelong theme in women's lives. Parents pressure their daughters to marry and children pressure their mothers to remarry. A woman is told she cannot live alone; someone, preferably a husband, must take care of her.

Single older women feel invisible, cut off from social contact. Even when they are included in social activities, many feel merely tolerated, even pitied. Their self-esteem and their sense of their individuality are under constant attack. As one woman of sixty-two pointed out, "There are two images of older women, neither of which is flattering – one is a little, gray-haired old lady and the other is a bleached blond, heavily made up, a grotesque caricature of a female sex object."

The goal of women actively searching for a male partner was to find men with whom they could socialize, men who would make them "authentic" women. There was widespread recognition that an older woman alone is somehow not a real human being; that she is superfluous; that she has outlived her function as a wife and mother. There is a

pervasive sense of uselessness, which often engenders feelings of panic and acute despair.

Despite all these pressures to curry social acceptance
as part of a couple, few women wanted another marriage.
For most, loneliness and even social ostracism were pref-
erable to marriage. Their overriding fear was that should
they marry, their husbands might become invalids, requiring nursemaids and housekeepers. Most of the women
cherished their privacy and their independence.

The Loneliness of Widows

There is an enduring myth of the merry, wealthy widow,
whose wealth is a form of social leverage. But in our society,
a widow, whether impoverished or financially secure, is
generally considered to be a social liability.

On one level, the widow is depicted as a woman deserving of compassion and support. In reality, most widows
experience acute loneliness and find life limited to social
contact with other widows, single women, and family
members.

Estelle became a widow when she was fifty-one.

I am luckier than most widows; my husband made
sure that I would be comfortable should he die. I own
my home, I have a car, and I have enough money to
travel. Friends and family started telling me at the
funeral that I shouldn't worry, I was still a young woman,
I was sure to remarry. I guess they meant well, but I
was very hurt that all they could think of at a time like
that was that I was a good candidate for remarriage.

In the weeks that followed, many of these same
people advised me to sell my home, to sell my car, to
take a small apartment because what did a woman
alone need with all these things. It was almost as if
everyone wanted to see me brought down, a little old
widow, waiting to be saved by a man who would take
over me and my affairs.

All I want is to live as normally as possible, to be

accepted as an individual. I guess I never realized how unacceptable a woman on her own is. Even my eighty-four-year-old aunt, whose husband is still alive, told me I should hurry up and remarry before it is too late.

Of course, I miss the companionship of my husband. If it were possible to find a good man I would seriously consider remarrying. But I don't know any single men; nor do any of my friends. The only men that seem to be around are older men, ten or fifteen years older. That is not what I want. On the other hand, I don't want a really young man either.

Since my husband died, I have spent most of my time with other widows. Last year I took a trip to Mexico with a friend. We stayed at a beautiful spa – it was really magnificent. What depressed me was that the entire place was full of widows in similar circumstances. The couples there never mixed with the single and widowed women. We were ostracized, almost as if we had diseases. I felt punished for being manless and somehow a failure. We didn't ask to be widows; we haven't done anything wrong; but somehow we all felt like our very existence is disturbing to the rest of the world.

I'm only fifty-three years old; I don't feel old and I'm not ready to be put out to pasture.

Sandra was widowed when she was fifty-six.

I guess because I had a happy married life, I felt it would be good to remarry. At least, that is how I originally approached my widowhood. Now I am not so sure that remarriage is quite so desirable.

My first attempt to socialize was quite disastrous. I went to a singles dance, where there were about fifty women to every man. I'm exaggerating, but, honestly, it felt like that. It was humiliating for all the women; we all felt awkward and a little desperate.

After that experience, I asked friends to introduce me to some eligible men. I've had two proposals of marriage and both times I had to say no. Both men were intelligent and financially secure, but neither man appealed to me physically or emotionally. You may find that a funny comment coming from a woman of sixty-two, but sexual attraction is something I consider very important.

One of the men who proposed considers himself quite a catch. He was very aggressive and tried to make me feel guilty about refusing his sexual advances.

Part of me wants to resume the life of a couple and to make a commitment to a relationship, but I am finding that I have an equally strong need for privacy. When I was a young woman I thought men were very special beings. Now I know they are just people. And as much as I enjoy their company, I don't want to become beholden.

When Lesley became a widow at forty-four, she found herself flat broke:

At first I fell to pieces, which didn't endear me socially, and I was dumped by all my married friends. People found me awkward to have around and feared I would become a social and financial burden.

Once I got over the devastation of my husband's death and took a job as a clerk, I found my family subtly suggesting that I remarry. But I had no desire to go out with men – I just wanted to breathe, to exist. I had watched helplessly as my husband died of cancer. He went steadily downhill over a two-year period, during which time I never left his side. I was exhausted and needed time to be alone.

Eventually, though, I started to think it would be nice to have a companion. I'm sixty years old now, and in all this time I have never met anyone I liked. I particularly remember one man. From the moment he met me he talked about his problems: how hard it was to find a good cleaning woman, how awful restaurant food was, and how ungrateful his children were. He had absolutely no sense of humor. I realized he was looking for someone to cook and clean for him in return for the dubious honor of being his wife. At the end of a very boring and awkward evening, during which he never asked me one question about myself, I patted him on the cheek and told him to keep his chin up.

What I want is a man with whom I share an intellectual and emotional rapport. Most of the men I've met are dull, frankly, and very self-absorbed. I've reached a point where I don't ever expect to find someone. The people closest to me are my pre-marriage girlfriends. Without these women, I would be truly lost.

Widows, however, are not the only older women who make people uneasy. Single older women, especially those who have never married, often find that people are disconcerted by their independence and self-reliance.

Paula has never married and, at sixty-three, believes that the possibility of finding a husband is quite remote.

I still go out with men and I expect I always will. But what I am finding is that my proposals now come from widowers, often from the husbands of old friends who have died. The whole thing really mystifies me. While my girlfriends are alive, in most cases, I have very little contact with their husbands. Then suddenly, shortly after the funeral, I receive a proposal. It is almost as if these men can't bear to be alone for one minute. I don't kid myself that they have suddenly fallen madly in love with me; they are looking for an easy replacement, someone who will take over where their wives left off.

I am no longer looking for Mr. Right, as some of my divorced and widowed friends are. I have always worked and managed to pay my bills and keep a roof over my head. Unlike a lot of women, I guess I feel entitled to something better than what is available. Women are really a lot nicer; it's easier to make a contact and to share with women. Men are so repressed and so demanding that I often don't think it is worth the effort to socialize with them.

What upsets me about being an older woman on my own is the attitude of couples. I generally don't get invited out with couples. I'm a pretty old broad now —

you would think that they would finally see me as a person, not as a threat. But I think that is a problem for most older women on their own, regardless of whether they have ever been married.

What these women have in common is the sense that their value as human beings has been drastically diminished by virtue of their manless state. They share a common fear that, by marrying, they may become merely housekeepers or nurses, recruited primarily to perform services. There is also the shared concern that such marriages are devoid of sexuality and emotional warmth, but are instead expedient financial arrangements. Even though being single in our society is an alienating, lonely experience, these women prefer their single state, and their privacy, to a loveless, sexless marriage. The thread of anger and outrage running through their comments centers on society's portrayal of them as pathetic and worthless.

Sexuality and Aging

The Sexual Disqualification of Older Women

If our society defines middle-aged women as sexually distasteful, old women who desire sexual relationships are viewed as obscene. In mid life, unmarried women are given an ambivalent message. They are expected to pursue marriage as the only possible lifestyle. However, since they have been labeled as unattractive, and hence not sexually desirable, there are few opportunities to conform to this expectation. The net result is often acute depression and a sense of worthlessness.

For old women, society provides a clear standard of behavior. The desire for a full, sexually satisfying life is improper and unacceptable. Old women are expected to return to the pristine state of early childhood, sexless and almost innocent.

When Olivia was eighty-nine, she was forced to give up her large farmhouse and move into a nursing home. She needed some help, but in the small town nearby and in the surrounding community there were no visiting home-makers or meals on wheels. Olivia was both sad and ter-rified at the prospect of living in a nursing home, but, much to her surprise, shortly after her arrival, she met an old high-school friend, Ernest, with whom she became very close.

Olivia's experience was related to me by her grand-daughter, Rachel.

Every other Sunday, the family visits my grand-mother at the nursing home. It became Ernest's habit to join grandmother at those times. He would lie down on grandmother's bed, put his arms around her, give her little kisses, often rub her neck, and occasionally hug and cuddle her. My relatives did not know where to look.

This situation continued for several weeks until my eldest uncle, who rarely visited my grandmother, an-nounced that he would give her a good talking-to and straighten her out. The idea that his eighty-nine-year-old mother was enjoying a loving and intimate rela-tionship was abhorrent and repulsive to him. When he confronted my grandmother, she laughed and told him to mind his own business. She would do as she pleased with whomever she pleased, and didn't need either permission or approval from any son of hers. My uncle was furious and threatened to have her de-clared mentally incompetent and removed to a psy-chiatric ward.

At this point, my mother, the eldest daughter, con-vinced the family to leave grandmother alone and let her and Ernest enjoy what time they had left. But then the nurses and doctors began to complain that my grandmother's and Ernest's behavior was inappro-priate for a nursing home.

When my grandmother and Ernest announced that they planned to marry, the nursing-home administra-tor told them the home had no facilities for married couples. He was running a home, not a hotel.

Ernest and my grandmother were undaunted. My grandmother sent a letter to my mother, formally requesting permission to marry. She also wanted my mother to help her shop for a wedding dress and trousseau. My mother realized that the nursing-home administrator would never change his mind, so she tried desperately, but unsuccessfully, to find a private housekeeper to take care of grandmother and Ernest.

In the meantime, Ernest and my grandmother became angry and impatient with the delays in their wedding plans. One night they crept out of the home and boarded a bus to the next town, where they took a hotel room. The nursing home called the local police when their absence was noticed the following morning, and the couple was picked up at their hotel.

My grandmother and Ernest are back at the home now, but my grandmother conspiratorily informs me that she and Ernest have not given up. They are making plans to escape again, but this time they are heading south to Florida, where they plan to make a new life without interference from doctors, nurses, or family.

Olivia is struggling to express herself as a sexually alive human being. Her behavior evoked strong censure from both her family and the nursing-home staff. Olivia has chosen to battle a societal taboo that denounces and forbids sexuality in older women. In our society, sexuality is considered to be the prerogative of the young, even though there is evidence to suggest that sexual arousal, desire, and performance remain part of a person's ability into the nineties, as long as physical and intellectual strengths are adequate.[13] Our stereotype is that older persons, particularly older women, may be affectionate, but certainly not sexual. In fact, older women run the risk of being stereotyped as having neither sexual feelings nor a need for sexual expression. Older men, however, are considered to have a valid need for sexual activity, if only to ensure good physical health.[14]

Not surprisingly, those older women who are sexually active often keep their sex lives secret. Many of the sexually active older women I interviewed were concerned that if their adult children ever found out about their sex lives, they would be shocked, upset, and disapproving.

Many adult children find sexual activity in their aging parents, especially their older mothers, disquieting or threatening. A mother's role, they feel, is primarily one of nurturing and responding to the needs of others. An older mother who enjoys sex is considered selfish. Older women whom I interviewed sensed this disapproval on the part of their children and frequently responded by becoming sexually inhibited.

We know and care so little about sexuality in older women that, until very recently, there had been no efforts to understand and to respond to their sexual needs. In an effort to collect data about sexuality in people sixty and older, a survey was undertaken of eight hundred older people in the United States. The results challenge many long-standing beliefs about the sexual interests and activities of older people, particularly older women. Sixty-five per cent of the respondents were women; 93 per cent of the respondents said they liked sex. The study revealed that respondents had a far broader scope of sexual expressions and held more liberal views about sexuality than popular notions suggest.

Older women, the study indicated, show enormous potential for sexuality in later years, but this potential may not be realized because society assumes that sex dies with age. Our cultural attitudes have prevented older women from expressing themselves sexually and have triggered unnecessary feelings of guilt, self-incrimination, and inadequacy. The notion that older women find sex both desirable and enjoyable is treated with skepticism and embarrassment. Many older women fear ridicule and come to regard sex as improper and absurd.

The study found that women who were interested in sexuality had not pursued the interest because their spouses had died or had become ill or impotent. It was apparent that there were not enough sexually active men to go around. Of those men who survived, the majority became sexually inactive because of impotence or the fear of impotence, nearly always resulting in an end to sex for their spouses.[15]

Older Women, Younger Men

The above study concludes that women have both the desire and capacity for sexuality in their nineties. Why have we not turned to younger men? All women are aware that a sexual association with a younger man is considered scandalous. A man of seventy who has fathered a child with a twenty-five-year-old is applauded and commended for his virility, but a woman of seventy who socializes with a younger man can expect negative reactions: puzzlement, embarrassment, and shock, or revulsion. The younger man may also encounter adverse reactions to his relationship with an old woman. He may be branded as neurotic, or gay, find himself an object of contempt and/or ridicule, and he may be accused of having a mother fixation.

Rarely is an older man involved with a much younger woman accused of having a daughter fixation. Even when a man marries a woman young enough to be his granddaughter, the relationship is not perceived to be either inappropriate or absurd. Indeed, the man's reputation is enhanced; he is seen as a man to be admired, as a man with immense sexual power.

A woman who has a relationship with a younger man breaks a taboo and cannot expect praise for her action. She is considered predatory, willful, selfish, and an exhibitionist. She could also expect to be pitied and ultimately assumed to be senile.[16] The only exceptions are public figures, for example, Mae West, who, in old age parodied her younger self. She defused a potentially dangerous situation and made it funny, and therefore acceptable. The danger she flirted with was the notion that older women are sexually powerful and can attract younger men.

Martha is a seventy-year-old widow whose husband died when she was fifty-five. When she turned sixty-five she decided to pursue a lifelong dream of becoming an artist.

I was miserable for those first ten years after my husband died. You are treated like a social problem, an embarrassment. I remember saying to my friends shortly after my husband's funeral, please don't forget me; please include me. But everyone drifted away and I found myself spending most of my spare time alone. I tried to go places on my own, but it was just too lonely.

I wasn't really interested in remarrying, since my

own marriage was a struggle and not what you would call happy or fulfilling. I wanted a companion to go to a movie with, someone to talk to, someone who would take an interest in me. I went out with many men for the first while, but if I didn't respond positively to their advances, I never heard from them again.

Well, after a while I became disgusted with all the cheap passes and decided that I would rather not bother going out with these dirty old men.

I had just about given up the thought of ever achieving a reasonable relationship with a man. Then during my first year at art school, I met someone much younger, a man of thirty-six.

I don't know, but I think we just were attracted to each other first because of our mutual interest in art. He used to work in the same room and often offered to drive me home when we stayed late. I knew that he ate most of his meals out, so I started to invite him over for the occasional meal. From there we began going out to the theater and to movies together. He made me laugh, he never mentioned the difference in our ages, and he seemed to genuinely enjoy my company. For the first time in years I felt good about myself; I felt attractive and vital. It was so good to be listened to and to be treated as a real human being, not a pathetic widow.

I guess I started to think of the whole relationship as natural and normal. Without stopping to think of the implications, I spontaneously invited my friend to a family wedding. I had thought that my family would be pleased that I had found someone to be my companion at the wedding. At the first opportunity, my older brother took me aside and told me that my action was creating a scandal. He insisted that my behavior reflected badly on the family; people would gossip. A woman my age should have more sense; society could not condone my running around with a man young enough to be my son.

I was so shocked that I simply walked out on the wedding. Since that time, I have never invited my friend to accompany me to family functions. He understands how I feel, but he can't understand how my family can be so cruel.

I have come to accept that in our society such a relationship is unacceptable. I am seen as an old lady, dried up, but I have this secret life with my young man. I realize that some day he will find someone more his own age, but for now I have a friend, and a companion, someone who likes and appreciates me for myself.

Martha's efforts to sustain a relationship with a younger man evoked both shock and outrage. To be attractive in our society, there is a presumption that a woman must be young. The image of aging as ugly and not feminine is strongly imprinted on our consciousness. As a result, older women are condemned to having no identity, value, or status. When confronted with a woman such as Martha, who at age seventy is still expressing her sexuality, the societal response is abhorrence. But women become more comfortable with their sexuality as they mature; their interest in sex peaks later than men's and declines at a much slower rate.[17] Martha is forced to keep her relationship a secret in order to retain her familial contacts. She is made to feel that her behavior is ludicrous and inappropriate for a woman of seventy. Her peers are much more comfortable and accepting of her as an aging, sexless widow. Martha's overt sexuality flies in the face of this passive, nonthreatening image. As a sexual being, she becomes potent, and somehow frightening, particularly to her older brother. The revulsion that her relationship evokes is "the cutting edge of a whole set of oppressive structures that keep women in their place."[18]

Against Oblivion

There is no age at which a woman does not require affirmation of her worth as a human being, but I found that women in their eighties and nineties are able to discard much of the emotional baggage that burdens them in middle age and early old age. A woman who lives to her eighties and nineties is generally waging a different battle, the battle

46

to live her remaining years with as much dignity and independence as possible. These women may have outlived one husband, or even two or more, and rarely have the opportunity to meet or to engage in social relationships with men. Yet they still need contact and physical warmth. Many see their families withdraw from them physically. The extreme physical expressions of age such as wrinkled skin, white hair, frail bodies, poor hearing, and failing sight frighten younger people. In our society, which is youth-oriented and youth-obsessed, there is a reluctance to accept or acknowledge physical aging. Older women suffer the brunt of these negative and discriminatory attitudes.

Many of the women in their eighties and nineties that I interviewed expressed a sadness that they are rarely touched or held; that their appearance is abhorrent to most people. "People don't look at your eyes when you are my age," a woman of eighty-three said. "They look through you and past you. It's almost as if you don't exist."

The consensus of opinion was that women in their eighties and nineties who retain their health and their independence are emotionally strong and resilient. Few are looking for spouses, but all are looking for social contact and physical warmth.

Jane is ninety-two. She lives in a senior citizens' building that provides one hot meal a day and on-call medical service.

It is not likely that I will marry again. The last thing I want is a sick, old man who expects me to wait on him hand and foot. I've had two marriages, one that was terrible and one that was not too bad. I don't think my experience is so much different from that of other women I know who are my age. We married originally because that was what women did in those days.

Now that I live in this senior-citizen building, I have made wonderful women friends. There are a number of widowers in the building, but I don't mix with them. Some of them are very unpleasant. One of them had a habit of grabbing women in the hallway. When he did it to me I told him that if he was looking for a woman he had come to the wrong place. Two marriages are more than enough for one lifetime.

I rarely see my son or my grandchildren. They are all very busy with their own lives. I would feel very lonely if it weren't for my next-door neighbor, Mrs. Walton. She and I look out for each other and she includes me when her family comes to visit. Often we cook a meal together and watch a program on TV. She has become my family and my best friend; we share so many of the same experiences and interests. Both of us wish we had more contact with the world outside the building, but it is hard to get around at our age and we are thankful that we have each other.

Breaking the Back of the Double Standard

While the twenties are hard and turning thirty is generally a crisis, by the time women reach their mid thirties, life often becomes more satisfying. Many of the women I interviewed who were in their mid thirties or late forties, especially those who had achieved some personal fulfillment and had developed a network of close and satisfying relationships, were concerned with their achievements rather than their looks. And even among much older women, there were marvelous exceptions to the rule of personal and sexual obsolescence. Life still held possibilities and the hope of emotionally and sexually satisfying relationships.

Age is gradually being perceived, by individual women, as it has always been perceived by men: as a measure of their success in developing their full potential as human beings. Age need not be a defeat; it can be the achievement of dignity, wisdom, and accomplishment. Admittedly, these women are not the majority, but they are redefining beauty and shifting attention from outward appearance to inner depth and maturity. They find that their value as human beings is enhanced by age because that value is based on achievement.

Eileen is a thirty-five-year-old lawyer who recalls with humor and pathos her earlier efforts to become an American beauty.

In my teens and early twenties, I spent an amazing amount of time experimenting with hair styles, makeup, and stylish clothes, all in the belief that this would make me more attractive to men. My weight, my complexion became virtual obsessions. I put myself through the torture of surgery to repair what I thought was an ugly nose. I was absolutely convinced that good looks were the key to attracting men.

It was horrible at the time, but it seems funny now. All my efforts were hopeless because of my big mouth. Every time I created the illusion of beauty I would ruin it all by being outspoken and argumentative. I was too forthright, too intellectual to be attractive and sexy to the boys of my generation. Every time I went out on a date I automatically paid my own bus fare: I paid for my half of the meal and my ticket to the movies. I couldn't understand that my desire to be independent conflicted with my desire to be seen as a sexy woman. It took me a long time to realize that my personality, not my looks, was what turned men off.

I now understand that I was threatening to those men of long ago: I refused to play the role of the helpless, passive female. I guess it was inevitable that I would not develop any long-term relationships with men, and I must admit that it was the men who generally broke the relationship off. When I was younger, I felt terribly rejected and asked several men why they left me. What it came down to was that I wasn't passive or submissive enough; I was too opinionated, too emotionally demanding.

About ten years ago, when I graduated from law school, I moved to a new city. I made a number of close women friends, and I started to think and read about women's issues. I began to evaluate the men I had known, rather than try to understand what they didn't like about me. For the first time I gained some insight into the world of beauty and I began to realize that what men found attractive was a compliant, nonconfrontational woman. With that realization, I came to accept that I would probably never marry and perhaps would never find a man who would love and cherish me.

I can't lie. I felt disappointed and angry, somehow cheated. Part of me was furious at men for not loving me. Today, ten years later, I am relieved that I have maintained my integrity. As a lawyer, I see a lot of damaged women my own age, women who are victims of brutal and debilitating marriages.

Occasionally I meet a man who interests me, but I am still told that I am too energetic, too expressive. There have always been women like me, I tell them, but they used to be burned at the stake as witches or they were pejoratively called spinsters. Men tell me I am cynical, but I am merely realistic.

People are always asking me if I am lonely and if I am afraid of growing old alone. It is my professional opinion as a divorce lawyer that the loneliest people in the world are married women. Much of my practice involves helping widows and divorcées to pick up the pieces of their lives.

I'm thirty-five now and I am looking forward to growing and developing. This is a good time for me and I know my life will become richer and fuller as I grow older.

Eileen is part of the postwar generation, a child of the baby boom. This generation of women, who are now between the ages of about thirty to thirty-eight, have had an enormous influence on how women are perceived. These women spearheaded the current wave of feminism, and have been instrumental in bursting the great youth bubble.

Enough of these women are educated, gainfully employed, and politically active to have had a serious impact on society's notions of beauty, youth, and aging. The image of the perpetual teenager is fast fading. For the first time in this century, there are women over forty, long past their first bloom and with the odd wrinkle, who are idolized as incredibly beautiful and accomplished. Gloria Steinem,

Diana Rigg, and Catherine Deneuve, to name a few, are portrayed as women in their prime, not over the hill.

There are several reasons for this change in the perception of older women's worth. One is that the baby boomers, many of whom are older than thirty-five, and who represent tremendous marketing power and the largest population bulge in North America at the present time, are exerting enormous pressure to expand the acceptable limits of what is defined as attractive and sexy in a woman. An equally important influence is most definitely the women's movement, which has articulated the fact that women are not going to allow themselves to be packed up and put on the shelf, as were women of their mothers' generation.

In addition, the prospect of divorce and/or remaining single is not generally as catastrophic to these women as it was to their mothers' generation. This is not to suggest that the baby boomers are immune to the devastating effects of unhappy marriages and the relentless pressure to marry. For significant numbers of these women, however, divorce is a period of reassessment and of potential growth, a period to take control of their lives and to make a number of fundamental changes. I interviewed women in their thirties and forties who were in the midst of divorce. Many of them sought out new friends who shared their values and interests. What became increasingly valuable was freedom to explore their potential and their privacy. These women also spoke of feeling better and looking better than at any other period in their lives. For the first time in their lives, they were treated as adult women, seriously committed to their work or to their education. As one divorced woman of thirty-eight said, "Finally I am listened to and respected as an individual."

A recent study from Brandon University, involving 285 women between the ages of thirty-five and fifty-five, found that more than half of the women discovered in maturity a new sense of their own worth, one they had not experienced in their youth. This was true for married and unmarried women, women with children and without, and those working and those without jobs outside the home. The researchers concluded that there appears to be an improvement in how most women experience the quality of

51

their lives. The researchers also concluded that the women in the study have been affected by the women's movement, which has struggled to redefine women's potential, especially from mid life on.[19]

I spoke with many women between the ages of thirty-five and fifty whose self-image was profoundly altered by exposure to feminist ideals and through contact with different aspects of the women's movement. The theme that ran through their comments was their confrontation with our society's standards of beauty and sexual viability.

Marnie, who at forty-three is a successful professional woman, analyzed her own maturation.

At thirty, I thought of myself as a middle-aged matron, married with three children, for whom life was over, for whom nothing exciting would ever happen. At forty, having shed two husbands, I celebrated, I felt wonderful, I felt my life was just beginning.

What happened was that I joined the women's movement and I made good female friends. My self-image took a giant leap forward.

I started to enjoy living on my own. And my work was and is very exciting because it involves traveling and meeting new people all the time.

I discovered that many men are attracted to me, and this time for the right reasons. They like my personality, my energy, and my independence.

Eventually I did meet a man who made me feel very sexy and very attractive. This is the best relationship I have had in my whole life and it happened after my fortieth birthday. Only a very mature and secure kind of man appreciates women like me, but those men exist and they want and are able to give of themselves. I think we are going to see a lot of changes in male-female relationships, both in my generation and the one just after mine. Women in our culture have started to demand, and to some extent to receive, a better sexual and emotional deal.

For Marnie, life has become richer and more stimulating after forty. Admittedly, she represents a small minority. Her quest is for a more personally satisfying and meaningful life in a culture that heaps negativity on older women and reinforces women's low self-esteem.

Other women I interviewed emphasized how important their relationships with other women became as they entered their thirties and forties. They found women nurturing and highly stimulating. As Julia, a feminist, clearly stated the case:

> I turned forty a month ago. It was not the crisis I had always feared. In fact, I am in a very good space. I started to realize that my most important relationships are with other women, both at work and in the women's movement. My feminism is what has made the transition to forty a time of celebration rather than a time of defeat. I have a wonderful network of nurturing and supportive friends. These are the friends I hope to have with me when I am a very old woman.
>
> My marriage is better than most and my husband tries very hard to share in the child-rearing and with the housework, but like most women I am the one who feels responsible. I imagine that when my children grow up, my marriage will become superfluous. Perhaps this sounds hard, but the older I grow the more I realize that I don't need a man to complete my life, to make me respectable. There is a wonderful social world of women out there that satisfies most of my emotional and intellectual needs.
>
> In every other area I feel I am growing. I feel more in touch with myself.

The goal of achieving the societal ideal of beauty was a topic that recurred repeatedly in my interviews with women older than thirty. Although many were still striving to achieve or maintain this elusive perfection, a significant number had rejected this concept.

Ruth explains her reasons for rejecting the societal ideal of beauty.

> I am forty-five, quite tall, and very well-endowed. Even now I have to fight against the image of the sexy

blonde. I want to be seen as mature and sophisticated, not a dumb blonde with big breasts.

I am less worried about my looks at this time in my life than I am about maintaining my health. Since I had my last child, I joined a health club with some of my close friends. It has been a very liberating experience for me to walk around in the nude with other women. Men have always seen each other nude, but it is something new for women. I see women who have pot bellies, big, unfashionable hips, sagging breasts, but they are proud and I find them beautiful. What you discover when you are surrounded by so many nude women is that the ideal woman who has boyish hips, large, firm breasts, flawless skin, and long, sexy legs, is the rarest thing in the world. In fact, at my club, where at any one time I may see as many as a hundred women in the nude, only one woman comes close to this ideal. She is a famous dancer who works out three times a day and admits to starving herself to remain thin. The thing that I find so uplifting is that these women are at ease with their bodies; they are proud and carry themselves well, and they make no apologies for not living up to some stereotype of the beautiful woman. My attitudes toward beauty have changed dramatically since I joined the club. What I appreciate in a woman is her character, her strength, and her energy. It is a shame that men in our culture define beauty so narrowly. They are missing out on some of the most sensual and lovely people alive.

It is limiting to ascribe to women only one physical dimension. The limitation becomes more destructive as we move from our forties to our fifties and beyond. The middle-aged woman has become the butt of cynical and crude jokes. She is often depicted as a suburban housewife in an empty home, who religiously keeps her weekly appointments at the hairdresser. She wears heavy makeup, and she diets all the time. Most of her energy is absorbed in an effort to look young. What she really looks like is a caricature of her former self.

At fifty Adriana believes she has achieved a healthy outlook on beauty and sexuality after a long, hard self-examination.

Most of my life I felt awkward and unattractive. I am tall, very big-boned, and certainly not this culture's idea of a classically attractive woman. I went back to school in my thirties and by age forty-four I had my Ph.D. Along the way I became a radical feminist and I finally realized that I didn't need beauty, big breasts, and tiny feet to feel worthwhile and attractive.

Now that I am fifty, I feel I could, if I had to, cope very well on my own. I have built up a marvelous support system among my women friends, who range in age from their early thirties to their sixties. I enjoy the mix of ages and it gives me an opportunity to give comfort to my younger friends and receive the benefit of my older women friends' experience and wisdom. I thrive on activity and involvement, but I feel my parts are starting to wear out and that I am slowing down. Like most women my age, I live in terror of ending up in a nursing home, shut off from the people I love and care about. In my efforts to avoid that eventuality, I have started to take much better care of myself. I exercise regularly, I have stopped smoking, I drink very little, and I try to eat three good meals a day. My children, who range in age from eighteen to twenty-five, have become very close to me in the past ten years. They have become my friends and are very proud of my achievements. I am especially pleased with my son's development; he is a new breed of man, sensitive, emotional, and very loving.

If my husband should die before me, I doubt very much that I would remarry. I have no regrets about having married and having had children — there are some very real and satisfying rewards — but I don't see any need for a husband in my old age. All those women who expected the companionship of a husband as they grew old are abandoned, divorced, or widowed. In the end, we are all alone. It is probably a very good idea to get used to the idea early and plan your life with that in mind. I have a tremendous advantage over my old

55

friends in the suburbs: I am growing and developing and meeting and making new friends all the time. I am not striving to create a youthful image: I just look as I am, a fifty-year-old woman, with gray hair and some wrinkles, all of which are signs of my maturity, not my decline.

These women who are in their thirties, forties, and fifties represent a particularly confident and enlightened minority. They have begun the difficult task of challenging accepted stereotypes of beauty and sexuality. They refuse to succumb to the self-hatred our culture foists on older women, a self-hatred that is translated into a shame for one's natural aging and involves time, energy, and money spent on makeup, surgical face-lifts, and breast reconstruction, dyeing of hair, and strenuous dieting. These women have begun to take issue with the double standard of aging by rejecting and fighting the influences that cultivate a fear of aging in women. Women are beginning to insist that their value as human beings be defined in terms of their personality, intelligence, maturity, and achievements, not their physical appearance.

These women derive strength and support from each other. Although their networking is quite informal, there is a sense of permanence about their relationships. That permanence sustains and nurtures them, much like the family is purported to do.

Many of the women I interviewed gained energy and vitality from exploring and analyzing the discrimination practised against all older women. The single most important realization was that the insidious societal pressure to preserve a youthful appearance destroys self-esteem and ensures a preoccupation with aging. This process drains and depletes the energy that should rightfully be used to promote personal growth and development throughout one's life.

But life does not end at fifty for the majority of women. We can, on average, expect to live on until our eighties.

I met very old women who insisted, as did some of the middle-aged women, that they were entitled to participate in all aspects of life. Milly was one of those women — endowed with sensuality and a zest for life.

I come from a long line of women who live well into their nineties. By those standards, at eighty-one, I have some good years left to me. Luckily, my health is very good and I plan to hang onto my apartment as long as I can. There are lots of things that I don't like about being an old woman, but the most important thing is that people try to make a baby out of you.

I am a professional woman and, except for ten years while I was at home raising my children, I worked most of my adult life as a children's doctor. When my youngest child was seven I became very restless and bored and I decided to go back to school and finish my medical studies, which I had interrupted when I married. My husband strongly opposed this move, but I am a very stubborn woman. I almost killed myself running my home, caring for my children, trying hard to be a good wife, while at the same time studying medicine. My husband's response was to start having affairs with other women. I thought of leaving him, but I really believed that one had to preserve the family at all costs; all the women of my generation believed that their first duty was to their family and that their own self-interest came second.

By this time, I no longer loved my husband and I was determined to finish medical school and then leave him. It is hard to explain, but I actually did not leave my husband until I was in my late sixties, a few years after my retirement. I am not and never was a pretty woman and I was sure that I would never find another man. The only thing that kept me going and made me feel like a worthwhile person was my work. I was a very good doctor and I loved the children who were my patients.

When I finally retired and I was forced to face my husband every day, I realized that we had nothing in common. He was still going out with other women, even then, but they kept getting younger and younger. The full force of my humiliation hit me at this point.

I decided that I wanted to spend my remaining years with some dignity. I was tired of people laughing behind my back as the woman whose husband was dallying with young girls.

The judge at the divorce hearing said to me, "Don't be foolish, a woman of your age doesn't divorce. After so many years, can't you go on for a little longer?" He was so condescending I thought I would scream. To everyone, even to my children, I was a silly old self-indulgent woman who had no right to make such a fuss and disrupt everything.

About a year after my divorce, I had a phone call from a man I had met in my thirties when I was a medical student. We hadn't seen each other in more than thirty years, but he had heard about my divorce and wanted to see me. This began a romance that has gone on for fifteen years. He is about ten years younger than I am, but that isn't important to either of us. We've had our share of problems, but somehow we've worked them out. In the beginning, he insisted that we marry or at the very least move in together. I explained to him that I had grown to love my privacy and my independence and that I had no intention of ever marrying again.

My children, especially my sons, have developed a new respect for me. The idea that their old mother is a sexually alive being was at first a foreign and even threatening idea. In time, though, they have grown to accept that I am my own person and that I have a right to some love and warmth in my life. I think my sons were a bit embarrassed that their old mother was having an affair at a time when most women are forced, mostly by circumstances, to give up any thought of a sex life.

Now that I am over eighty, people are a bit scandalized by my arrangement. Up until eighty, I was still perceived as young enough to have a man, but eighty is a magic number. We are supposed to take to our rocking chairs and never express our sexuality. But you know, inside I feel like a young girl; I don't feel old. I have been very lucky to find a lover at a time when I thought such a thing was impossible.

2

Older Women and Health:
The Hazards We Face

From puberty on, women increasingly risk becoming "perpetual patients." Mary Daly, the author of *Gyn/Ecology*, very graphically points out that the bodies and minds of many of us "are constantly invaded by foreign objects — knives, needles, speculums, carcinogenic (cancer-inducing) hormone injections and pills, sickening self-images, festering fixations, and debilitating dogmas."[1] Gynecologists, psychiatrists, and general practitioners in particular, exercise tremendous control over our lives and deign to offer expensive advice and often risky intervention.

Too many of us are intimidated by doctors. We accept their pronouncements unquestioningly. High status and huge incomes help foster our perception of doctors as godlike and infallible. But we are rarely treated by doctors as intelligent consumers who are capable of participating in decisions about our own health. As a result, our bodies and our minds are frequently perceived by doctors and researchers as fertile fields for exploration and experimentation.

Many of us believe that this sexist and condescending attitude toward women has led to a situation in which modern medicine creates at least as many illnesses as it cures. The problem becomes compounded as we grow older by doctors' distaste for aging and its attendant chronic problems.

Breast Cancer: There Are No Definitive Answers

The treatment of breast cancer is an extremely disturbing example of doctors' insensitivity to women's fragile self-images and their dogmatic approach to women's health. When our breasts first develop, most of us are very affected by how they look. Our culture places enormous value on female breasts as an intricate part of our sexuality. Most women develop a self-consciousness about their breasts at a very early age, and few of us completely outgrow this self-consciousness.

This preoccupation with what breasts look like has nurtured a thriving medical business — breast enlargement and breast reduction. Women who choose breast "beautification surgery" aspire "to appear more desirable to men or more like the stereotyped images of society as a whole."[2]

When a doctor tells a woman she has a suspicious lump in her breast that may require radical surgery, she will likely become emotionally upset at the prospect of a life-threatening disease, and also at the possible mutilation of her breasts. Medical diagnosis of breast cancer is rarely concerned with the potential emotional devastation of the proposed treatment.

Having been taught that breasts are essential to femininity and sexuality, most women are terrified that operations for breast cancer may "desex" them. The speed with which doctors are prepared to lop off breasts indicates a basic disregard for women's self-esteem and sense of worth.

Breast surgery is one of the oldest operations in modern medicine. Despite controversy about its effectiveness, the procedure has acquired a kind of sacredness that many doctors are reluctant to challenge. Western medicine has an almost mindless devotion to the "surgical answer" to human problems, without considering its emotional impact.[3]

Cynthia is fifty-two years old, and her family has a history of cystic breasts.[4]

I am a very conscientious person. Every month I routinely examine my breasts for any lumps or changes. I've been doing this for fifteen years, and in that time I've discovered three lumps. Each time I was frightened, but luckily they have been benign lumps.

It is a very nerve-racking business and my experience with surgeons has been none too pleasant. I have been careful to read the consent forms when I enter the hospital, making sure that the surgeon removes nothing but the lump. I have heard enough horror stories of women waking up and finding that they have had a radical mastectomy without realizing that, by signing the consent form, they have given the surgeon permission to proceed with any surgery he thinks necessary.

I am not very well liked in medical circles, probably because I ask so many questions and request that I be consulted every step of the way. After I had the last lump removed, I visited the surgeon for a check-up. Once the examination was over, he leaned toward me and said that he would strongly advise me to have both breasts removed immediately. I was so shocked that I could barely speak. I asked him if he had discovered cancerous lumps in both breasts. He hesitated a moment and said no, but he added that I was a high-risk case and the best way to proceed would be to completely remove both breasts as quickly as possible.

I told him that I would have to think about his suggestion and that I would let him know my decision. He frowned and said that there really was no choice for a woman with my condition.

I left his office dazed, worried sick, but not totally convinced. Fortunately, I was working as a secretary in a large hospital and was on friendly terms with a number of doctors. I asked the three I knew best — two were surgeons — what they thought of my doctor's advice. All three seemed surprised; one said that he would never allow his wife to have both breasts removed in a similar situation.

You know, I have always worked around doctors and I have come to realize that as a patient you have to be very careful and treat the profession with healthy skepticism. Women who don't have my experience are really at risk when dealing with knife-happy doctors.

The unresolved controversy over the various methods of treatment for breast cancer is a widely discussed issue. A range of surgical procedures is used, from a radical mastectomy, in which the breast, the underlying lymph nodes, and the pectoral muscles are removed, to less drastic surgery, such as the partial, modified, simple or subcutaneous mastectomy.

The radical mastectomy was first devised by William Stewart Halsted in 1882. At that time tumors were more massive by the time they were treated than they are now. Halsted's radical mastectomy quickly became the standard operation for breast cancer in North America. In *The Hidden Malpractice*, Gena Corea reports that although there has been no proof that the Halsted radical is superior to more moderate procedures, no controlled study of the various procedures was undertaken until 1970. In 1970, the National Cancer Institute tested seventeen hundred women to compare three treatments: the radical mastectomy, the simple mastectomy, and the simple mastectomy followed by radiation therapy. After two years, patients with all three treatments had approximately the same 15 per cent disease-recurrence rate. The evidence suggests that the medical profession does not really know what treatments are most effective, since there is no proof that a radical mastectomy does any more good than simply removing a lump.[5]

Dr. George Crile, author of *What Women Should Know About the Breast Cancer Controversy*, takes a more extreme view. He reported that many surgeons in North America and most of those in England now agree that there is no longer any place for the mutilating radical operation. "If the cancer is so advanced that it cannot be removed by an operation less than radical mastectomy, it has already spread throughout the system and is incurable by surgery."[6] But when American physicians detect a cancerous tumor in the breast, 90 per cent of them perform a Halsted radical mastectomy. In Britain, half as many radical mastectomies are performed per 100,000 population as in the United States.[7]

Many doctors criticize the findings of the National Cancer Institute. They point out that the women tested must be followed for a number of years before any firm conclusions can be drawn. Dr. Crile counters that for too long surgeons have assumed the entire burden of deciding how their breast-cancer patients should be treated. "Since there is no agreement on treatment," he says, "the surgeon has an obligation to inform the patient of the facts. Only when the patient is allowed to participate in the decision can she accept an operation on her breast with what can be known ethically as 'informed consent'."[8]

To promote early detection of breast cancer and reduce the incidence of radical surgery, the American Cancer Society and the National Cancer Institute set up twenty-seven Breast Cancer Detection Demonstration Projects across the country in 1972. Voluntary early detection tests were offered to women over thirty-five. Since 1972, the screening programs have aroused intense controversy among scientists and doctors. Radiation specialists have argued that the female breast, which is probably the most vulnerable organ for X-ray-induced cancer, should not be routinely exposed to a known carcinogen. It is their position that X-rays might do more harm than good, especially to women under fifty.

An equally serious concern arose as a result of a National Institute of Health investigation, which revealed that hundreds of women had been treated with some kind of surgery, usually radical mastectomy, for types of breast cancers that rarely, if ever, invade the rest of the body and kill the patient.

A special investigating committee that met in 1977 recommended that all women treated for such cancers be notified as quickly as possible that they were not at risk. Since their surgeries might well have been unnecessary, the committee felt that it was imperative that they, their daughters, and their sisters be informed that the women had not had a virulent, life-threatening disease.

The problem for these 2500 women is that they still do not know if they have relatively minor breast cancer or a life-threatening variety. These women are caught in a legal morass. Lawyers with the Department of Health, Education and Welfare have concluded that the federal government cannot tell the women their diagnoses, because the screening programs were set up as a voluntary program, for detection only. If a woman's mammogram (breast X-ray) revealed something suspicious, a notification was sent to her physician. At that point, the National Cancer Institute was no longer involved. The matter became a doctor-patient issue.

However, as a result of the controversy, the National Cancer Institute decided to inform the individual screening centers which women did not have cancer. Then the director of each center notified individual physicians that they had performed unnecessary surgical procedures on their patients' bodies; that their patients did not have breast cancer; and that the daughters and sisters of those patients are, therefore, not at higher risk as they probably feared.

Quite obviously, the federal government cannot and will not force the physicians to invite malpractice suits. And it is probably impossible for a patient to win such a suit because pathologists insist that microscopic diagnoses are interpretive and subject to variations of judgement. No physician is prepared to go to court even when he is almost certain he will win. Consequently, most of the women who underwent breast surgery because of diagnoses from the screening program still do not know whether they did, in fact, have breast cancer.[9]

Medically Old at Forty

In our society, women are deemed "medically old" at age forty. The "disease" to which all women succumb, according to the vast majority of members of the medical profession, is menopause. Considering that forty-year-old women can anticipate approximately forty more years of life, it is difficult to accept that we have been stereotyped as "aging" when forty-year-old men are perceived to be at their vigorous best. The prognosis regarding our mental and physical health becomes increasingly negative as we pass from forty to fifty and beyond. We are increasingly at risk, too, from controversial surgery, potentially dangerous medication, and premature institutionalization.

The process begins with the prevailing image, nurtured by many in the medical profession, that menopausal women "are expected to have emotional breakdowns, lose their sexual appetites, experience hot flashes, and sprout little moustaches. Their breasts and vaginas are supposed to shrivel up."[10] And it can end with a malnourished old woman, shunted from doctor to doctor, ingesting as many as thirty pills a day, labeled senile, when, in fact, she is over-medicated, and ultimately placed in an institution.

These are bleak images of the medically defined old and aging woman. An "aging" woman may be subjected to hysterectomies, radical mastectomies, antidepressants, tranquilizers, estrogens, and psychiatric care. It is true, of course, that aging brings a slowing down and a greater risk of fatal and chronic disease, but "equating aging with disease (especially in women) inhibits the development of any preventive approach to health maintenance that could slow down aging processes and limit debilitation from chronic disease."[11]

The medical profession, in fact, has promulgated a destructive attitude toward older women. We all have a vested interest in exploring those attitudes and behaviors of the medical profession that place our health in jeopardy, reinforce negative self-images, and interfere with the full enjoyment of half of our lives.

Menopause Is a Rite of Passage

Women have been conditioned to expect something horrific to take place at menopause, which has been defined as "the most serious endocrinological disorder next to diabetes,"[12] and as the "death of womanhood."[13] Dr. David Reuben, in his book *Everything You Always Wanted to Know About Sex*, asserted that a menopausal woman was "not really a man, but no longer a functional woman [living] in the world of intersex. . . . Having outlived their ovaries, menopausal women may have outlived their usefulness as human beings."[14]

Feminine Forever, written in 1966 by the respected American gynecologist Dr. Robert A. Wilson, went one step further. Wilson described a menopausal woman as "living decay. . . an individual who can't be entrusted with decision-making jobs."[15]

But most women continue to produce sufficient amounts of the female hormone, estrogen, to be well and functioning. Just as we emerge from our child-bearing years and are finally free to live less confining lives, we are defined as medically and psychologically unfit. The fact is that "menopause refers only to the termination of menstruation, the subtle changes in sex hormones which underlie it, and the end of fertility."[16] Menopause is a biological event. We must remember that fifty years ago, it took place shortly before death. Today a woman may live for another twenty-five years. A woman defined as old and inept at forty is sentenced to living many unproductive years.

Reports from physicians who treat menopausal women indicate that only 10 per cent experience symptoms so severe that they are incapacitated. The other 90 per cent are victims of cultural attitudes toward older women, not of biological realities. In medical journals, menopausal women are often perceived as physical and emotional wrecks, beset by wrinkles, stringy hair, and dull eyes.[17] It is not surprising that many women are horrified at the prospect of reaching menopause, and often develop symptoms based upon what they have been conditioned to expect.

The San Francisco Women's Health Center prepared a list of symptoms women have experienced during menopause. None is life-threatening and most are temporary (lasting from six months to four years). The most common occurrences directly associated with the decrease in estrogen production at menopause are hot flashes[18] and tissue atrophy or dryness of vaginal tissues. (Hot flashes are not fully understood. They may be the result of the body's attempt to achieve a new hormonal balance. Or they might be a result of estrogen deprivation or withdrawal. When the body adjusts to new estrogen levels, the hot flashes cease.) Other reported problems include insomnia, change in weight, headaches, lack of energy, general anxiety, and an inability to concentrate. Few women suffer from all nineteen reported symptoms, and approximately 40 per cent never have any, except the cessation of menstruation.[19]

Dr. Barbara Joans, an anthropologist at San Jose State University in California, discovered that there has been very little medical research on menopause. Medical research concentrates on males; things female are devalued. No culture actively celebrates menopause as a rite of passage, but our culture openly views menopause with fear and distaste. Dr. Joans maintains that, unlike being born, puberty, giving birth, and death, menopause is not ceremonialized, because we do not wish to acknowledge its occurrence: it indicates that our status in society is threatened. In all cultures we are viewed as wives and mothers; we are defined in terms of our relationships with men and our subsequent fertility. It is not surprising, then, that we are reluctant to draw attention to the end of our fertility. In Indian and Chinese societies, a woman's status grows as she stops menstruating. But Dr. Joans found no ceremonies, public announcements, or rites of passage. These women gain freedom of movement, but they lose their most important role, that of child bearer. When it becomes an honorable and venerated thing to be an older woman, perhaps we will begin to create proud ceremonies of menopause.[20]

Youth in a Pill

Gillian was still menstruating regularly in her early forties.

> I found that I was irritable and more tired than usual. I knew that women were supposed to go through menopause at about that time, so I assumed that I "had menopause." My knowledge of what menopause was supposed to be and how it should be treated was very limited, so I consulted my gynecologist. When I explained my symptoms, he told me, without an examination of any kind, which I thought was strange, that I definitely was going through menopause. He explained that the normal treatment was estrogen pills, which he prescribed in the highest possible dosage. I remember that the pharmacist was surprised at the high dosage and called the doctor to make sure that the prescription was correct.
>
> At the time, I was quite happy to take the estrogen, since I felt better almost immediately. I now believe that the whole thing was psychological. However, I took the estrogen for more than three years, until I began to have break-through bleeding between my periods. I became alarmed, but the doctor assured me that a lower dosage of estrogen would solve the problem.
>
> At about this time, I visited a friend, who told me that when she began menopause her doctor sent her

to a psychiatrist. She was so distressed at having her problem treated as a form of neurosis that she went to the library to see if she could find any information on menopause. She found an article published by a women's health collective that convinced her she wasn't crazy but simply going through a natural change. Listening to her, I realized that I was blaming menopause for personal problems. My marriage was in trouble and I had no real interests to absorb my time.

I decided to see my doctor and tell him that I wanted to stop the estrogen pills. It also occurred to me that unless I discontinued the estrogen I would never know when my periods would end. The doctor was very matter-of-fact and brusquely told me that I could stop using the estrogen if I wished, but he personally would not advise it.

It was remarkable. I felt nothing when I went off the estrogen; there was absolutely no change.

Just about this time, I read a series of articles in a magazine about the link between estrogen and cancer. I was in a panic, so I contacted my doctor again. He seemed very angry and annoyed. He told me that all the publicity about the dangers of estrogen was ridiculous — it was all premature. The only women that need be concerned were those with histories of breast and uterine cancer in their families. He said that the press was irresponsible, causing him and his colleagues a lot of bother. Apparently many of his women patients had called him in a similar panic.

I guess I lost my temper. I told him that if he had bothered to take my family history he would know that my mother, sister, and grandmother had all died of breast cancer. He just hung up.

Gillian's experience is far from unique. The arrogant and careless manner with which her doctor prescribed estrogen is indicative of the low level of interest many doctors have in menopause.

Too often, menopausal women are dismissed as neurotic, bothersome, and boring. It is easy to misdiagnose or overlook underlying problems even in a thorough examination, but a menopausal woman runs the risk of not being examined at all. The response to our symptoms is frequently a pat on the shoulder and a package of estrogen pills.

Charlotte's periods stopped when she was fifty-one.

I don't recall having any symptoms. I felt fine. In fact, I felt very free, relieved to be finished with menstruating. At any rate, in the last year I noticed some vaginal discharge along with a burning and itching sensation. It was a bit uncomfortable, so I decided to have a checkup with my gynecologist. He gave me estrogen for the itching and burning. I had no idea that it was a controversial drug and he said nothing about it. I come from the generation that doesn't ask questions: if a doctor gives you a medication, you assume he knows what he is doing and you take it.

My daughter, Karen, had read about estrogen and was upset that I planned to take it. She pressured me into asking my family doctor about it.

I explained to the doctor that my daughter had read that women who take estrogen have a greater likelihood of developing cancer. "I am sure that your daughter means well," he said, "but I know for a fact that the rumors about estrogen are untrue and that you can take these pills without any side effects. If anything," he declared, "estrogen is a marvelous drug that will stop the itching and dryness and make you much more comfortable."

When I told Karen what the doctor had said, she became quite agitated and read me several articles and chapters in books on the dangers of estrogen. As I listened to her, I became upset as well. My husband is angry that I decided to listen to my daughter rather than to the doctor, but I am satisfied that I did the right thing. I ended up using my mother's old remedy — douching with vinegar — and the itching and burning are gone. You could say that I have lost all faith in doctors.

It is true that many of us become depressed in our forties.

But it is not because we are going through menopause. Our children are leaving home. So many of us have no aspirations or ways to fulfill ourselves as human beings. We are discouraged and thwarted by a society that considers us obsolete, emotionally unstable, and physically unattractive.

The medical professionals do not deal with the causes of our depression and its attendant physical symptoms. Instead, they generally have two extreme and unacceptable views: that this aging process must be retarded with the ingestion of the female hormone, estrogen; or that menopausal women are neurotic and should be tranquilized or ignored.

Women have been given estrogen replacement therapy (ERT) for more than forty years. But between 1965 and 1975, prescriptions for ERT nearly tripled. In the United States, six million women were taking estrogen. Some of these women started taking estrogen in their thirties to prevent aging.[21]

As early as 1947, a link was made between uterine cancer and the use of estrogen. The medical profession prescribed the hormone less until 1966, when Dr. Robert Wilson published his book *Feminine Forever*. Wilson's theory was that menopause could be averted and aging allayed with ERT. He claimed that the hormone pill could reduce or totally eliminate twenty-six symptoms of menopause including nervousness, irritability, anxiety, hot flashes, and vaginal atrophy. But no scientific body has ever approved ERT as a preventative to aging. In fact, estrogen levels are naturally high in women between twenty and forty, yet during those twenty years women age considerably. Estrogen is not a magic cure for aging.[22]

The consequences of treating menopausal women with ERT became apparent in 1975 when Dr. Donald F. Austin, the chief of the California Tumor Registry, reported "that from 1969 – 1973, the rate of invasive uterine cancer in California rose 80 per cent among white women fifty years and older." He linked the rise in cancer to the increased use of ERT. (The United States estrogen market had grown from seventeen million dollars in 1962 to sixty-nine million dollars in 1973.)[23]

In 1975 the prestigious *New England Journal of Medicine* published two studies showing that post-menopausal women who take estrogen are five to fourteen times more likely to develop cancer of the uterine lining than are women who do not use estrogen.[24]

The debate continued, but estrogen has remained on the market. It is estimated that, in the United States, twenty million prescriptions for estrogen are written annually.

In January 1979, the *New England Journal of Medicine* published a new study on thirteen hundred menopausal women conducted by Dr. Paul Stollery at Johns Hopkins Medical School in Baltimore, Maryland. Stollery found that estrogen users had five to six times the incidence of cancer of the lining of the uterus than women who did not take estrogen. The study also condemned the form the therapy took — three weeks of taking the hormone, one week off — which Stollery found to be as risky as continuous use of the hormone.[25]

New evidence, although it is not yet conclusive, links ERT to other types of cancer. There is a growing concern that ERT might cause breast cancer.[26]

In September 1979, the United States National Institute of Health and the United States National Institutes on Aging co-sponsored a conference called "Estrogen Use and Post-Menopausal Women." The conference indicated that ERT is not an effective treatment of psychological problems. Apparently there is no present justification for prescribing estrogen for relief of depression, anxiety, fatigue, irritability, or insomnia.

For years, drug-company advertisements in medical journals suggested that menopausal and post-menopausal women with emotional complaints could be "cured" by estrogen therapy. A typical ad would depict a middle-aged woman slumped in a chair holding a plane ticket. The text would read: "Bon Voyage? Suddenly she'd rather not go! She's waited thirty years for this trip and now she just doesn't have the bounce. She has headaches and feels tired and nervous all the time. And, for no reason at all, she cries." And, in large type: "Estrogen Deficiency? [Brand of Estrogen] can help improve her sense of well-being." Such advertisements are extremely misleading.[27]

A study done at St. Michael's Hospital in Toronto suggested that menopausal women need emotional support, not hormonal drugs that promise to alleviate symptoms. The study administered estrogen to one group of menopausal women and a placebo to a second group. Both groups received counseling from the medical staff and took part in discussions. Results showed that the support rather than the drugs was the effective element. The women on the placebo did as well as the women on estrogen.[28]

Despite so much information debunking the exaggerated claims for ERT and pointing out its hazards, estrogen use is still widespread. The pharmaceutical companies' promotion, which implies that menopause is an abnormal or pathological state, is partly responsible for continuing sales. The ads have convinced doctors and millions of women that menopause is a disease caused by estrogen deficiency, which leads to unhappiness, a loss of femininity, and accelerated aging. Their arguments are so compelling and information on the dangers of ERT is so poorly disseminated that estrogen continues to be widely prescribed.

Hysterectomies Are Big Business

About ten years ago, at forty-seven, Madelaine was having her yearly examination at the gynecologist's.

> He advised me that I needed surgery to lift my bladder. He briefly explained that my bladder had fallen during five pregnancies and that very minor surgery was necessary to repair the situation. He asked if I planned to have more children. I thought it was a strange question, since I had five children in their teens and had neither the desire nor the energy for more. As far as I know, I was not going through menopause. I had no symptoms and my period was regular. The women in my family all continue to menstruate until their late fifties. We are long-lived and extremely healthy women.
>
> I consented to the bladder operation, expecting to be in the hospital for a week at the most. My family doctor came to see me almost immediately after the operation, and told me that the doctor had given me

72

a complete hysterectomy. I was very upset. When I asked him why, he told me it was standard procedure for women my age. It would protect me from the possibility of cancer of the uterus. It's hard to explain how I felt – outraged, depressed, desexed. But what could I do? It was out and supposedly for good reasons.

As Madeleine's family doctor pointed out, it is standard practice to remove the ovaries as well as the uterus of a woman older than forty-five.[29] Although consumer and health advocates have campaigned vigorously against unnecessary surgery and for the need for informed consent, many women still share Madeleine's frightening experience. Madeleine was angry and humiliated by being told about her hysterectomy only after it had been done; however, like many women, she was not prepared to confront her doctor whom she feared and felt in awe of. In the end, Madeleine convinced herself that her doctor knew best.

At fifty-six Nancy found herself in a new city as a result of her husband's promotion.

Shortly after we had settled, I discovered that I had a vaginal discharge. The wife of one of my husband's colleagues recommended a doctor, and claimed he was one of the best in the city.

The doctor was a very tall man, extremely overweight, and very surly. He led me into the examining room and told me to prepare myself for an internal examination. We did not discuss my medical history. I was very tense and ill-at-ease, but I did as I was told. While the doctor was examining me, he asked in an ominous voice, "How old are you?" I answered, 'Why? Do you suspect something?" He showed me the speculum and the discharge. He seemed repulsed and irritated. I was quite frightened and asked if he suspected cancer. He answered that he didn't have microscopic vision, but he would immediately arrange for a hospital bed so I could have a hysterectomy.

I replied that I could not consent to any type of surgery without a second opinion. His face became flushed and he angrily retorted, "Well, go get one then!" He literally threw me out of his office.

I immediately went to another doctor who told me that a hysterectomy would have been inappropriate. All I had was a vaginal infection that would easily clear up with antibiotics.

Although discussing the prevalence and perils of unnecessary surgery is a recent phenomenon, they have been serious problems since the nineteenth century. A century ago it was believed that women had no capacity for sexual feeling. If a woman did develop the "illness" of sexuality, which was called "nymphomania," physicians cured her with a variety of techniques, including cauterizing (burning) or removing the clitoris.

Removal of both ovaries (called an "ovariotomy") was a nineteenth-century "cure" for female sexuality and "nonconformity." American historian G.J. Barker-Benfield reports, in the book *The Horrors of the Half-Known Life*, that the medical symptoms for ovariotomy included: neurosis, insanity, troublesomeness, eating "like a plowman," masturbation, attempted suicide, erotic tendencies, persecution mania, or anything "untoward" in female behavior.

The name for the surgical removal of the uterus is "hysterectomy." Its root word is "hysteria," which literally means "a disturbance of the uterus." Hysterectomies are performed on women who have uterine cancer, inexplicable menstrual bleeding, small, nonmalignant tumors, menstrual cramps, and vaginal laxness (a condition in which the vaginal walls lose their firmness, often as a result of childbearing).

More cautious doctors believe that most of these symptoms should be treated by rest, relaxation, or scraping of the uterus (called dilation and curettage or D&C) yet the hysterectomy is one of the most frequently performed operations in the United States. Only tonsillectomy, hernia repair, and removal of the gall bladder are more common. In the past thirty years, the hysterectomy has come to be regarded by many gynecologists as a simple answer for everything from backache to contraception. It was once considered a radical means of contraception, but it is now called "the only logical approach to female sterilization."[30] Moreover, it is standard practice to remove the ovaries as well as the uterus of women over forty-five.[31]

Doctors frequently bully women into believing they need hysterectomies, ignoring the fact "that the death rate from hysterectomy itself. . . is, in fact, higher than the death rate from uterine/cervical cancer."[32]

The number of hysterectomies performed in the United States increased by approximately 60 per cent between 1965 and 1973, far in excess of population growth. In 1976, a Federal Drug Administration (FDA) bulletin reported that the rate of hysterectomies had been rising in the past decade to the point that almost one in three American women had surgical, not natural, menopause. Many women who underwent hysterectomies had not presented symptoms prior to surgery. United States medical audits performed in 1976 showed that in many regions more than 40 per cent of the hysterectomies and ovarectomies involved the removal of normal, healthy organs. The women were also exposed to the risks involved in any operation: anaesthesia reactions and complications such as pneumonia, blood clots, and infection. The chance of dying from a surgical complication is one in five hundred. When a hysterectomy is followed by an unnecessary and highly controversial drug such as estrogen, the patient may be at far greater risk.[33]

The hysterectomy is an expensive operation: it costs between fifteen hundred and two thousand dollars. (This is five to seven times more expensive than a tubal ligation, a simpler form of sterilization, which involves tying off the tubes.) It generally takes about four to six weeks to recover from the operation. Most experts agree about what makes the hysterectomy business so lucrative: the hospital-oriented, fee-for-service U.S. medical system.[34]

In Canada, the rate of performance of hysterectomies is twice that of England and Wales, and increased by 40 per cent between 1968 and 1972. Particularly notorious incidents of unnecessary hysterectomies were reported in the province of Saskatchewan. An increase of 75 per cent in the provincial rate of hysterectomies between 1964 and 1971 was brought to the attention of the Saskatchewan College of Physicians and Surgeons. The college appointed a special committee which, in 1970 and 1973, classified hysterectomies at selected hospitals as "justified" or "unjustified." Rates for "unjustified" hysterectomies ranged from 1.7 per cent to 58.6 per cent.

Hospitals with low rates of unjustified hysterectomies were commended. Those performing unjustified operations were given five recommendations, including: "unnecessary surgery should cease," and tissue committees (which examine all tissues removed by physicians) should take a renewed interest in their responsibility. The committee reported a 50 per cent reduction in the rate of hysterectomy in the city with the highest unjustified hysterectomy rate and an overall provincial reduction of 13 per cent, which they attributed, in part, to the review.[35]

One reason why hysterectomy rates are so high is that physicians remove the uterus in cases other than uterine cancer. Increasingly, hysterectomies are performed to prevent the possibility of cancer. In fact, many gynecologists believe that the healthy reproductive organs should routinely be removed when a woman reaches "a certain age" to prevent the development of cancer of the uterus and ovaries.[36] A hysterectomy will, of course, prevent cancer. If you don't have a uterus, you cannot develop uterine cancer.

In *Seizing Our Bodies*, Claudia Drefus reports that the United States Planned Parenthood Association is taking issue with what they call "hacking preventively." The absurdity of this form of surgery is clear, Planned Parenthood argues. "Preventive lobotomies for young people at statistically high risk of developing violent psychoses at some future time have not been suggested by physicians writing in psychiatric journals."[37]

Some doctors completely avoid the issue of which medical symptoms warrant surgical removal of the uterus. They endorse the hysterectomy as a means of sterilization. They have even changed the name of the operation to "hysterilization." The alternative, they argue, is to leave a useless uterus in which cancer might develop and to prolong menstruation in women in their forties. In hospitals throughout the United States, by 1970, sterilization by hysterectomy had become a routine operation for women with normal

pelvic function or minor abnormalities that would not jus-
tify a major procedure.[38]

Ninety-two per cent of all American physicians are male.
In 1970, *Medical World News* published a report on a cancer conference. The assembled surgeons agreed that they
rarely hesitate to remove an ovary but think twice about
removing a testicle. The doctors readily admitted that the
viewpoint arises from the fact that most surgeons are male.
Said one of them wryly, "No ovary is good enough to leave
in, and no testicle is bad enough to take out."[39]

Use and Abuse of Drugs

Medicine for women emphasizes birthing and birth control, and good services are difficult to find for menopausal
or post-menopausal women.[40] Rather than receiving indi-
vidualized care, older women are stereotyped as silly, self-
indulgent, and superstitious.[41]

When a woman enters a doctor's office, she is twice as
likely as a man to receive a prescription for a mood-altering
drug. (These drugs are called "psychotropics.") For medical
professionals think that women have weak central nervous
systems or are psychologically inadequate, and tranquilizers will make up for this defect.[42]

Dr. Linda Fidell, the author of a 1975 California drug-
use study, pointed out that North American men are encouraged to be stoical, to endure hardship rather than to
ask for help immediately. Our culture encourages women
to express emotion, to admit their pain, and to ask for help.
When confronted with a woman who describes vague symptoms at length, the doctor, who has been programmed to
believe that women's ailments are often psychosomatic, may
consider her problem an emotional one rather than a physical one. So, Dr. Fidell concludes, the doctor prescribes tranquilizers.

Drug advertisements also tend to foster these sexist assumptions. A five-year study of advertising in medical journals concluded that the ads tell physicians that men have
"real illness," women have mental problems.[43]

In a famous survey, mental-health clinicians were asked

to describe a healthy, mature, socially adjusted, competent man, woman, and adult. Regardless of the sex of the clinician, traits of a healthy adult were less likely to be attributed to a woman than to a man. The clinicians' concept of healthy, mature men did not differ significantly from their concept of healthy, mature adults; but their concept of healthy, mature women differed significantly from those of healthy, mature men and adults. The clinicians, irrespective of their sex, believed that healthy women were "more submissive, less independent, less adventurous, more easily influenced, less competitive, less aggressive, more excitable in minor crises, less objective, more easily hurt, more emotional, more conceited about appearance, and less interested in math and science." The analysis of a healthy woman, the survey concludes, is a powerful negative assessment of women. If a man and a woman present the same set of symptoms, the man is less likely to be dismissed with a prescription for a tranquilizer.[44] Clinicians programmed to expect women to have psychosomatic afflictions are likely to overlook women's serious illnesses.

As early as 1971, the high use of psychotropic drugs among women began to surface. Yet there has been little response from the medical profession. Doctors are reluctant to refer women patients to agencies outside the health-care system, although much of the anxiety and many of the genuine emotional problems that women experience are associated with marital, housing, and financial difficulties. Doctors do not allow women to express their fears and anxieties; instead, they prescribe drugs that diminish anxiety for short periods of time.

Moreover, a prolonged, high-dosage use of psychotropic drugs often leads to addiction, and doctors are given very little training in pharmacology or the problems of addiction. In a 1976 article in the Canadian Medical Association *Journal*, Dr. Eugene Vayda observed that "physicians need continuing training in clinical pharmacology . . . including teaching the properties of individual drugs and an understanding of the measures used to determine therapeutic effectiveness."[45]

Canadian research has also found that women and the elderly are more likely to be prescribed tranquilizers than are other population groups. One Canadian study found that, when asked what drugs they had taken in the past two weeks, about 20 per cent of the women questioned replied that they used psychotropic drugs, mostly tranquilizers. At any time, one in five Canadian women is ingesting mood-altering drugs.[46]

For many years, the drug industry has aggressively promoted psychotropic drugs for women. The drug industry's profits have exceeded those of all other manufacturing industries. The markup on the tranquilizer Valium, for example, is astounding. When stamped into pills, Valium sells for one hundred forty times its manufacturing cost. The manufacturer of Valium, Hoffmann-La Roche, spent two hundred million dollars during a ten-year period to promote the drug, and commissioned some two hundred doctors each year to produce scientific articles about its properties.[47]

Sylvia is forty-eight years old. She is happily married and has been working successfully as a real-estate agent for ten years.

During the past two years, my life has been one long round of doctors. I have been treated like a neurotic, crazy lady. I had a whole range of physical symptoms, but no one seemed to take them seriously after they asked my age. The first doctor I visited looked bored; his eyes actually glazed over as I spoke. When I finished telling him of my headaches, loss of appetite, insomnia, and irritability, he yawned, stretched, and in a condescending manner said, "What do you expect at your time of life?" He prescribed tranquilizers, which he told me would make me less of a misery to myself and my family. I ran out of his office in tears, wondering if perhaps he was right and I was just another middle-aged, depressed woman.

I am lucky. My family is very supportive and insisted that I consult another doctor. This time my husband accompanied me, because he wasn't feeling well either. I was astonished at the treatment he received. He was given a battery of tests, and when they proved negative, the doctor asked him to come in regularly so that he could observe any changes. Under the care of the same doctor, I was given no tests, but told that I needed tranquilizers for my nerves. After this particular visit, my husband joked that perhaps the doctor thought he was more important than I was.

I ended up taking tranquilizers for two years. They took the edge off my feelings of anxiety and irritability, but they did nothing for the rest of my problems.

At times I tried to stop the pills, but I found myself going into a panic — feeling edgy and desperate. As time went on, I needed larger and larger doses to achieve the same effect. The doctor asked no questions; he just upped my prescription and sent me on my way.

After two years, my whole life began to revolve around my tranquilizers. I could not get through a day without them.

I still had headaches and insomnia and I was underweight. My husband and my children noticed that I was becoming withdrawn and vague. They all encouraged me to see another doctor. My son quite openly kidded me about being a drug addict: "Mom can't get going without her hit of Valium."

Finally I acknowledged that it wasn't a joke. I was addicted to Valium and I needed help. I made very careful inquiries and found a female gynecologist who has a good reputation for being very thorough in her examinations. She was about forty, with three children of her own. She was also the first doctor who took me seriously and showed an interest in my symptoms. She took many tests, very carefully examined me, and asked detailed questions. It was a great relief to be treated as a human being. And as it turned out, I am apparently a borderline diabetic. Without treatment, my condition could have become much worse and seriously threatened my health.

It was very hard for me to stop the Valium, as my new doctor urged me to do. It took me six months in a self-help group of women similarly addicted.

Sylvia's addiction to tranquilizers is partly due to doctors' attitudes toward middle-aged women. Without even a cursory examination, she was diagnosed as neurotic and menopausal. This off-hand approach to women's health severely hampers and often precludes effective treatment.

Little addiction research has been done to learn about women's use and abuse of drugs. The literature that does exist "abounds with myths, sexism, patriarchal notions, and double standards."[48]

As we move beyond middle age into our later years, the probability of being prescribed a psychotropic drug increases. In 1976, 44 per cent of sedatives prescribed by Canadian doctors in private practice were for patients older than fifty-five.

Many health professionals do not look for the causes of our anxiety and depression; instead, they sedate us. Unfortunately, very few doctors are trained in geriatrics; most tend to view the old as incurable, and they show a lack of concern and respect for old patients. The real problems — boredom, loneliness, fear, poverty, and malnutrition — tend to be ignored.[49] Sandra is a nursing practitioner who worked with older women for twelve years, both in nursing homes and in private practice.

It is my experience that older women, especially those older than sixty-five, do not receive medical treatment that takes into account the risks they face as they age. Most of the doctors I have come in contact with view older women as neurotic and troublesome. You must remember that to be a good patient you must show evidence of getting well. Unfortunately, older women have complex ailments that take time and patience. I have seen many older women diagnosed as senile and locked up in nursing homes when, in fact, they are suffering from some form of physical degeneration such as a brain tumor.

The problem is further complicated by the socialization of older women. Most were taught to believe that doctors are gods and have all the answers. Even if they are worried that they are receiving inadequate or indifferent treatment, they rarely complain.

The older women who end up in clinics suffer particular indignities. They can't afford to pay a specialist, so they are forced to agree to have students practise on them. The whole exercise can be humiliating and degrading to the women. I have seen women older than sixty-five stripped to the waist while young male medical students gather round to gawk and peer and poke at them.

Unfortunately, I don't see anything changing. Doctors receive incredibly poor training in geriatrics, and most avoid the area like the plague. I once worked in a nursing home where patients with minor ailments were sent to the hospital because doctors refused to come to the nursing home to provide treatment. It was my impression that they found the patients, particularly the older women, a nuisance not worthy of their attention.

Anne was a geriatric nurse for twenty-five years. When she turned forty-five, she left the nursing profession to take her doctorate in history. That was ten years ago. Today she is an associate professor at a large university.

Toward the end of my nursing career, I was head nurse on the geriatric ward of a chronic-care hospital. We had several hundred patients, 70 per cent of them were women. Before there was medicare for the elderly, my patients received very little attention from doctors. I guess there was very little money to be made from attending to the needs of older women. But when medicare came in and doctors were permitted to bill for various procedures, women who had been ignored for as long as twenty years were suddenly fascinating patients. The doctors performed painful and often unnecessary procedures. Older women in institutions are sitting ducks for a whole range of potentially dangerous medications and procedures.

I have the distinct impression that older women use confusion as a defense mechanism and as a mild form of rebellion. It is not hard to understand, when so many of them have lost everything: their homes, their families, their incomes, and, most of all, their dignity and self-respect. What they are saying is, "You, the institution, are defining my reality, a reality that I don't accept."

Three quarters of the women under my care were designated confused or difficult by the doctors, who prescribed large doses of tranquilizers. Once they are zonked with drugs, they totally lose their dignity and seem to forget the reason for their original rebellion.

Every year, final-year medical students received two hours of instruction in geriatrics – from a nurse, not a medical professor. It demonstrated how contemptible the medical profession felt the area was. There is no other area in medicine that is taught by a nurse.

I was also very concerned by the amazing deficiency in treatment and research in geriatrics. Most older women who require frequent medical care are on fixed incomes. Doctors make most of their money on consultations and surgery, not by providing aid, comfort, and chronic-care treatment. Younger women in their child-bearing years are the real money-makers for doctors. Older women are literally not worth the time.

Post-menopausal women, especially those sixty-five and older, are particularly likely to be labeled confused or even senile as a direct result of overmedication or prolonged use of medication. Drugs frequently precipitate episodes of acute agitation or depression and generalized disorientation. The iatrogenic, or drug-induced, diseases that may be caused by health practitioners are alarming and their number is extensive. Medical research is just beginning to accumulate data on the effect of one drug on another, and the field of insidious drug toxicity or poisoning is largely uncharted.[50]

Older women, who often suffer from a number of chronic ailments, are the recipients of a bewildering variety of drugs. An estimated one in ten hospital admissions for older people are related to adverse drug reactions. Older women in chronic-care hospitals or nursing homes are the prime candidates for drug abuse. The "spaced-out" grandmother, oblivious to her surroundings, lost in a medicated fog, is surprisingly common in an institutional setting. Studies exploring what happens when medication is stopped show that "the patient is rarely worse and may be much improved."

Because gerontology is a field in which there is opportunity for drug research, older people may unwittingly become the subjects of medical experimentation. This experimentation can expose patients to the risk of serious drug reactions and might lead to unnecessary hospitalization. Obviously, patients should be protected from drug abuse and human experimental research. But many older women participate in medical studies without understanding the nature of the experiments or the risks involved. They are incapable of giving genuine informed consent.[51]

Nutrition and Older Women

Mabel is seventy-seven. She lives alone on her government pension.

> The thing I skimp on is food. Once I am through paying the rent and my utility and phone bills, there is very little left.
>
> I was once considered a gourmet cook. With a family of six you learn all about good nutrition. At that time my husband was alive and making a good living. But when he died, ten years ago, there was no money left. He died of a rare blood disease, and we spent all our savings on doctors. We traveled all over – to clinics in Europe, to Latin American hospitals – looking for a cure that would save his life. My husband had been self-employed as a plumber, so there was no widow's pension.
>
> I don't want you to think that I regret anything, but now I find my life very difficult. I try to economize on food, which means that I eat a lot of starch – canned beans, spaghetti, bread, and so on. You wouldn't believe it, but I used to be quite slim. In the last ten years I've gained twenty pounds. I don't have much pep any more and my blood pressure is too high.
>
> I admit, too, that when I get depressed I eat too many cookies. It is the only treat I can afford. The lean meat, fresh fruit, and vegetables the doctor keeps tell-

ing me to eat would be much better for me. I know that, but the price of these foods is too high.

I am too embarrassed to tell the doctor that I really can't afford his sensible diet. He tells me he has a lot of trouble with his "old ladies," that we all eat way too much starch. He probably just assumes we are weak-willed, self-indulgent, silly old women, with money socked away under our mattresses. That *is* what people think, isn't it?

One of the most serious health problems older women face is poor nutrition, which makes one susceptible to physical and mental deterioration. The main cause of poor nutrition is poverty. Two thirds of all women older than sixty-five are not able to eat nutritious, well-balanced meals because their incomes are well below the poverty line. Even women with adequate incomes often eat poorly because of their "isolation, purposelessness, and a damaged self-image."[52]

Many older women replace milk with tea, and whole-grain cereal and eggs with bread; pastries are substituted for fruits and vegetables; and candies and other sweets are fillers. This diet, which is too high in cholesterol and other fats, sugar, and refined grains, leads to tooth decay, arteriosclerosis, obesity, diabetes, and heart disease.[53]

A woman attains her maximum weight between the ages of fifty-five and sixty-four. Women who are obese tend not to lose weight until they are in their late sixties and seventies. Twenty per cent of women aged eighty or more are overweight.

The subclinical form of malnutrition that so many older women suffer from may lead to depression, confusion, and disorientation. There are no reliable figures on the numbers of undernourished older women who have been diagnosed as senile, but it is believed that the percentage is quite high.

What we do know is that diet is related to the age at which women die. Those whose diets are rich in ascorbic acid (citrus fruits, vitamin C), low in fat, and high in protein live longer. Unfortunately, few older women eat well enough to enjoy even moderate emotional and physical health.[54]

The Misdiagnosed Older Woman and Alcohol

Middle-aged and older women are becoming increasingly cross-addicted to alcohol and mood-altering drugs. Cross-addiction is synergistic, which means that the same amounts of, say, alcohol and Valium have a greater effect taken together than they would have when taken separately. Doctors are aware that the prognosis for alcoholism is poor, so they often avoid dealing with the problem. They are not taught much about alcoholism; nor do they usually ask their female patients about their rate of alcohol consumption. Many women will not talk about their drinking because society is particularly shocked by female alcoholics. But women who tell their doctors do not fare much better: many doctors prescribe tranquilizers to reduce tension, in the belief that alcohol consumption will diminish with the anxiety. Instead, the drugs also become addictive. When tranquilizers do not cut down alcohol intake, women are often sent to psychiatrists who frequently prescribe even more powerful psychotropic drugs.[55]

Alcoholism is routinely misdiagnosed in younger and middle-aged women, so it is not surprising that few doctors know when women older than sixty-five are alcoholics. Moreover, most women over sixty-five were brought up in an era when alcohol was associated with sin and evil, so the problem remains a family secret.

Older alcoholics have not been studied extensively. The few existing studies, conducted by individual social agencies and institutions, suggest that alcoholism among the old is more prevalent than is indicated by nationwide surveys.[56]

A 1976 Ottawa study demonstrated that older drinkers differ from younger drinkers. Alcohol abuse in the old is often mistaken for senility or chronic brain malfunction.

It is difficult to determine the extent of the problem because many treatment centers have an unofficial policy of not treating alcoholics older than sixty-five. The centers are designed to rehabilitate alcoholics, and old people are an extremely low priority.

Dr. Sarah Saunders, a medical consultant at the Addiction Research Foundation in Toronto, developed the only treatment center for the old in Canada in 1974. The center is located at Toronto's Castleview-Wychwood Home for the Aged. Dr. Saunders believes that elderly alcoholics are generally neglected or simply go undetected.[57]

When it becomes obvious that an older woman is an alcoholic, Saunders points out that often the woman's relationship with her family is severed. The woman becomes isolated, and her physical health begins to deteriorate. Nor is it uncommon for the alcoholic older woman to suffer from malnutrition.

Alcoholism often starts because of the despair and loneliness to which older women are susceptible. It is conservatively estimated that between 8 and 10 per cent of women older than sixty have alcohol-related problems. These women are essentially invisible; unlike older male alcoholics, they are rarely seen on the streets. The women and their families are embarrassed by alcoholism, and try to hide it. They rarely seek medical or psychological treatment. Alcohol adversely affects every part of the body, especially as one grows older. As a consequence, the life expectancy of an older female alcoholic is considerably lowered.[58]

Doctors treat women patients with an arsenal of psychotropic drugs and carcinogenic hormone injections; they recommend questionable or unnecessary surgery. And women who *are* in need of medical help run the risk of being misdiagnosed or neglected.

Many women are intimidated by doctors and find it difficult to question or challenge treatment. But a distinct minority is approaching doctors with a healthy skepticism. Fortunately, the field of women's health has attracted an outspoken, informed, and critical consumer lobby, especially within the women's movement.

For more than a decade, women's health advocates have been researching and writing, trying to expose the most flagrant medical abusers. However, their efforts to publicize their findings have met with only limited success. For example, despite all that has been written about the dangers of estrogen, it is still prescribed, and millions of women continue to take it. Health advocates have challenged the combined power and authority of the medical profession, the drug industry, and, in the United States, at least, the private-hospital lobby. These groups work as much for their own financial self-interest as for their patients.

But as we learn more about the dangers of drugs and surgery, and as more women take greater control over their bodies and health, the demand for powerful drugs and dangerous surgery will diminish. For the present, our only defense is to approach doctors and medicine with extreme caution.

3

Living at the Edge:
Older Women and Housing

Warehouses of Death

Each year at least thirty-five thousand men and women, aged sixty-five and older, run away.[1] This figure was compiled by the Travellers Aid Association of America and represents only those older runaways who sought the association's assistance. The real number of older runaways, which would include those who become street people and those whose disappearance never shows up in official records, is considerably higher.

At eighty-one, Emmie broke her hip while in the hospital recovering from a cataract operation. Three years later, after being shunted from one institution to another, she packed her few belongings, found a cab, and returned to the home she had lived in before her operation.

What I hated most about the nursing home was the lack of privacy, the lack of dignity. A typical day at the home would begin with breakfast on a tray. It was brought by very nice young women who unfortunately could not speak English. Perhaps this is petty, but it is enormously lonely to begin the day in silence. I would have my breakfast and then I would start waiting, waiting for someone to bring me water for a sponge bath. Often I waited until eleven o'clock. The staff couldn't help it; I understand that. They were so few and we were so many. But things were so bad that I wore the same nightdress for up to three weeks.

It was almost impossible to keep yourself clean. There was one nursing assistant for seventy-five patients between midnight and seven in the morning. Three or four people wet themselves every night and this poor woman would dash about trying to change all the bedding. It was a bit much for one woman alone.

What I realized very quickly was that the home is a place where people go to die. Everyone around you is old. Aside from the staff, you rarely see a young person. It's all very depressing. All day long people watch TV or sit and stare into space.

Even eating became an awful ritual. The first time I was able to go to the dining room, I was horrified. People were shoveling in their food, eating in total silence. I asked a nurse why no one talked. She asked me why I didn't take the initiative and start talking to one of the other residents. So I started. I turned to the woman next to me and asked what I thought was an inoffensive question, "Have you any grandchildren?" "Forty-one," she hissed. I thought she misunderstood me, so I repeated, "Have you any grandchildren?" She almost shouted, "Yes, forty-one grandchildren and eleven children and not one of them has a bed for me." I was so upset by her anger and bitterness that I never went back to the dining room.

I realized that unless I escaped I would go mad. And so I approached the head nurse and asked her what I had to do to qualify to leave the home. She told me that I must demonstrate that I could care for myself on my own — wash, dress, make a simple meal, and so on. Well, I was able to do all those things and more. I pointed this out to her and demonstrated. When I had done what was required, I said, "Now can I go home?"

She just looked at me with a wooden stare. She would not commit herself to a yes or a no. Afterwards I found out that she had a load of paperwork because I walked out. I suspect that her paperwork meant a great deal more to her than my potential freedom.

That was two years. Today, age eighty-six, Emmie leads a full and satisfying life. She works part-time at the library, exercises at the local Y to keep fit, follows a special diet for diabetes, and she is involved in an amazing number of local activities, from conferences on rape to volunteer work at nursing homes.

Not so many years back I could paint my own home. Now I need help and I have found it. I have a visiting homemaker who comes several times a week to mop my floors, water my plants, wash the dishes and clothes – the tasks that I no longer have the strength to do. I guess my house could be more spiffy, but I'm comfortable with my books and magazines.

I am luckier than most – I have my own home. Older women cannot afford the frightful rents they must pay. If it wasn't for my husband's pension I would be in the same position. Mind you, when my husband died I was only entitled to half the benefits and a veteran's pension that only amounted to a couple of thousand dollars. I was very insulted. After all, they had this money all those years and they had the nerve to dole it out in dribs and drabs.

Still, even with my own home and two pensions, I live very modestly. I can't travel often and I don't have many clothes. But imagine women who live on government pensions – they must struggle terribly. It's no wonder they end up in nursing homes. It's society's way of getting rid of us, tucking us away. I may not have much longer, but I am determined to live here in my own home, in my own way. Nothing short of force could induce me to go back to the nursing home.

Emmie sums up the entire problem. Where older women live is determined by their economic status. Most older women have been homemakers, have raised their children, and have helped their husbands. They were financially and emotionally dependent in their younger years; that same dependence characterizes their old age. With limited financial means, many old women find themselves unable to maintain their homes or pay the rent on an apartment. Subsidized senior-citizen apartments are limited and often poorly located. Rooming houses often have dubious safety standards and can be in squalid condition.

When a woman's health fails, her options are even more

limited. The vast majority end up in chronic-care hospitals or nursing homes. Studies have shown that as many as 40 per cent of older persons (most of whom are women) now in nursing homes do not need to be there on a permanent basis, but there are no alternatives available.[2] It is predicted that one quarter of all persons older than seventy-five (again the majority are women) will be in either chronic-care hospitals or nursing homes before they die.[3]

Jean is a sixty-four-year-old widow who found herself institutionalized. Ten years ago she started to go blind. About two years ago she lost her vision completely.

I initially lost interest in living. My formerly active social and cultural life was almost totally impossible. My greatest fear was the stove — I imagined I might set my hair or clothes on fire. Although I tried to manage with visiting homemakers and volunteers, I found they were not reliable. The visiting homemakers were nice enough, but they never worked after four o'clock and they were not available on weekends. Meals on wheels only came twice a week with hot meals. None of these programs is really adequate for a handicapped woman like myself. I was becoming an enormous burden to my family and my friends. My only alternative was institutional care, a home for the aged blind.

I'm here in this tiny, abysmal room — I know it's abysmal even though I can't see it. I feel like a horse in a corral; I'm ready to kick out the fence. I hate institutional life — the regulations, the public washroom, and the lack of privacy. The institution does not allow the "inmates" to bring in their own furniture. The nurses just walk right in; they never knock. Meal times are the worst. When I first came they allowed you ten minutes to eat a meal. All around me the waitresses were slamming down plates, urging everyone to hurry up and get done, so they could wash the dishes.

I'm afraid that the older women here are like little dogs crouched in a corner, afraid they will get kicked. Most of them were born blind and have lived in institutions most of their lives. They are browbeaten women who have had their spirits broken. They live in terror of the matron, who is quite a tyrant. I guess this sounds like something out of Charles Dickens.

Perhaps because of this pervasive sense of hope-lessness, the institution focuses on sports and crafts to fill in time. There is nothing here for the mind. I have complained continuously about this, but have gotten nowhere. I would like to try for a Bachelor of Arts degree, but I don't trust volunteer readers to keep their commitment to me. My experience with volun-teers is that they tend to let you down. They can cause a lot of heartache to shut-ins who are pathetically de-pendent on their goodwill.

I don't belong here, but I have no place else to go. I want a more meaningful life. Sometimes when I wake in the morning, I can't think of a single reason to get out of bed. I come back from breakfast and realize I have nothing to do; I have no challenge in my life.

As an "inmate" I have very little say in how this institution is run. Ideally, I would like to live on my own or with a roommate, but I don't leave, because I'm afraid I'll get stranded. What I need is reliable, guar-anteed help, someone to cook my meals. The other chores I can do on my own. I would become active in the community again, have friends in for a meal or tea, go to school, come to life again.

Emmie is more than twenty years older than Jean, but in our society both are deemed old women whose appropriate homes are institutions. Both think institutional life is regi-mented, distasteful, and grim. Neither of these women could be classified as financially destitute or mentally impaired. They found themselves institutionalized because of phys-ical limitations. Emmie at eighty-six has managed to create a life on her own; Jean at sixty-four is still confined to the home for the aged blind.

Admittedly, institutional life varies. I have visited homes for the rich that resemble expensive hotels or country clubs. At the other end of the scale are the public and private nursing homes, where four women share one room that is furnished with only iron beds, chrome and plastic dressers, and hard-backed chairs. But both rich and poor suffer from an erosion of autonomy and self-direction. Institutions reduce residents to total powerlessness. For most women, institutional care is a last resort. Even if they find themselves miserable in the institutional setting, there may be no place else to go. Once a woman signs the "permission-to-treat" form, she may find herself institutionalized for years, or until she dies.

Life becomes regimented. There are no self-administered medications: some institutions allow no alcohol or cigarettes and certain foods may be prohibited. A woman cannot choose for herself when to get up, when to go to sleep, when to eat, or what to eat. Her personal possessions, individual clothing, and furniture may not be allowed. And there is an overwhelming sense of dependency, depersonalization, and low self-esteem. These deprivations are often further compounded by a lack of freedom, crowded conditions, and the sense of being regarded as a desexed infant.[4]

Studies that evaluate what residents do in institutional settings yield these statistics: "55 per cent of their waking time is spent doing nothing; 20 per cent of their time is occupied with bathing, dressing or grooming; another 20 per cent of their time is taken up watching TV or socializing; but only 2.1 per cent of their time actually involves any medical or nursing activity of any kind."[5]

Canada has one of the highest rates of institutionalization in western society: 8.4 per cent of the population sixty-five and older are in some form of institutional care, as compared with 5.1 per cent in Great Britain and 6.3 per cent in the United States.[6]

The Burden of Guilt

Older women's daughters often find themselves responsible for their mothers' welfare. It is assumed in our society that daughters, rather than sons, will care for an aging mother; it is a natural extension of a woman's role as a nurturer.

Tensions and misunderstandings can destroy the possibility of dignified living for mother or daughter. If mother and daughter have separate living quarters, if each respects the other's privacy, if each enriches rather than diminishes the quality of the other's life, this arrangement can and does work, but only as long as the mother's health allows her to be independent.

Marie was thirty-five, married, with two children younger than ten, when her divorced mother had a serious heart attack.

I felt very confused and full of guilt. My mother had divorced my father when I was two, and she had worked hard to put me through school. I felt I owed her a great deal, but I knew that my husband would not like the idea of my mother coming to live with us. I admit my mother is a very strong-willed and difficult person; she likes her own way and is not very considerate of other people's wishes. She had a hard life and struggled to make a living, but in the end she was a success as a designer of women's clothing.

I finally convinced my husband that if my mother came to live with us it would alter our lives, but not too drastically. Our house is of average size — there's enough room for our family — so we placed the children together in one room and gave my mother the room next to the bathroom.

Before my mother moved in, my husband and I had a serious discussion with her about how we would live together, and about respecting one another's privacy. We even asked a social worker to sit in on our discussion so that issues that we might miss could be brought to our attention. We thought we had come to an understanding.

I don't know exactly what went wrong. Maybe it is impossible for people to live together in a house meant for one family. My mother seemed to think that I was there to do her bidding. She had me running morning, noon, and night. I understood that she was ill, and I made allowances; but it became impossible. She began inviting all her old friends around; they came all day long and stayed for lunch and dinner. Often in the evening a new batch would appear. It was a madhouse, with dirty plates and glasses in her room and in the living room.

My husband became tense and irritable, especially

after supper, when he tried to read the newspaper in the living room. He felt that we had lost control of the house. He warned me that unless I could convince my mother to do her entertaining during the day, he would have to ask her to leave.

I was caught between my desire to see my mother's last days happy ones – doing what she wanted, enjoying herself with her friends – and my need for a family life, some privacy, some time alone with my husband. I adore my mother; I admire her courage and strength to continue to live fully. Part of me felt I owed her for her sacrifices, for being my mother and taking care of me when she must have felt burdened by a young child. She was very beautiful when she was my age and could have had an exciting social life. But she chose to spend most of her spare time with me, taking me to the circus and on little trips. I remembered all those things and kept asking myself why I couldn't do the same for her when she needs me.

I kept putting off confronting my mother about the chaos she had created in my home. I kept hoping things would settle down. But things just became worse. My husband finally told me that he would move out, unless my mother stopped having her friends over or found another place to live.

With that ultimatum I spoke to my mother. Her response was shock: she said she was terribly hurt. I tried to explain that some compromises were necessary, that perhaps her friends could come only in the afternoon, so that my family could be alone in the evenings. My mother insisted that she would find an apartment on her own, with some part-time help. She said the idea of being confined to her room in the evening was intolerable and humiliating.

In the end, my mother moved out. For a while she refused to speak to me. Now, my husband and she are very cool to each other, but the children have resumed their old affectionate way with her.

For the moment, she is managing, but I am over there almost every day. I worry that she may fall and hurt herself, but she insists that this arrangement suits her very well. I don't really know what I will do when her condition deteriorates and she needs constant care. She has told me that she will never enter a nursing home, that she will kill herself first.

Neither Marie nor her mother is the villain in this particular situation. The house they tried to share was too small and was never meant to accommodate two different lifestyles. The bad feelings and tensions that erupted are not a reflection of a lack of love or a lack of caring. But an older woman who wishes to enjoy what is left of her life and a young mother of two have different priorities. What evolved was a strained, unhappy household, husband and wife close to divorce, mother and daughter locked in conflict.

Some daughters of older women never attempt to live with their mothers. There are many reasons: limited space, unwilling husbands, dual careers as homemakers and working women, and the legitimate fears of being unable to provide physical and emotional comfort without totally altering their own lives.

Yet these daughters often find themselves in a different predicament. They spend half their lives managing their own homes and the other half visiting and caring for their mothers in nursing homes. This is not simply a way to assuage guilt because their mothers are not living with them. Daughters of older women often fear that their mothers are being mistreated by both doctors and nurses. Their constant vigil becomes a form of advocacy on behalf of their mothers — a frustrating, seemingly endless effort to ensure that their mothers are properly fed, clothed, and treated. Even if these basics are provided, the daughters often watch despairingly as their mothers totally withdraw into themselves, radiating the message that they have been dumped, abandoned, and rejected. The relationship between a mother and daughter who were formerly warm, loving, and intimate may deteriorate dramatically in an institutional environment. Both mother and daughter feel diminished and powerless.

Marian recalls her situation.

I was working full-time and both my children were

still at home. My mother lived around the corner in a very nice one-bedroom apartment. For years this arrangement worked. I helped her with the shopping, washing, and cleaning. She often complained of loneliness and boredom, but she seemed happy most of the time, baking, visiting with her grandchildren, having her friends over, knitting, and so on.

I admit I was disappointed with my two brothers. They visited occasionally and helped out financially, but they never were very involved in her day-to-day life. I was the only daughter, and they assumed that I would take over primary responsibility for my mother.

When my mother turned eighty her health began to fail. She became quite frail, and I was worried that she might fall and hurt herself. I realized that she needed more help than I could provide, so I arranged for a visiting homemaker and meals on wheels. It never worked out; sometimes they showed up, but sometimes they didn't even bother to let me know they were unavailable. With the rare exception, most of the people who came round were not very interested in sick, old women. I felt trapped, torn with guilt; I was in a state of constant anxiety. There was no room in my own home at the time, and my brothers refused to take my mother into theirs.

My mother must have sensed my concern because she inquired about placement in a nursing home. The social worker who was assigned to her persuaded her that she was too dependent on me and should spend an experimental six weeks in a nursing home. What the social worker didn't explain was that part of the experiment involved not seeing me, supposedly to break the dependency. My poor mother never understood; she was terribly hurt that I never visited. After the six weeks were over, my mother decided that her only option was permanent placement in the nursing home. The social worker, without my knowledge, went with my mother to the bank, emptied her account and safety-deposit box of her life savings, a little more than five thousand dollars, and turned over my mother and the money to the home.

Although my mother was frail, her general health was very good. She was bright and clear-minded, with full use of her faculties. I believe that she went into the home to avoid becoming a burden to her children. I suppose her room wasn't bad. It was utilitarian, clean, sparse and hospital-like, with an iron bed, a built-in dresser, a cupboard with a key, and a private toilet.

My first sense that all was not well came when I arrived up the back steps, unnoticed, and heard a nurse yelling at my mother. On another visit I noticed that she had started to stagger, and she seemed drowsy all the time.

They moved her to the special-care floor, where she became noticeably more alert. When I asked the head nurse about her condition, she replied, "We don't over-drug them here like they do on the fifth floor."

My mother was sent back to the fifth floor, after a few weeks. The whole atmosphere was depressing. None of the women talked much; they all seemed to be waiting — waiting for their children to visit, or perhaps waiting to die. Eventually my mother turned almost totally inward. She tearfully explained that *they* had robbed her of her dignity. She was not stupid, just old, yet *they* insisted on treating her like a baby or a mental incompetent.

To cheer my mother up, I would bring her bright clothing and special soap and cologne. Initially she was pleased, but before she could enjoy these gifts they disappeared. I suspect it was the staff, but I could never prove it. Gradually my mother lost interest in her appearance and wore old housedresses.

My life was one long battle with the bureaucracy. She developed an eye irritation that did not go away. The nurse ignored my requests for medical attention for more than six months. Finally I created a scene and threatened to go to the director unless a doctor was called. A doctor was quickly summoned. He cava-lierly informed me that my mother had cancer of the eye, but that we were lucky — it was still treatable.

My major bureaucratic battle was over the head nurse's decision to place my mother on the senile ward, known as "death row." I insisted that my mother's withdrawal was not senility but overmedication complicated by sadness and despair. In the end, I got her transferred to the special-care floor again.

Whenever I complained to the director of the home about my mother's treatment or lack of treatment, he threatened to discharge her. He knew that my mother needed regular nursing care, care that I could not provide. I kept searching for alternatives and looked into other homes, but each one seemed worse than the last. And I worried that my mother would not survive another move.

My mother died almost exactly six years after she entered the home. During her last two years, I quit my job and spent several hours every day at the home. Whenever I left my mother I felt like a traitor. She seemed so tiny, so helpless, so resigned, like a caged bird.

The process by which Marian's mother became a resident of a nursing home caused pain, dislocation, and unhappiness for both women. However, as Marian points out, there were no real alternatives.

To be advocate and protector for a parent in a nursing home is more the norm than the exception. It is rare that the responsibility for an aging mother or father is shared among all family members. The sole responsibility usually becomes that of the middle-aged daughter.

Judith's mother was in her late sixties when she suffered a stroke that resulted in brain damage.

My mother was a very active woman. In her thirties she was tragically widowed, left with four young children — myself and three younger brothers. She worked very hard in a factory to provide for us. I managed to finish high school and then went to work to help put my three brothers through university. Two became successful lawyers and the youngest is a well-known and respected gynecologist.

I married and my husband, a businessman, became very successful. I wanted to ensure that my mother lived a comfortable life. I was very grateful to her for the sacrifices she made for us when we were kids. Until her stroke, my mother lived alone in a beautiful apartment. She entertained, did volunteer work in the community, belonged to an exercise club, and participated in an amazing number of intellectual and cultural activities.

I realized that my mother needed special care. Most of the time she was perfectly well, but at times her brain damage caused her to become incontinent and unable to communicate. I spent several months investigating various facilities and ultimately decided on one my mother had worked in as a volunteer.

When I told my mother of the arrangements I had made, she looked stricken. Very quietly, she said, "Judith, I would never do this to you." Although I was very upset, I saw no other choice. Her safety was my primary concern.

Even though she had a private room (which cost seventeen hundred dollars a month) and was allowed to bring in all her personal belongings and furniture, she became acutely depressed. She had always been a very independent person, accustomed to doing things on her own. She felt stripped of her freedom, and she felt a pressure to be pleasant to both the staff and other residents.

What further depressed and angered her was that her belongings started to disappear. When I questioned the staff, they ignored me or accused my mother of misplacing things. But when half of her wardrobe and her fur coat disappeared, I knew the situation was serious. I complained to the director, but he refused to investigate the matter. He said he would not insult his staff by introducing spot checks as they left the building, that it would jeopardize the morale of the entire institution. His reaction puzzled me, but I let the matter drop rather than cause my mother embarrassment or bad feelings on the part of the staff.

To compensate for the loss of half of her wardrobe, I had a dressmaker come in to measure her for a new outfit. When it was finished I placed it on her bed while she was in the dining room. I left the room for a moment and when I returned everything had disappeared. I ran to the nursing station, explained what had happened, and requested that they help me find the clothes. They turned their backs and continued their conversation.

I guess all my pent-up frustration and anger exploded. I raised my voice, demanding attention. The head nurse suddenly appeared, and asked me why I was making a scene. I told her about the theft and insisted on a search. She tried to calm me down, but I yelled for everyone to hear, "I will call the police if one of you doesn't return the clothes."

The head nurse very quickly summoned a security guard and one of the doctors to restrain me. It was a nightmare. They tried to give me a hypodermic to knock me out, but I struggled free. I was crying. "I'm not sick or crazy, I'm angry. Don't touch me. Just give my mother back her clothes."

I was determined to see the director. He found endless excuses not to see me, but I persisted. Our meeting was very tense and unpleasant. I told him the details of the theft, but he countered that I should be grateful to the home for taking my mother in and providing her with the best possible medical care. I kept insisting that he deal with the theft of my mother's belongings.

By this time I had found out from a nurse who the thief was, and told the director. He abruptly terminated the meeting, but the very next day my mother's new outfit mysteriously reappeared in her closet.

Apparently, most of the nursing staff are aides, not registered nurses, and they earn the minimum wage. Many are single parents struggling to make ends meet. To them, old women like my mother have no need for beautiful clothing, jewelry, and furs. I can understand their resentment.

The bureaucracy chooses to ignore the high rate of theft, as if it's a perk of the job that compensates for low wages. When a resident or relative complains, the bureaucracy threatens to throw the resident out, knowing there is no place to go.

My mother is still in the home and I still try hard to protect her, but it would be much easier if my brothers would help. They can't accept that their once-vibrant, self-reliant mother is old and frail and in need of their affection and attention. They only come to see her on very special occasions. Their discomfort and embarrassment mortifies my mother. She makes superhuman efforts to please, hoping that her agreeable behavior will encourage them to come more often.

My brothers' callous attitude has ruined my relationship with them. Their financial contributions are not enough. I need moral support, I need their time and involvement. But in their view it is a daughter's duty, not a son's, to care for one's mother.

Judith's wealth and devotion cannot ensure that her mother's dignity is not eroded. Although her mother is ensconced in a private room in a luxurious nursing home, she endures a more polite variation of the indignities suffered by patients in a public nursing home. The real issue is that nursing homes are institutions that establish a total twenty-four hour dependency relationship. Resident older women are not able to direct their lives and rapidly deteriorate physically, mentally, and spiritually. They feel they have been dumped because they have outlived their usefulness. They become depressed and withdrawn. With limited and unsatisfactory alternatives, a daughter unwittingly compounds her mother's sense of lost dignity and autonomy by being obliged to assume a parental role.

Outside the Custodial Circle

Approximately 8 per cent of older women live in nursing homes or chronic-care hospitals. How are the other 92 per cent managing their lives? When studies specifically refer to older women, they focus primarily on women living in institutions. Thus, old age is generally equated with infirmity and infantilism. Institutions are a goldmine for researchers on aging. They limit the variables to be considered; they provide a homogeneous population; they separate the incapacitated, allowing the researchers to make generalizations about old age based on the behavior of few. As a result, we have biased models: we think of old women as frail, dependent, infantile, infirm, and mentally incompetent. This stereotyping often becomes a self-fulfilling prophecy.

Undoubtedly, greater attention should be paid to that 92 per cent who are not and may never be institutionalized. Their circumstances are far from ideal; they, too, experience poverty, isolation, understimulation, and rejection. But women who live on their own have a hope of ordering and directing their own lives. There is at least a possibility of retaining some dignity in the aging process.

Of all the older women I interviewed, Janine was the most fiercely and successfully independent. She is in her early nineties; she has outlived two husbands and two daughters, and has one sister, who is in her late eighties.

Janine has lived for more than forty-five years in a converted schoolhouse on a quiet street that has become part of the suburbs. She is half a mile from transportation and the shopping plaza, but finds the distance perfect for a walk in good weather.

I never expected to live this long. My health is quite good, but my hearing, sight, and strength are somewhat diminished. My housekeeping was never perfect, but I keep things tolerable. I do what I feel like: I clean a little, I make all my own meals, I garden, and I even hold regular dinner parties. Maybe I've lived this long because I'm curious and active. I still enter my flowers in horticultural contests, I sing with a choir, and I entertain quite a lot.

There has been considerable pressure on me by my family, my doctor, and even my minister to give up my house and move into a senior-citizens' apartment. But I would feel so boxed in. I understand that some are nice, but the ones I have visited are very tiny and dark. Besides I want to be with people of all ages, not tucked away with only older people.

I guess if I become very ill I will have no choice but to give up my house. At the moment, I'm managing very well. I have one special friend whom I've known for fifty-two years. It is difficult for us to visit, since she lives on the other side of the city, but we talk every day on the phone. It's our way of checking up on each other, making sure everything is all right. Women, especially as they age, can become very close and dear friends. One of my grandsons teases me about these daily phone calls, implying that we are silly old gossips. He is wrong. We were both teachers and we enjoy discussing politics, books, music, gardening, and the like.

I really feel angry about how the world views older women. All my life I've worked hard, struggled alongside my two husbands to make a living, and I've endured the sadness and pain of watching my loved ones die. At ninety you really are your own person, yet I know I am perceived as a little, frail, dotty, old lady. There is no use grumbling; it's not in my temperament. When you live this long, you learn to adapt. It's having my own home that keeps me alert. I'm a woman with property, and people respect that.

Janine defies the stereotype she describes. She exudes vitality. She has successfully integrated her life into a meaningful whole, adapting to and compensating for her altered and weakened sight and hearing. Unlike older women in institutions, she has control and direction over her life. She has built her own informal network of friends and contacts who provide reinforcement and assistance in the event of an accident or illness. She is acutely aware that her dignity and self-reliance are fragile and would be destroyed if she became incapacitated. "This house," she said, "is not very special to anyone but me. It's old and a bit run-down — much like myself — but as long as I am able to remain here, I can maintain a life of my own."

Many older women are engaged in a desperate battle to remain at least partially independent in the face of illnesses and dwindling resources. Often they must overcome familial, medical, and governmental opposition to retain even a modicum of independence. The rush to institutionalize older women at the first sign of deterioration, either physical or mental, is very compelling. Part of the problem lies with the paucity of home-care services and other forms of alternative support. Institutions often become a dumping ground for older women. Society's guilt is assuaged, since institutional care supposedly provides the basic necessities – food, board, and health care – and is better than the alternative: old women, alone, hungry, ill, and living in substandard housing. Both images are true in large part, but they do not consider the widely varying needs and capabilities of older women.

Edith's efforts to avoid spending her remaining years in a nursing home approach the heroic.

In my mid seventies – about ten years ago – I had a stroke. It weakened me, but I did not become a cripple. After spending six months in the hospital, where I was repeatedly urged to give up my apartment and enter a nursing home, I was released, considerably weakened. During my stay in the hospital I persuaded my only son to allow me to buy a house that I would share with his family. He was very enthusiastic, since his financial position made the possibility of buying a home extremely remote.

I guess I was naive, but I thought it could work if we found a house big enough to allow for privacy. The house we chose was beautiful, spacious, and ideally situated near transportation and shopping. Since my daughter-in-law worked, I managed the house, with some help, and took care of my eight-year-old granddaughter.

It just didn't work, although I tried very hard. My daughter-in-law resented my presence. I felt like an unwelcome intruder, and finally, after three months, I could not stand the tension.

Rather than prolong the unpleasantness, I found a room in a house owned by a man about my age. He lived there with his bachelor son. It worked out very well; they were both good company and very kind and considerate. For four years I lived there, happy and comfortable. We became very close, sharing meals and often entertaining jointly. I felt closer to my landlords than to my own family. They treated me as a capable, intelligent woman.

Unfortunately, after four years my health went downhill, and I needed some help on a regular basis. It became too difficult to cook and shop. I was terrified that I would have no choice but a nursing home. My son, my doctor, and a social worker all urged me to accept that I was incapable of living outside an institution. I had almost capitulated when a friend told me of a day-care center that had a reputation for helping people to live on their own by providing daily lunches and dinners, physical therapy, and other medical services.

I put an ad in the paper for a roommate with similar needs to share an apartment near the center. And I found one – a woman about my age with almost identical medical problems. We found a two-bedroom apartment a few blocks away from the center, but discovered that we were both too weak to walk the distance. Fortunately, the center had a little bus, which picked us up in the morning and took us home after the evening meal, or later if we wanted to participate in an event or activity. We were happy with the arrangement – we had both privacy and the help we needed.

Two years later, I had another stroke. I was left with some paralysis on my left side, but I can talk, walk, and do most things myself. However, the day-care arrangement wasn't adequate. I had anticipated that my health would decline further, so I investigated the apartment building adjacent to the day-care center. It provides meals and access to medical staff in emergencies. This facility is unique. Every resident has a bachelor suite, with a galley kitchen, a full bathroom, and a large room with space for a table and chairs, couch, bed, and dresser. It's all very clean, modern, and functional. There is a cleaning staff who keep the apartments spotless.

I've been here for three years now. It's a home until the end, God willing. I have made many friends, especially one woman who has welcomed me into her family. We are very close. If one of us is feeling poorly, the other brings food and books, and alerts the staff.

I can live a reasonable life here. I close the door and I have privacy. Friends can visit and I can offer hospitality — tea, cake, a piece of fruit, even a meal when I am in the mood. Oh, the furniture is plastic and not my taste, but my family sold all my things during my last stroke. They assumed that I was heading for the nursing home. What can you expect? They see me as a very old lady in need of constant care. I'm not an invalid. I need help, I admit, but I don't need to be suffocated by a nursing home. As long as I draw breath, I will live somehow on my own.

Edith was a prime candidate for a nursing home ten years ago, when she suffered her first stroke. With little encouragement or assistance, she found alternative living arrangements to suit each stage of her aging process. She is unique in that she was far-sighted enough to investigate and to plan for her changing needs. Her desire to remain independent was so intense that it empowered her to withstand the pressure to capitulate to institutional care.

Edith's case raises fundamental questions. Why are there so few alternatives and why are they so difficult to find? They should be readily available, not hidden, to be discovered by only the most tenacious and strong-willed. Edith is one of a very small assertive minority. Most older women, often with less serious disabilities, find themselves in nursing homes, either because they are unaware of the alternatives or because there are no alternatives in their communities.

The Final Option: Older Women and Rooming Houses

They are called by many names: rest homes, retirement lodges, lodging homes, and boarding houses; I call them rooming houses. There are a small number of excellent rooming houses offering reasonable food, medical care, laundry, housekeeping services, private bedrooms, and private baths. But the quality of housing can more often be compared to nineteenth-century slums — dark, grim, overcrowded firetraps. To create a clean, warm, and cheerful environment, rooming-house owners must be both caring and responsible. Sadly, such owners are the exception.

For the reasonably healthy older woman living on a government pension, rooming houses are one of the few kinds of affordable housing. Older women put up with incredible squalor in buildings in substandard neighborhoods rather than move to subsidized housing in the suburbs, because the emotional pull of a neighborhood is so strong. Familiar people and places become increasingly important to older women as their own lives erode, and the women are prepared to pay exorbitant rents for shabby accommodation to remain where they have always lived, even if the neighborhood has become rundown and dangerous, even if the women are forced to scrimp on food and nutrition.[7]

May is eighty-three years old. She is hard of hearing and has poor eyesight. She has lived in a rooming house for the past five years. Her room is little larger than a closet; her one tiny window overlooks a parking lot.

I could not maintain my home; it was just too much money. I live in the same neighborbood I grew up in, married in, and now I guess I will die here. My health is not what it once was, but I am better off than most women my age.

As you can see, this is not much of a place. The toilet only works half the time, so I am forced to use a potty. I have trouble getting down to the first floor, where the toilet works somewhat better. I cook my meals on this little hotplate. I don't really need much more, since I just heat up beans and some tea most days. The fridge in the hall leaks and smells quite awful. I'm afraid that nothing would survive long in there. The one thing I can't bear is that the owner rarely cleans the halls. Sometimes you can't get down the steps – people just pile up garbage and old newspapers and magazines. In the winter, with all the snow and slush, the steps become dangerous. One old man broke a leg last winter when he slipped and fell down a full flight of steps. I guess he is lucky it was only his leg.

I don't know, I guess you just get used to a place. When I first came here, I had just turned seventy-seven and I was used to a much cleaner place. I'm too old to keep after the old men in the house to flush toilets, clean out the tub, and put out the garbage. I did that for my boys, but that was different.

I tried calling the health department when I first moved in here, about the bugs everywhere. The owner threatened to evict me if I ever did that again. It didn't matter anyways – no one from the health department did anything. I finally decided that I would just take a sponge bath in my room in this pot. I can't face the bugs or the dirty tub anymore, and I haven't the strength to clean the tub out.

I have this army cot, the chair, and this bridge table. I guess it serves my needs, but it isn't very cheerful. I've wandered around looking for other places, but most of them are the same. The ones that are a little cleaner and have better furniture are too expensive.

What I worry about is that I will fall or become very ill and no one will come. All the people in this house keep to themselves. They are all tired out and depressed by life. I just don't think anyone would come if I needed them.

Look at the older women around you. Two out of three are poverty-stricken. More than 8 per cent live in nursing homes or chronic-care hospitals, often because they cannot sustain their independence without support services such as housekeeping, medical care, and meals. (You might find that these support services are not available in your community, or they may be unreliable.) Most of these old women are residents of public facilities. The "lucky" ones are in private nursing homes or hospitals, where they must follow a bewildering number of rules and regulations that destroy their autonomy. In public and private institutions, residents are overmedicated, intimidated, and even physically abused. From the luxury-hotel environment of private homes and hospitals to the austere, crowded, barracklike atmosphere of public facilities, the goal is rarely to promote independence and dignified living, but rather to provide a waiting room for death. "There is no such thing as a civilized institution in which to be old."[8]

110

But to live without custodial care is often a desperate struggle to remain independent. Women might live in their own homes, in apartments, or in single rooms, but it is difficult for them to cope with failing health and inadequate pensions. Those who choose subsidized housing are usually uprooted from an old, familiar neighborhood; they trade their quality of life for cheaper rent.

The preoccupation with maintaining a semblance of a home drains older women — their poverty is a constant source of anxiety and humiliation — but it is often better than the alternative: institutionalization, which means the end of their independence, the destruction of their dignity, the wait for the end.

4

Violence Against Older Women

When I began my research it occurred to me that, as violence in the home and on the streets is such a serious problem for younger women, it must also be a problem for older women. About the same time, I was invited to participate in a conference on violence against women. I asked the organizers of the conference if they were planning to include a session on older women. They seemed puzzled by the suggestion, admitting that they knew nothing about the subject and had not designed the conference to include older women.

In the course of collecting my case studies, I began to notice a number of things: the older women living alone generally had more locks on their doors than did the rest of the population; most of the older women I interviewed expressed a fear of leaving their homes after dark; and they continually and repeatedly alluded to violence or fear of violence in institutions, among members of the family, and on the streets. Yet when I attempted to ask specific questions about their fears, I rarely received a satisfying response. These older women were ready and often eager to talk about housing, health, and income problems; they would discuss their sexual and emotional experiences; yet almost none would discuss violence. I sensed a deep-seated embarrassment about the fact that they found themselves victims or potential victims of such abuse and violence. As a result, I had great difficulty in finding case studies in this area more than any other.

I did a thorough review of the literature, including a library search and a computer search of the *New York Times*. These searches yielded very little information. In fact, the computer search produced only twelve articles that dealt specifically with abuse or violence against older women. I also wrote to a number of feminist publications, requesting information or assistance in locating relevant articles or studies. I received several short bibliographies, but few of the articles and books cited were helpful. A letter from *Aegis*, a magazine about violence against women, accurately assessed the literature: "Unfortunately, we have not published anything on this important subject and have no other suggested sources for you."[1]

I also interviewed professionals in the field of violence. Although they were aware of violence against older women, they admitted that the focus of their work was on younger women.

Most of the reports and studies focusing on older women were primarily impressionistic or were based on what is described as "extensive clinical experience." Very few studies presented conclusive data in case studies or survey results, and when they did, the samples were often depressingly small. I could only conclude that we have an appallingly small amount of research in an area that is in desperate need of inquiry.

I then tried to define and analyze the specific issues of concern to older women. Through talking with women, I was able to isolate and categorize four problems: familial abuse, institutional and social-services abuse, crime, and wife-battering.

Violence in the Family

When the subject of the abuse and neglect of older women by family members is raised, many women hark back to some mythical "good old days" when the old were respected and revered. However, the average life expectancy in the eighteenth century was only thirty-five years. By the turn of the twentieth century it had risen to fifty.[2] Many women died in childbirth or shortly after menopause. Today, for the first time in history, women have an average life expectancy of more than eighty years. This longevity has brought with it "a new social phenomenon, the care of aging parents."[3]

But, long before parents may require actual physical care, they often seek shelter and financial assistance, especially if they are widows or divorcées. Tensions and strains can develop if several generations are living together in crowded and inadequate housing. Such living arrangements tend to drag on, and tensions intensify. For older poor women, in particular, there may be few or no housing alternatives.

At fifty-seven, Rita emigrated to Canada to be with her only daughter. Both her daughter and son-in-law worked full-time, leaving her alone during the day to babysit three children younger than six years of age, to cook the family's dinner, and to clean the apartment. Rita spoke to me through an interpreter.

I was alone in my own country, widowed, without any living relatives. Life was hard for me and I thought that I could be useful in my daughter's home. She wrote me pleading letters, explaining that she and her husband had to work to support the family but that they couldn't find a good babysitter. When I came, I expected to help out with the children and some of the housework, but I never expected to become so trapped, so cut off from the world. I don't blame my daughter. She is totally under the control of her husband.

I came with just my belongings. I spent my savings on a plane ticket and some presents for my grandchildren. In the four and a half years that I lived in my daughter's home, I never received any money. I was totally dependent on the family, even for my clothing and necessities.

At first I was happy to be there, to be helping my daughter. I wanted to meet more people and have some time to myself, but I was prepared to do what I could to make life easier for my daughter and her family.

Serious problems began when my son-in-law had an accident at work. He was in bed for a few weeks and then insisted that he couldn't work any more because he had too much pain. He hung around the house all the time and he started to drink.

When my son-in-law was drunk he started to hit

me. At first he hit me only on the arms, but soon he began to beat me, hitting my face, my breasts, my stomach – all over. While he beat me he always swore in terrible language. Many times he locked me out and I had to wait until my daughter came home from work before I could get back into the house. I never talked back to him or really tried to defend myself. I hoped that if I stayed very quiet and uncomplaining, he would realize how terribly he was behaving.

He beat me for four years. It is hard to believe now, but it is true. Many times I had to go to the doctor because I was covered with welts and cuts, and I was afraid something was broken. Once I needed an operation on one of my breasts – he caused such an ugly lump. The doctors always accepted my stories: that I had fallen down, walked into a door or something.

My daughter tried to stop her husband, sometimes actually putting herself between us during his rages; but she was really powerless. He was her husband, the father of her children, and he never beat her. Just me and sometimes the eldest son.

I never told anyone about it. I was too embarrassed. My neighbors could hear what was going on, but they never said a word to me or to my daughter. But it became too much for me. I felt such anger inside; it kept growing until I could barely breathe.

After four years I told one of my women friends at the church. She told me to come to Angela here at the clinic. I didn't want to start trouble, I couldn't stand it any more. But I was afraid to leave. I had no money. And I was afraid that once I left the house he would beat the children. As long as I was there, I felt, maybe I could protect them.

One day, though, my sadness and anger were too much and Angela helped me move out when my son-in-law was away from the house. Now I stay with a friend. She is seventy-one, I am sixty-one; but we come from the same village. I have a room and my own kitchen.

Angela helped me get welfare. I am too sick and too depressed to work. Anyway, who would hire an old woman like me? I used to do farming in the old country — that is all I know. It was a big fight to get on welfare. They didn't believe me; they thought I made everything up. They kept telling me to go back to my daughter's, where I was useful and taken care of.

I am not happy, but at least I am not beaten any more. I miss my grandchildren and I worry about them all the time. My eldest grandson tells me his father beats him more now that I am gone. My daughter doesn't tell me what is happening at home. I'm afraid to visit her and I have never seen my son-in-law since I left.

My life is very lonely now. By talking to other women, I have found that my problem is not so unusual. Many of the women I know are thrown out by their children. Some of the older women become ill and can't do as much work in the house, so the children find them a burden.

I don't feel that I will live very long. I have lost my health and I don't have much reason to live any more. But I would like to see my grandchildren away from that place and out on their own. My daughter accepts everything, even the beating of her own children. She never complains and I think she will stay with my son-in-law. I hope he doesn't beat her, but I don't know.

Rita feels her life is over. Her dignity and self-esteem have been battered as badly as her body. Her experience, as she points out, is not uncommon among her contemporaries. Her shame and humiliation were echoed by the women who agreed to be interviewed.

Clare is seventy-six, fifteen years Rita's senior. Her fragile health and low energy frustrate and enrage her family. Unlike Rita, she is not physically able to provide services in return for her keep. Like many older battered women, she requires constant physical care.

When my husband died, I came to live with my son and his family. There was really very little choice, since I had too little money to keep my apartment and I was terribly lonely.

This is an awful thing to talk about, but I want

people to know that women like me can be treated cruelly simply because we are old and not useful any more.

I was seventy-four when I went to live with my son; my health was fairly good, but I didn't have the strength and energy to do very much. Once I was settled, it was made clear to me that I was to help out in the house. For about a year, this arrangement worked out quite well, although I now realize that there was a lot of tension. My daughter-in-law was polite in the beginning, but not very friendly. The children were teenagers, so they had their own lives and were not around very much.

I found it difficult to keep up with my son's and daughter-in-law's expectations after the first year, because my health began to go down: a touch of arthritis, lower-back problems, and maybe just old age. My son and his wife became annoyed when I dropped things or did things very slowly. They began to berate me for being clumsy and for taking so long to do ordinary tasks.

I felt humiliated. Every time I tried to explain that I was doing my best, my son exploded. He said he wasn't asking for much, considering how expensive it was to feed another mouth.

The more my son yelled, the more clumsy I became. The simplest things, like washing the dishes, were more than I could manage. I was nervous all the time and filled with anxiety. Part of me knew that I should leave, but I didn't know where to go.

All this lead to a heart attack, which put me in the hospital for about two months. Around the doctors, my son and his wife acted full of concern. The minute we were alone, he would tell me that the only solution was a nursing home. I cried and pleaded with him to let me come home, and I promised to work harder than ever. I was terrified that if he sent me to a nursing home that would be the end of me.

The doctor finally shamed my son into taking me home. He said that I was weak, but not so old and incapacitated that I needed a home.

The next few months were a nightmare. I was supposed to take it easy, but my son insisted that I get out of bed and get busy in the house. When I found myself tiring, he would shake me very hard and tell me that I was lazy. But all the drugs I was taking made me dizzy and sleepy all the time. I lived in constant fear of my son's rages. My daughter-in-law never physically abused me: she ignored me. She said I was a foolish, useless, old woman, and that she didn't have time to be bothered with me.

About four months ago, my son came home from work in a terrible mood. I hid in my room. He started yelling that he couldn't stand having me around any more, that I was ruining his life. I started to cry and shake, but this just infuriated him. He came running into my room and started to beat me and yank me around. I guess I lost consciousness, but when I came to I found I was covered with bruises and welts.

I was terrified, but I didn't know where to turn. I was too ashamed to call the police; I felt guilty that I made my son behave in such an outrageous way. In a way, I thought it was my fault: if I were stronger, or had a bit of money, I would never have ended up this way.

For the next couple of weeks, my son kept my door locked. He sent in one meal a day with his wife, who looked very concerned and frightened. My bruises finally healed and my son let me out of my room, but he warned me that my laziness and bad behavior would not be tolerated any more.

I guess, having hit me once, my son found it easy to slap me around after that. At the slightest thing, he would start to beat me. I would cry out and plead with him to stop. His wife sometimes tried to intervene, but he just pushed her aside. I began to wish I was dead. Even my grandchildren began to notice that I was always in my room and trying to hide my bruises.

That year, my son decided that I would not be allowed to join the family on Christmas day. He insisted that I remain in my room, and I am sure he did something with my medication because I spent the day in a haze.

By this time I felt and looked awful. My doctor couldn't understand why I wasn't responding to treatment and finally conceded that I should enter a nursing home. My son won, and here I am. No one ever thinks a child of hers will behave so badly. When I was younger and healthy, my son was always very kind and considerate to me, but after my husband died, it was as if I ceased to exist, except as a burden and a bother.

Court records, newspaper articles, and books make it clear that violence in the family is basically perceived as a problem experienced by younger women. The references to older women are rare. Admittedly, this is an extremely difficult area to research, because it threatens the sanctity of the family — just as the notion of child abuse did twenty years ago. But the abuse of older women in the family is even more difficult to identify than child abuse, since older women tend to be more isolated from the public. And people tend to ignore or simply not notice the comings and goings of older women. Even when medical and social-service professionals are confronted with abused and neglected older women, they usually do not recognize the problem, unless the evidence is unmistakeable and overwhelming.

The problem was first discussed in Britain, where medical professionals coined the terms "granny bashing," "granny battering," and "gran-slamming." Although geriatricians were aware of incidents of violence against older women, they had no sense of how large and pervasive the problem actually was.

In 1975, Dr. G.R. Burston, a geriatrician at the Southmead Hospital in Bristol, wrote to the British Medical Journal about the physical abuse of older women by their families:

> Hardly a week goes by without some reference in the national press or medical journals to baby-battering. We should realize that the elderly, at times, are deliberately battered. . . . In my own experience, I know of cases where it is possible to confirm that elderly

patients have been battered by relatives before admission to hospital and in which there has been no doubt that the battering was deliberate. In other cases, assault at home was suspected but could not be confirmed. I wonder how many who are supposed to have fallen down frequently are the victims of assault? I don't condone it – but I think this is just another manifestation of the inadequate care we as professionals give to elderly people and to their relatives who are left with the task of coping with them unaided and unsupported.[4]

The few tentative references in medical journals to abuse of older women were printed by the popular press, but the general response was incredulity. The public simply could not believe that the beating of helpless, vulnerable older women was a widespread and pervasive problem. The medical profession, with few exceptions, voiced the same disbelief. Doctors and other medical people did not even think about "granny-bashing," let alone ask questions of the victims. Older women who come into hospitals and clinics with broken bones, welts, cuts, and bruises are not generally asked questions about possible violence. It is assumed that old women – who are perceived as frail and unstable – fall and bruise easily.[5]

A major Canadian study was begun in 1979 in Manitoba by the Manitoba Association on Gerontology and the Manitoba Council on Aging. More than four hundred cases of abuses were reported by professionals who come in contact with older people. The study found that financial abuse headed the list, followed by psychosocial and physical abuse. The cases included: "cashing and withholding pensions and social insurance funds; theft of funds or property; verbal/emotional abuse; isolation and confinement; physical assault; rough handling; denial of food, personal care and medical care; overmedication, and gross neglect."

The study also found that two thirds of the victims were women who had lived with a family member for ten years or more. The women were most frequently between the ages of eighty and eighty-four. Unlike British and American research on abuse, which points to mid-life daughters as the most common abusers, the Manitoba study showed that 60 per cent of the abusers were males, usually sons.

No official or legal action was taken in three quarters of the documented cases. Ninety-nine per cent of the professionals interviewed had "no set directives" for coping with cases of abuse.[6]

In the United States, there is no accurate assessment of the number of older people who are beaten, abused, or exploited by their families. The few studies that have been attempted indicate that older women, not older men, are the principal victims.

A study conducted in Cleveland in 1978 concluded that out of 404 cases of abuse of older persons, 76 per cent were older women who had at least one major physical or mental impairment. In a 1979 Massachusetts study, one thousand social, service providers for older clients were questioned about their caseloads. Fifty-five per cent reported abuse of clients during an eighteen-month period; of these, 80 per cent were women who were being abused by people they lived with. The study also found that 85 per cent of the victims were related to their abusers.[7]

A widely quoted 1979 study undertaken by the Center on Aging at the University of Maryland yielded two hundred returns from eight hundred questionnaires sent out. Of these two hundred responses, only twenty-six were actual case studies. The other respondents did not know of cases, or did not want to report them. From the sample, the researchers drew a number of conclusions. They found that the abusers of the elderly were adult children, spouses, grandchildren, and other relatives. The victims, whose average age was eighty-four, were in ill health, unable to do certain tasks for themselves. The victims were generally white, disabled, middle-class, and female. In fact, 81 per cent of the abused were women. Most abuse occurred repeatedly, and seemed to be psychological rather than physical. Attempts to seek help were generally not successful.

The study found that the abusers think of their victims as "too senile to matter." They punish the elderly for not being strong, for behaving in a manner that the abusers describe as "improper." The victims become dehumanized, the study indicated, and therefore risk further abuse. The study defined physical abuse as blows resulting in bruises and welts and included slaps, shoving, and shaking. However, the greatest abuse was psychological: lack of personal care and lack of adequate supervision. There were extreme cases involving beatings, fractured skulls and bones, and tying the victims to beds or chairs. Psychological abuse centered on verbal assaults, threats, fear, and isolation. Material abuse involved theft or misuse of money or property. Medical mistreatment included withholding medication, eyeglasses, and false teeth.

The study estimates at least one million cases of abuse in the United States, a figure that represents 4 per cent of the senior population.[8]

Other studies have found more extreme cases of neglect: in not providing adequate or appropriate food, oversedating, and placement in nursing homes or other institutions.[9] There are also reports of attacks with knives, guns, or other lethal weapons.[10]

The Maryland study is significant, for it has attempted to identify the victims and the kind of abuse they suffer. Nevertheless, it is based on only twenty-six case studies, all from the articulate middle-class. Poor and minority women are harder to reach and perhaps even less willing to talk, so this study only scratches the surface of the problem.

A question follows from these preliminary studies: Why are older women the main targets of familial abuse? There are several theories. Older women are often financially dependent or poor, and many must rely on their families for financial assistance. The family may consider their older female relative a financial burden or a source of additional stress. As well, people think that older women are no longer effective or productive members of our society. And for older women, there are few shelters and services to provide for their needs.[11]

In many respects, the battered older woman is like the battered child. Both are dependent, vulnerable, and in need of care. People assume that children and old women will be protected by their families: the natural response of families should be to love them and treat them with kindness and gentleness. However, both old women and children may become the sources of emotional, physical, and financial stress to families.[12]

But battering and abuse are not confined to frail, sickly, old women. Healthy older women are also in danger of exploitation and abuse. These women babysit, clean house, and cook in return for room and board. Their interaction with the community outside the home is severely restricted. When tensions develop in the household, they may suffer the brunt of verbal and physical abuse. Many of the women I interviewed felt profoundly ashamed that their children or in-laws treated them badly.

All abused older women have limited options. Most victims suffer in silence because they fear retaliation or abandonment if they report the abuse to the police or to medical or social-service professionals. They often prefer familiar torments to the prospect of an unknown situation. More fundamental is the humiliation that victims would experience by admitting that their relatives are capable of such behavior. For many, there is simply no place to go if they leave the family home; others fear they will end up in nursing homes.

In the past, relatively few women survived to old age. Today a woman may live into her eighties and beyond. As she ages her health may decline. Longevity has brought with it a new social phenomenon: the care of aging parents. And this can be expensive. Illness may wipe out a parent's savings, and drastically deplete the next generation's financial base.[13]

Another phenomenon is the disintegration of the extended family. In previous generations, the few women who lived to be very old could reasonably expect that their immediate and extended families would care for them in their old age. Today's nuclear family is often neither willing nor financially or emotionally equipped to care for its aging women.

Although the abuse of older women is deplorable, society cannot self-righteously point an accusatory finger at the care-givers. The burden of care generally falls on the nearest female relative, who is also expected to look after her own family and house while attempting to generate income through part-time work. Not surprisingly, many care-givers express feelings of frustration, anxiety, depression, and anger. This can lead to highly charged emotional situations that provoke acts of abuse and neglect.

An unpublished dissertation on "Granny Battering" prepared by Kathryn Painter in Coventry, England, takes a humane and compassionate look at the unrealistic expectations placed on female care-givers. In her research, Painter found that society expects care-givers to be stoic. Over time, as aging relatives require more help and attention, the care-giver suffers from enormous strain, which they are not equipped to deal with. They often do not understand the nature of their older relatives' illnesses. As well, doctors, nurses, and social workers, instead of offering advice and assistance before a battering incident erupts, tend to ignore signs of abuse.

Moreover, care-givers also often experience restrictions in their lifestyles. According to Painter, many care-givers are resentful because caring for an aging relative precludes pursuing a career. There is often serious financial hardship and deprivation within the family. The care-giver's family is accorded less and less time as the needs of the parent or relative grow. This can precipitate stress, and the aging relative may become the focus of disagreements and arguments. But all members of the family pay a price in worry, reduction of social interaction, and financial expenses.[14]

Granny battering will become more commonplace in years to come, unless society provides desperately needed support services for the care of the old. We need day centers, respite care, properly trained home help, social workers, doctors, and nurses; these services are expensive. If our response continues to be to let families take care of their own, and if we insist that granny battering is an aberration rather than a widespread cause for concern, we are, in fact, creating greater and greater strain on families. We cannot ignore this latest manifestation of family violence; we have an obligation to search for humane responses. All of us are potential victims of abuse in old age, and many of us may also spend many years as care-givers.

Abuse in Nursing Homes

For most older women, a nursing home represents a depressing and frightening end to life. I spoke with residents, their relatives, and friends, and I was inundated with stories of physical and psychological abuse and neglect. Although the gerontological literature is sparse, and tends to be very conservative, there are numerous newspaper and magazine reports of poor care, substandard accommodation, crowding, indifference, negligence, and vicious abuse.

Since older women make up the majority of the nursing-home population, they tend to be the principal recipients of negligence and abusive treatment. Most nursing homes are run for profit, and demand for beds exceeds supply. This imbalance invites the exploitation of vulnerable older women. I found a wide variation in the quality of nursing homes, even though they are supposedly governed by stringent rules.

One of the basic problems plaguing nursing homes is the chronic, industry-wide shortage of people trained in geriatrics and willing to work in a nursing home. Laura is a geriatric nurse who has left the profession because of what she describes as "insensitive and cruel treatment of the residents."

Old women in nursing homes — and let's face it, most of the residents are women — are treated as beds without personalities. It was my experience in three different homes that the staff never has or takes the time to sit down and talk to the residents. Conversations consist of a series of directions or orders.

Over the eight years that I worked in homes, I saw what happened to residents that the staff thought of as difficult or hostile. Very powerful drugs are given to them, drugs that make you dopey, that give you the shakes and cause you to drool. The effects are very similar to Parkinson's symptoms.

It doesn't take a lot to get yourself labeled a "bad patient." It's simple things, like refusing to eat your supper because you find the food unappetizing, or disobeying a rule. One woman was constantly drugged because she complained to the staff about the inflexible and to her mind illogical daily routine. Her inappropriate behavior was insisting on taking a bath in the evening rather than in the morning. It was her way of saying, "Look, I'm an individual and I have some preferences."

What terrified me about this whole phenomenon is that once patients are put on these drugs, they very often are diagnosed as senile. Patients are never allowed to display emotions, to express their likes and dislikes. The patients who fare the best are the passive, uncomplaining ones who smile sweetly and do exactly what they are told.

The whole system is insidious. No one wants to complain because we are all afraid of reprisals. The residents know that, if they tell their relatives and friends, and they, in turn, complain to the staff, there is a strong likelihood that the residents will get known as troublemakers and will run the risk of receiving worse care than before.

When I criticized the way homes are run, I found that I was quickly isolated and given difficult workloads all the time. It eventually became too much for me. My conscience was always bothering me, but I didn't feel I could change things by taking on the system alone.

I have left the profession, but I know that things haven't changed. I believe that most nursing homes do irreparable damage to people. A person comes into a home and it is assumed she is retarded. It's a terrible shock to most people. You suddenly find that your identity is wiped out; you are just another frail, old lady, sitting in the corridor while people shout at you as if you are deaf. You become confused. For some people the experience is so destructive that they go downhill very quickly.

Most of the people who work in nursing homes don't like or respect old people. In fact, I believe the workers are sometimes afraid of them because they represent what could possibly happen to all of us. This fear leads to real cruelty. I have frequently seen a staff

126

member stuffing a diaper into a resident's mouth because she wet her bed and berating her for her "disgusting" behavior. On more occasions than I like to admit, I have seen staff handle residents in a physically abusive way: very rough handling, shaking, shoving, and, in extreme cases, slapping and hitting.

All this goes on routinely in homes considered to be among the best. I have no idea what happens in the really scuzzy places – I'm sure it's even worse because of the crowding and critical shortage of staff.

Nothing will change unless we change our attitudes toward the old and the sick. You can't expect people who are depressed and repulsed by old people to provide dignified, humane care. Nursing homes just reflect how the rest of society feels about old people. We don't want them around and we really don't respect them, so we dump them when they can't fend for themselves.

A 1973 Ph.D. thesis written at Northwestern University investigated a sixty-five-bed hospital in the suburb of a large midwestern city. The writer found that the problem of abuse is directly related to securing and retaining adequate staff. A job in a nursing home is marginal and carries little status because the wages are low. Most of the non-supervisory positions are held by poor minority women who are either divorced or widowed and have little education, training or skills. The study also found that some of the employees were ex-mental patients or drifters, and several had criminal records or were former alcoholics. In addition, some of the staff were currently suffering from mental illness, such that they exhibited bizarre behavior. Since these non-supervisory employees did not develop strong commitments to their jobs, there was an exceedingly high annual rate (500 per cent) of turnover and absenteeism.

Although the nurses were responsible for the care the patients received, the study showed that they provided little of this care themselves. Their time was taken up with administrative duties, organizing, co-ordinating, and directing the activities of the aides.

The study indicated that the nurses were cynical about

their work and adamantly believed in and practised custodialism. They distrusted the aides and orderlies, whom they saw as "unreliable, untrustworthy, dishonest and immoral." The nurses also believed that tranquilizing drugs were necessary to control the residents, to prevent the disruption of daily routines, and to keep residents from escaping or injuring themselves. As well, many relatives refused to let nurses restrain residents. (The nurses wanted to restrain patients to avoid accidents and to prevent escapes, which reflect badly on the nurses.) Complaints about care seemed, to the nurses, to indicate ill-will on the part of the relatives. The residents frustrated and irritated the nurses, as well, by constantly breaking rules and complaining to their relatives.

The nurses particularly emphasized the hopeless position of the patients, their enfeebled mental states, and the need to control them with drugs and cloth restraints. The nurses focused on keeping the home and the residents clean and orderly. This form of care was dubbed "pediatrics senior grade" by the study.

The study found, however, that physical abuse was meted out by the aides and orderlies, who worked on their own with little supervision. If a resident became difficult, it was not uncommon for an aide or orderly to use physical force. The nurses chose to ignore this abuse, claiming it was random and infrequent. But the study found that physical abuse was a "patterned response by the aides and orderlies to their recurring problems of controlling residents."[15]

If relatives complained to the nurses about physical abuse, the nurses responded that the resident was a troublemaker, or crazy, and was not to be taken seriously. The staff thought the residents were unreliable because they could not take care of themselves in the outside world; therefore, they were incompetent and helpless.

The study concluded that workers in nursing homes think residents have a low social worth, are powerless, have a poor prognosis for recovery, and have low credibility. As a result, treatment is defined as custodial rather than therapeutic. This, in turn, encourages hostility and mutual antipathy between residents and staff. Control of the residents is seen as central, and psychological and physical abuse are ways of trying to maintain that control.[16]

Very few women manage or direct nursing homes or chronic-care facilities. This hierarchical system mirrors the job market — most women are at the bottom, in dead-end, low-paying jobs; a few are in lower- and middle-management positions. It is estimated that of all the women who work in nursing homes, only 3 per cent hold senior management positions. In effect, women have little or no input into the policy and direction of these facilities, even though we are the overwhelming majority of residents.

Angela was rare: she was the director of a private nursing home, one of a network of moderately priced homes. In the sixty-bed home she administered, she introduced innovative changes. She emphasized restorative care, and wanted the residents to take as much control of their lives as they could. The results of her efforts were quite dramatic — the mood, tone, and atmosphere of the home completely changed, and many of the residents were able to move out. Her superiors were impressed, and she was promoted. She became a senior administrator at headquarters, and was responsible for a region.

Angela began her new duties with enthusiasm, but she very quickly realized that her advice and opinions were resented by the male directors over whom she had authority. She received a curt note informing her that her performance had been assessed as inadequate and was relieved of her job, with two weeks pay. She was to vacate her office by noon of that same day. When she attempted to confront her boss with her bizarre dismissal he refused to see her, as did all the senior executives.

Angela has decided to take the matter to court. She is charging her employer with unjust and wrongful dismissal.

I am fighting a large and powerful company with vast resources. My chances of success are good, but only if I can afford the costly and time-consuming litigation. It's strange; they originally hired me for my unique approach to nursing-home care and now they are, in effect, firing me for the same reason. The tragedy is that the residents, the majority of whom are women, are paying for care that only hastens their deterioration. The home is structured in such a way that the residents are over managed – their physical disabilities are overemphasized while their social and spiritual needs are neglected. The system I worked in is the epitome of the worst of custodial care. In most of the homes, about 25 per cent of the residents are restrained in beds, chairs, and wheelchairs. The whole atmosphere is oppressive and gloomy. There are no activities that are meaningful to the residents. Most are waiting to die, but unable to articulate their fears and needs.

Regrettably, there are not many Angelas. Her courageous, new approach to nursing-home care was short-lived, and she lost her job. But the rumblings of discontent are there. Many women will end their days in nursing homes or chronic-care hospitals; their goal should be a dignified, humane environment in which the recipients of care have a real input into the policies and management of the institutions.

The abuse of residents in nursing homes stems from a basic disrespect for and antagonism toward old people. All the older women who were still managing on their own said, "I don't want to end up in a nursing home." They added, "But I don't want to be a burden to my family."

At the moment, old and sick women have few choices; their vulnerability is pathetic and tragic. Homes, by their very nature, are breeding grounds for abuse, from condescension and benign neglect to physical maltreatment.

Abuse in Home-Care Services

Obviously, one of the alternatives to institutions is to keep people in their homes as long as possible. But for this to work, social-service agencies must provide reliable, affordable, high-quality support services. To date, the record for home-service care is uneven and at times abysmally poor. The system relies heavily on volunteers, who are often meeting their own needs rather than those of the recipient. The few paid workers generally receive low wages and little training to sensitize them to the needs of older people. It's a patchwork, make-shift structure that invites abuse.

At one point in my research, I volunteered to work for a meals-on-wheels program run by a large inner-city church. The director was always in a high state of anxiety, forever juggling routes to compensate for volunteers who were unable or unwilling to meet their commitments. As a result, people often received their lunches and dinners late – and cold. But what particularly upset me were the judgments passed on people who received the meals. The director said that some of the women "lived like pigs," and that some were former welfare recipients. The director preferred clean, well-behaved, middle-class women who were sick or in reduced circumstances. Most of the volunteers I met shuddered with horror when they told me about the hovels they visited and how senile and disgusting some of the old women were.

Of the many old and needy women I met while I worked as a volunteer, one woman epitomizes the humiliation this program can engender.

Seventy-year-old Matilda is partially blind, which makes her very dependent on homemaker services.

I need help, but I get very little. A woman from homemaker services comes for two hours a week to clean my place. She knows I can't see well, so she doesn't do much. But I'm afraid to complain. You get known as a big mouth and they cut you off. If I can't get homemaker services, I know they will put me away in a nursing home. They could force me to move because I don't own my home; I live in a special housing project.

Sometimes I get fed up. This woman from homemaker services is always putting me down. If she sees that I have some nice fruit or a piece of cheese, she wants to know why I am eligible for meals on wheels. If I buy myself a little trinket, she lets me know that she thinks I don't deserve nice things.

But the volunteers are much worse. I find them bossy, demanding, and very nosy. I pay part of the

131

costs for cleaning and meals, but they act like they are doing me a great big favor.

Once the director of the meals-on-wheels program came to deliver my meal because she couldn't find anyone else to come. It was Christmas time and I was out shopping with my daughter. My son-in-law was home, so he took the meal and put it in the fridge. The next day she called me to ask about the young man in the apartment, implying that something fishy was going on. When I explained that my daughter and her husband were visiting from out of town, she quite bluntly told me that my guests should cook my meals. Her program was only for needy people who appreciated the service.

I wanted to tell her to stop interfering in my life, but she has a lot of power over me. All she has to do is write a report saying that I'm dotty and not able to keep myself. She did that to a woman I know. It's true her apartment was dirty, but so what? It's her business and her home. Without warning, they came and got this woman. She had no family, so they took all her things as well. When my sight gets worse, they might do the same to me.

Because I am very outspoken and not two-faced, I turn the volunteers off. They like nice, grateful little grannies. I don't see well; I need someone to take me shopping, to take me to the doctor and to the bank. Because I've been critical of the services, they always put me off. Still, even though I feel no one really gives a damn, and I worry that they will take me from my home, some days I wake up singing. I keep hoping that things will change for people like me.

Matilda depends on the goodwill of support services to help her retain her independence, yet she is the victim of condescension. She is afraid she will be institutionalized unless she is appreciative of her helpers and volunteers. If she speaks up, she might lose the services that make her life more tolerable. Although she pays for every service to the best of her ability, she is made to feel that she is the recipient of charity.

Some women are able to purchase home-care services such as housecleaning and personal nursing care. But these women do not necessarily command quality care. The negative attitudes toward the old and sick defy class boundaries. The rich and the poor can be victims of condescending and abusive home-support service.

Ten years ago, Nora (who is now sixty-one) discovered that she had multiple sclerosis. For the past four years she has been dependent on homemaker services to enable her to continue to live in her furnished apartment, which is equipped with all the latest aids for the severely handicapped.

I am very stubborn, and I am determined to remain on my own as long as possible. My experience in nursing homes was highly unpleasant. The most vivid memory I have is of a very old lady who was slapped by an aide because she passed gas and wet her bed. The poor thing was so sedated she didn't know what she was doing. That incident made me so angry and frightened that I have worked very hard to remain on the outside.

My disability pension and my own savings have made it possible for me to hire all the services I need. I am finding, though, that few of the people who come here are properly trained. The quality of care is going from bad to worse. So many of the homemakers are callous and uncaring.

I'm pretty outspoken, but at times I feel quite helpless. One of the nurses who used to come was really cruel and full of hatred. I become angry and frustrated, but I was afraid to alienate her. When you are as physically dependent as I am, you have to be careful not to antagonize your helpers. I suppress my feelings and swallow my temper.

I have found that a lot of the people who work as homemakers or visiting nurses are sick, almost sadistic people. One told me that I can't be helped and I should just accept my condition. I don't need such a negative attitude; it doesn't help. Other homemakers are terribly condescending and imply that I don't need nice things and should be in a home.

A lot of my frustration stems from trying to get the homemakers to do the things I think are necessary, like washing my back and my hair. They tell me they don't have time and I shouldn't be so fussy. Surely it is up to me to decide how often I want to wash. You have to be careful about complaining because you run the risk of getting blacklisted. There are very few good people around who like to work with sick and old women. I try not to be unreasonable, but I don't think the services are particularly good or reliable.

Nora is an educated, affluent woman. But, like Matilda, she finds that homecare-helpers are condescending and abusive. She feels just as vulnerable and degraded even though she has the financial resources to buy all the services she needs.

As long as homemaker services are viewed as essentially volunteer or benevolent, the recipient will remain open to abuse. Poorly trained home-service workers who earn small wages have neither the incentive nor the skills to deliver uniform, quality service. This system promotes insensitive and abusive treatment of the people it serves.

Crime and Older Women

Although violence against older women takes many forms, the fear of random physical violence on the streets is the fear most often voiced by older women. The older women I interviewed agreed that it is unsafe to be outdoors at night. They perceive themselves as especially vulnerable because they know they are stereotyped as "physically weak, emotionally distressed, fearful, and incompetent" by muggers, robbers, rapists, and con artists.[17]

Nobody knows the extent of violent crime against older women. Incidents are not often reported, and reports are frequently not believed. Many professionals who work in the field of crime prevention claim that older women are a timorous, paranoid lot who exaggerate crimes committed against them or fabricate stories to evoke sympathy and attention. But many researchers feel that older women do not report crimes because they fear reprisals, and because they are embarrassed. Rape is a special problem: an older woman must confront society's attitudes regarding aging and sexuality. She is keenly aware that a complaint of rape or sexual assault may not be taken seriously.[18]

Older women are paralyzed with fear. It is their perception that it is dangerous to walk on the streets, during the day or at night, especially in the run-down, high-crime areas where so many older women live. In effect, the combination of their fears and the reality of their circumstances powerfully reduces or totally eliminates their freedom of mobility. Too frequently, older women barricade themselves behind multiple locks.

A British voluntary organization called Age Concern has devoted considerable energy to an examination of crime against the elderly. Their research shows that the elderly, older women in particular, are easy victims of crime. The particular vulnerability of older women is exacerbated by their acute poverty, which forces them to live in unsafe and often deteriorating neighborhoods. Older women are victims of petty crime, vandalism, fraud, cons, harassment, and assault.[19]

Dolores had a dream that if she could make a little money, her life would be a little more pleasant. She could take a trip, upholster her sofa, and help out her divorced daughter and her grandchildren.

You'd think, at seventy-three, I would know better. I had a friend who kept calling me and telling me about a way I could make some money. She told me that she knew an accountant who charged high rates of interest on money for loans he gave his clients for short periods of time. His clients were apparently businessmen who had overdrafts and needed cash at certain times in the year. It made sense to me, and I was assured that there was nothing illegal about it.

I was slowly sucked in. At first I put up $2,000, which was repaid with a profit of $500 a month later. As some of my small investments matured, I needed a place to put them. I finally met with the accountant, and was impressed with his ease and assurance. I carefully explained to him that I relied on my little income for meeting my monthly expenses. He told me that he had a number of clients like myself, older women on small incomes who were looking for a good return on their savings. He said they were very satisfied with this arrangement, since they were earning a good profit, far better than the interest they would get from the bank.

So I went along with it, thinking that I was very lucky to have such a good way to invest. For more than a year everything seemed fine, and I was very pleased. The accountant called me one day to tell me about a deal he had in mind that was very lucrative. He said he had called me first, giving me preference because we had become friends. I was very excited at the prospect of making some real money, so I scratched around and cashed in everything I had. I even borrowed money from my sister. Since I had to tie up my money only for a month, I wasn't really concerned. All in all, I gave him $34,000 – my life savings – plus a $5,000 loan from my sister.

Ten days later, I heard that he had gone broke. All this time he lived like a lord, taking expensive trips, buying three cars and a beautiful new home. He had also gambled away a good portion of the money in Las Vegas. There were no clients or deals. I discovered that there were twenty-five older women like myself involved. What he did was borrow from one to pay to another until eventually he went broke. He ended up owing $350,000.

At first I was in a daze, but then I became angry and consulted a lawyer. He contacted the police, but of those twenty-five women, only seven were prepared to come forward. I guess everyone was embarrassed, and I heard that a lot of the women didn't want their children to find out. You feel like a fool when something like this happens.

It's been suggested to me by well-meaning friends that I was greedy to fall for such a con. Is it greedy to want to live a little better, to want to help out a daughter who is struggling to raise three kids on her own? I don't think I will ever recover my money and I am worried that the other people involved in this swindle will settle for what the accountant's lawyer is offering us. All of us received a letter from his lawyer offering us thirty cents on the dollar over a period of four years – if the accountant can meet this arrangement. In very fine print, the agreement also stated that if we sign, we can't make any further claims. The lawyer also glossed over the accountant's behavior, claiming illness and business problems.

I have refused to sign. I am being pressured to give in by most of the other women involved; but I don't want to. I want to hold out and see if we can do better.

I still can't quite understand that someone who posed as a friend could come into my home and swindle me out of all the money I had. He knew I lived modestly and that I had worked all my life so I would have a little in my old age. I know why I did it. I was scared that inflation was eating up everything I had. Every day, prices went up, and I thought that unless I did something drastic, I would have to move and sell most of my things. I wanted to live out the rest of my life with pride and dignity; I wanted to pay my own way. My health is fine now, but I was really worried that if I got sick I wouldn't be able to afford the medical expenses. This has happened to a lot of my friends. I have seen them wiped out entirely by one bad illness. I never wanted to be a burden to my daughter, or to my sister, who is quite wealthy. It's funny now, but I had faith that no one would want to cheat an old lady.

Research has shown that older women are easy victims of frauds and cons. Their isolation and their financial insecurity make them particularly receptive to a con artist who befriends them and promises to help them make some extra money.

The National Association of Victim Support Schemes was begun in Britain, in 1974 to help people like Dolores. Their specific goals are to repair the damage caused by crime and to reduce unnecessary suffering. They recognize the lack of concern or response from relatives, friends, neighbors, and the community at large. The victims, they discovered, feel neglected and ostracized. The association offers advice about compensation, insurance, the future security of homes, and referrals to other services, such as psychiatric counseling, social workers, and doctors.[20]

In North America, there are a few services available to older victims of crime. But much of the crime that older women experience is the result of unsafe housing, dangerous neighborhoods, acute poverty, and social isolation; thus individual programs have a limited impact. Crime against older women is part of the larger problem of our society's neglect and indifference to the needs of its older citizens.

I live in a room above a store; I share a bath with five men. The place is full of men who drink and carry on all night, so I can't sleep. But I'm afraid to complain to the landlord. He runs the store during the day and leaves at six o'clock every night. All he cares about is getting his rent. What goes on after he leaves doesn't interest him.

Everything is wrong with me. I go to six different doctors and they all give me different pills. Most of the time I walk around in a fog. Before I became sick, I worked in a knitting factory downtown. I made enough to get by, although it was rough. I'm only fifty-seven, but I feel a hundred.

I moved into this room because I was short of money. From the first day I had a feeling that I was in for trouble. One of the men is more than six feet tall. He's always asking me to run out and buy him cigarettes and sandwiches. I'm afraid to say no; I just do what he tells me. I've seen him beat up the other men; he's mean and violent.

I try to mind my own business and I always keep my door shut and locked. All those cigarettes and sandwiches were eating up my money. He never paid me for any of them, not one cent.

One night this big guy started to pound on my door at eleven o'clock, demanding that I get him some sandwiches. I told him all the stores were closed, except the donut shop. He started to swear and kick the door. He finally pushed the door in, breaking the lock. By this time I was crouched in a corner, with my hands over my head. He picked me up and threw me down on the floor. He said that if I told anyone about what he did he would beat the hell out of me. My back really hurts now all the time, and for a long time I had a big, ugly bruise.

The next night he came back when I was out and went through my things. I don't have much, but he took my winter coat, my boots, and all my food. I never complained to the police or to the landlord because I don't think they would believe me or protect me. This big guy is a bully and he knows he can get away with it. It's easy for guys like him to push old women around because he knows we can't protect ourselves.

If I move, the next place will be just as bad, maybe worse, but I'm always afraid now that he will really hurt me. I don't know, he could be into raping and things like that. I don't wish anyone any harm, but I wish they would put him away.

No one is easier to bully and terrorize than a frail older woman. One American research project (the San Francisco Victim/Witness Assistance Program) found that older women are particularly shaken and demoralized by crime and are prone to feelings of shame. Moreover, many end up blaming themselves for the crime. As a result, some older victims decide they cannot ask for or accept help – that, in fact, they are unworthy.[21]

Louella suffers from arthritis. At sixty-two she lives on welfare because she is no longer able to work.

I can get around, but very slowly, and I need a cane and braces. Since my condition became so bad, it is really impossible for me to work. A waitress has to be fast on her feet to keep up with the orders. I haven't worked for about three years now and I was forced to move into this low-rental building for old and sick people. It's a terrible area; there are lots of drunks and

139

tough kids roaming around day and night. I can't just sit in the apartment all the time, so I go out to the store across the street to buy milk and groceries. The city sends around someone once a week to clean up, but for the rest I am pretty much on my own.

I have been assaulted twice now, once in the lobby and once just outside the building. The first time some drunk threw me across the lobby for no reason. I was in braces and came crashing down. I was a bit bruised, but not really hurt. A couple of people stood around and watched, but one very old lady came up to me and tried to help me. The drunk just sauntered out of the building, singing to himself.

Since I wasn't hurt, I decided to go about my business. I never reported it to the police. But the next time was very serious. One night at about seven o'clock, I needed some milk, so I decided to go to the store across the street. As I left the building, a young boy, maybe eighteen, came running up from behind and started to punch me. He grabbed my purse and rifled through it. He was furious when he only found five dollars. By that time, I had pulled myself up and had started to move away, back to my building. He came after me and belted me so hard in the face that my glasses broke. I tried to push him away, but he was just too strong. He kept on shaking me and pounding me.

I was crying hysterically and pleading with him to leave me alone. Luckily the man from the grocery store had seen the whole thing. He came running up, shouting, "She hasn't done anything to you. Leave her alone." The boy must have been frightened because he bolted down the street.

The police came and took all the details. I was taken to the hospital because I was covered with welts. Luckily he didn't break any bones. For weeks after that I was black and blue, especially around my eyes.

About two months ago, I went to court to testify against the kid – the police caught him doing the same thing to another woman. This other woman and I have laid charges of assault, bodily harm, and attempted

140

theft. I'm now scared to death that this kid will come and get me when he comes out of prison. His girlfriend lives in the next building, and she stopped me on the street and told me that I better watch out.

I'm terrified all the time now. I don't even go out to the store past five o'clock in the evening. I've asked for police protection against this kid and his friends, but the police told me that I should just relax. Threats don't mean much. They think I am exaggerating about the threats. I've asked to be moved from this building, but there are no vacancies in the other low-rent buildings. When my friends ask me to visit for supper, I refuse. I can't take the chance. I've become so nervous that the doctor has given me pills to calm me down.

I'm very worried about the future. I think things will get worse. Without real protection, women like myself are open to robberies and attacks and even worse. We're easy marks because we are old and lots of us are sick and can't move fast.

Louella took the difficult step of laying charges against her assailant. She now lives in terror of reprisal once her assailant completes his prison term. Her fears are dismissed by the police as the paranoid delusions typical of older women. Her experience is not extraordinary; unfortunately it is shared by many older women.

At eighty-five, Virginia lives in a bachelor apartment in the center of what she describes as a very dangerous neighborhood.

I really don't have much choice with the amount of money I have to live on. The rent is affordable and I am close to my friends and near my church. I don't feel very happy about staying on here now, though. Since the robbery, I am more nervous and frightened than before.

About six months ago, I was sound asleep when two masked men broke into my apartment through the windows and started to beat me with clubs. All the time they were beating me, they demanded to know where I kept my money. I refused to tell them, even though they began to choke me. They pulled me from the bed and threw me roughly on the floor. One of them kicked me and swore at me. The next thing I remember was waking up tied to a chair.

The men were still in the apartment, destroying everything in sight. They pulled apart my mattress and yanked everything out of my drawers, throwing my things all over the apartment. They took my TV, my radio, my wedding rings, and my gold watch — everything that was of any value. When they were through, my apartment looked like a whirlwind had hit it.

The landlord finally found me, hours later, when he came to collect my rent. I guess I was lucky it was rent day — otherwise I could have remained tied up for who knows how long.

I was in terrible shape. My body was covered with cuts and bruises and I had a bad concussion. I stayed in the hospital for more than three weeks. The doctors have told me that the dizziness I feel most of the time is permanent. At my age, you don't come back like a young person would, and I am afraid that they will put me in a nursing home.

What I can't understand is why no one in the building heard all the commotion and noise when these men were pushing me around and throwing things on the floor. I guess people don't want to get involved. One of my neighbors told me that he thought I was having a fit of some kind.

I guess people think old ladies like myself are a bit off, and they don't take much notice of us. But I'm frightened now. I used to think that I had to look out when I was on the street, but now I am terrified of being robbed and beaten in my own home. No place is safe any more.

Since the robbery I have bought locks for the windows. I don't know if it will do much good. The police never found the robbers and they don't hold out much hope that any of my things will be found. One of the officers told me that an old lady shouldn't live in this neighborhood, that I should move to a better area. I would like to know how he expects me to do this on my income. It's hopeless. I feel like a sitting duck, waiting for someone to do it again. Only I am not sure I could pull through it again.

At eighty-five, Virginia describes herself as a "sitting duck," waiting to be robbed and assaulted again. She feels unsafe both on the street and in her own home. Her situation is intolerable, but her fixed, low income dooms her to a run-down and crime-ridden neighborhood.

Priscilla is eighty-three. She lives in a small shack about fifteen miles from the city.

I don't have heat or running water because this place was left to rot a long time ago. When I was seventy-five, my husband died and I didn't have any place to live. We had both worked the farm that we rented most of our married lives. When Tom died, I couldn't stay there. I didn't have enough money and I wasn't well enough to keep up with the work.

The landlord knew of this old shack at the end of his property, which he said I could have for very little money. There is a pump outside and I have an out-house at the back. I use gas lamps and I burn wood in the old pot-belly stove to keep warm. It's a good place for me to live. I can grow a few vegetables, and up until six months ago no one bothered me.

Now things are very bad for me. A gang of teenaged kids from the city have started to come out here. I guess they came on my place by accident and now word has spread that a witch lives out here. That's what they call me. At first all they did was taunt me and call me names. I admit I was good and scared, but I just locked myself in and hoped they would get tired and go away. I didn't call the police because I figured that would make trouble all the way around.

These kids drink a lot of beer. They started throwing beer bottles and stones through my windows, chanting "Come out, witch!" I hid under the bed, but it was dawn before they finally left. They became much bolder after that. They started to come in large gangs every Saturday night. About two months ago they became so drunk and crazy that they broke down the door and began to throw things around. I was so angry that I forgot to be frightened. I picked up my hammer and started to wave it. One of the kids grabbed me and pushed me so hard that I fell against the bed. Another kid started to hit me and shake me. By the time they were through, they had ransacked the whole place. It was a terrible mess, and so was I. My face and arms were black and blue and I had cuts and welts everywhere.

My landlord, who doesn't like to get involved, was so upset by this episode that he called the police. He found me lying on the floor, crying and all beat up. I was very sore, but I'm a pretty tough old bird; it would take a lot more than a bunch of punks to do me in. Anyway, the police came real quick and they took all the details. These kids had stolen my savings, which I kept hidden under the mattress. It wasn't much, but it was all I had.

The police said they would take care of everything. I felt a lot better, but the next night the kids came again, yelling and screaming, threatening to kill me this time. Since the break-in, though, the kids haven't come in the house. I guess they know there is nothing left to steal. The police have come out a few times, but they only arrested one kid, the one who beat me. He spent three weeks in jail, and now he is out there again, almost every night now, making my life miserable.

People ask me why I don't leave. I tell them I'm determined to stay. This is where I spent most of my life, and no bunch of rotten kids is going to push me out. But I'm really scared that one day they will become so loaded up that they might take it into their heads to kill me. The police said they can't be out here all the time protecting me. They want me to move into an old-folks' home in the city, but I'm not budging. I keep hoping the kids will get tired and leave me in peace.

These cases portray the terror experienced by older women, the victims of random and violent crimes. It is common knowledge that many older women live alone and in deteriorating, unprotected neighborhoods. Rapists, muggers, robbers, and con artists can exploit their vulnerability.

What is clear is the permanent effect of crime and the fear of crime on the physical and psychological well-being of older women. They feel that they have relatively little control over their lives, and that at any moment they may be victimized. Too frequently, their response is to become virtual recluses. Certainly, women of all ages live with the fear of crime, but for older women, this fear is translated into a reduction of independence. The quality of their lives is drastically diminished.

The following case of the rape of a sixty-three-year-old woman was related to me by a female crime-prevention officer named Marsha.

I still shudder when I think about this case. During my twenty years on the force I have seen a lot of violent crimes against women, but never anything quite like this. We normally don't get very many complaints from older women about rape.

This woman was widowed, worked part-time in a dry-cleaning store, and lived in a very run-down neighborhood. I don't know much about her except that she comes from a farming community and doesn't have any family around. The social center for her was the church.

One day when she had gone shopping in the afternoon, two men grabbed her and pulled her into a car. She says they ripped off all her clothes. She struggled very hard, and in the scuffle hurt her shoulder. She believes that at one point she fainted. When she came to, the two men were taking turns raping her, laughing all the time. They had guns and kept threatening to kill her. She thinks the whole thing only took about an hour, but she's not sure. In the end they dumped her in a parking lot where the attendant found her unconscious and covered with welts and bruises.

She was taken to the hospital and checked over for internal injuries and then questioned by the police. I met with her several months later when she came to the station to ask if we had found her assailants. We hadn't, and we never did. What struck me was how pale and nervous she seemed. She told me that she had been going to her doctor with all kinds of physical problems since her rape, but the doctor told her that everything was in her head, that nothing was wrong with her. She kept wringing her hands and saying how sick she felt. I knew of a woman gynecologist who I thought might be more sympathetic, so I called and made an appointment.

The woman called me several weeks later and told me that she finally feels clean. I asked her what she meant. Apparently she and the doctor had a long talk and worked out the basis of her pain. She felt clean again because the doctor treated her with dignity and explained that what happened was not her fault.

This case affected me very strongly. I realized that if the intent of rape is humiliation, and I think it is, the assailants certainly succeeded in this case. I suspect that rape for an older woman is particularly devastating, perhaps even more so than for a younger woman who may have the strength to heal.

For more than a decade, rape-crisis centers in North America have been created in response to the general indifference, ignorance, and even brutality that women encounter when reporting rapes to police, lawyers, and doctors. As the number of centers has grown, the public has become educated about what constitutes rape and who is a probable victim. However, most rape-crisis centers are understaffed and financially strapped. Although there is an awareness that older women are victimized, the majority of rape-crisis centers have neither the financial resources nor the special counseling skills to help significant numbers of older victims.

One center, called Sexual Trauma Services, in San Francisco, has a specific grant to work with older women. What they have found is that older women have special needs. The expertise rape-crisis centers have developed for younger women is neither adequate nor appropriate. Older rape victims are likely to suffer a decline in their physical health. Quite frequently, the Services' research indicated, older women are vulnerable to flu and pneumonia. Even more than younger women, older women feel acute embarrassment and shame. Often their experiences trigger a period of disturbing confusion and disorientation. And, to work through their trauma, older victims may need a much longer period of therapy than younger victims.

Sexual Trauma Services workers realize that the attitudes of the police toward older women are not helpful. The police think sexual crimes are perpetrated almost exclusively against young and attractive victims, despite overwhelming evidence to the contrary. In San Francisco, workers have allotted time and resources to educating the police, so that officers will refer older victims and be more aware of the possibility of sexual crimes against the old.

The program has also discovered that victims older than seventy tend to suffer more internal injuries, abrasions, and lesions. A significant number of older victims sustain such severe injuries that the program is beginning to classify the crime as attempted murder.

Sexual Trauma Services provides a unique and innovative approach for older victims – one that recognizes the inappropriateness of traditional counseling methods. Older victims fear most that their families will put them in a home if they are informed of the rape or sexual assault. To relieve this anxiety, the program has a strict policy of respecting their clients' confidentiality.

As awareness of the program spreads, the number of older victims seeking treatment has risen. The statistics compiled in 1981 show that only 3 per cent of the program's caseload are older women; however, Sexual Trauma Services believes that this is just the tip of the iceberg.[22]

Older Women and Wife-Battering

In the past few years, the subject of wife-battering has become a big issue in North America. There has been a proliferation of books, films, and studies that show that wife-battering cuts across class, race, education, and income levels. Once again, older women, in this instance women from their fifties on, have been excluded from such analyses. Surely there is no reason to assume that an abusive and violent husband miraculously stops beating his wife when she turns fifty. Nevertheless, the literature only briefly mentions older women, focusing almost exclusively on women between the ages of eighteen and forty-eight.

I am not for a moment minimizing the plight of young women and their children. I acknowledge that their needs are not being met; there are far too few temporary shelters, and these women have inadequate and ineffective legal protection. Women are locked into marriage by virtue of their economic dependence; researchers claim that wife-battering is reported less often than rape.

Barbara has worked in a shelter for battered women for six years. She says that the average age of the women who seek refuge in the shelter is twenty-eight.

Our shelter, like most of the others, only accepts women with children. We have a maximum capacity of thirty-two people and we are always bursting at the seams. The oldest woman we've ever had was forty-seven; she had relatively young children.

Other shelters serve desperate, derelict women. Their women must leave at nine in the morning, and can't return until 4:30 in the afternoon. They attract a very transient population of alcoholics, ex-psychiatric patients, drug addicts, and bag ladies.

I think those shelters do very important work; they serve a population of desperate women who are homeless. But it's not an environment that would attract older battered wives, who would be forced to wander on their own during the day.

I know that older women suffer from battering, but I don't know how widespread it is. Our shelter often receives calls from older women, but all we can do is be sympathetic and refer them for legal and medical assistance. I get the impression, from talking to these women, that they originally stuck it out for the kids, and they now feel bitter and abandoned. These battered women are suffocatingly dependent on their grown children. This alienates their children so much that the women become quite isolated.

There really is no place for these women to turn.

The support groups and hostels are geared for the needs of younger women. Relatives and friends generally drift away from any battered wife, so I can only speculate that an older battered wife is especially isolated.

If it's so hard for younger women to break out of an abusive home, it is even more difficult for older women. The ones I and my colleagues have spoken to over the years are painfully embarrassed to admit that they are battered wives. Their abuse has generally gone on for so long that their self-image is irrevocably damaged. They are even less sure than their younger counterparts that they will be believed.

The more I work in this area, the more I realize that we have only scratched the surface of the problem. I do a lot of public speaking to help make people aware and sensitive to the issue. For the past few years, I have spoken to quite a number of businesswomen's groups, in which the women mostly are between fifty-five and sixty-three. During my presentation, there are normally few questions, but afterwards, invariably, some privately confide that I could have been describing their marriages.

The older women are so beaten down. It's much harder at sixty or seventy to leave a marriage, even a violent one. You can tell a younger woman to get out because she has the rest of her life ahead of her. What do you tell a woman of seventy?

Barbara is aware that older women have been ignored and discounted as battered wives. Her perception is that acute embarrassment at their situation and an appalling low self-image have prevented older women from publicly declaring their victimization. She also acknowledges that when older women seek assistance, they generally meet with disbelief and find that there are no temporary shelters to help them.

I suspect that the battering and abuse of older women by their husbands is a chronic and widespread problem — but is a problem that nearly everyone has overlooked or ignored. Although many of the older women I interviewed admitted that they had lived with violent husbands, only two women were prepared to discuss their experience. As

I listened to these women, I was affected by their pain and profound sadness.

Pearl sat dejectedly in her tiny apartment as she explained to me why she remained with her alcoholic and abusive husband.

At seventy-two, where am I going to go? When I was younger I used to think that, when my two girls were on their own, I would get a job and find my own place. But somehow I just stayed with my husband, and now I can't leave.

My husband has always beat me, particularly when he is drunk. He worked as a shipper for a big company until he retired. It was better when he worked, because then he only hit me on the weekends. Now he is home almost all the time, except when he goes drinking with some of his buddies. He has nothing to do, so he gets surly and picks a fight with me almost every day. It's always the same: he calls me names and then he begins to punch me and shove me. You would think I would be used to it by now — it's gone on for more than fifty years.

When I was younger, I left him a couple of times and went home to my parents' place. My father always told me that a wife belongs with her husband; if a husband beats a wife, it is because she deserves it. I guess my father didn't want to get stuck supporting me and my kids.

The last while, I have tried to keep out of my husband's way. Right after breakfast, every day, I leave while he is in the shower, and I wander around the city. I go to the library and I spend a lot of time in the shopping mall. On Sundays, I ride this one bus up and down for hours. Most of the bus drivers know me; I guess they think I'm just another crazy old lady. When I get tired of the bus, I drink coffee at this one place where they don't mind me sitting around for hours. I always try to come home in time to make his supper. He never hits me while I am cooking, but he's always yelling for me to hurry up.

In the evening, right after supper, even though I

am terrified of going out, I visit an old friend who lives around the corner. She's a widow, so it's pretty quiet and peaceful over there. That is the best time of the day for me. The two of us have a cup of tea and watch TV together. My friend knows about my husband, but we don't talk about it much. I'm stuck; I don't have enough money to leave, and I am too old to work now.

Once I went to speak to a lawyer, but he told me that I had better stay where I am. After that, I decided I would have to make out as best I can. It's not much of a life, riding the bus and hanging around shopping malls, but it's the only way I can get away from him. He's so drunk most of the time that I don't think he notices I'm gone.

The doctor tells me that my health isn't too good. I tried to tell him about my husband, but he doesn't want to know. He gives me pills to calm me down and other pills to help with my depression. Even when I needed an operation to stop internal bleeding from a really bad beating, the doctors in the hospital never asked me any questions. They just patched me up and sent me home.

My two girls know that their father is always hitting me, but what can they do? They are busy raising families now and they don't have a lot of time to visit. Besides, they know what goes on and I think they hate coming over.

Even if she were prepared to seek refuge in a shelter for battered women, and even if a shelter were prepared to accept her, Pearl would encounter a number of problems.

The shelters I visited in Canada, the United States, and Britain are not set up to accommodate older women. Older women find the stairs difficult to negotiate, the fire doors cumbersome and heavy, and the noise level generated by young children overwhelming.

Most shelters survive on a combination of government grants, private donations, and fund-raising events. Their resources barely cover the needs of younger women; they have no money to help older women.

All my life I have worked in a bakery. They finally let me go last year, when I was sixty-five, because I just wasn't as fast as I used to be.

You see this scar on my cheek? That is what it was like to live with my husband. He gave that to me more than a year ago.

My husband was always a difficult and fussy man, but never what you would call violent. He swore a lot, and when the kids were young, he used to yell all the time. It was only when he retired that he started to nag. This was about five years ago, when I was still working. The moment I would walk in the door he would begin to complain that the house was dirty, that I was a lousy cook, and so on. I just told him to knock it off in the beginning, but he would turn purple and start to throw things. This scar is from a milk bottle that hit me in the face. I was bleeding so badly that I had to go to the hospital. He came along to be sure that I didn't tell anyone how it happened. When the doctor asked me questions, he answered for me, telling them I wasn't watching where I was going and walked into a door with a glass window.

Until I retired, I just took it. I was scared to move out because we worked hard all our lives to own a house and I slaved to make it comfortable. He warned me that if I got it into my head to leave, he would make sure I got nothing. I was always tired and tense. Not a day went by without him nagging me. In time, he became much bolder and he started to hit and kick me. I tried to push him away, but he is a very big and strong man for his age.

I finally decided that I couldn't take it any more, especially after I retired. He was driving me crazy. I reached my limit when he loaded his gun and threatened to kill me. He walked around the living room, pointing his gun at me, telling me I had better listen to him or I would be dead. I was trembling so hard I could barely breathe, but eventually he put the gun down and went to sleep.

I ran to the bedroom and threw a few things together and just wandered around for a couple of hours.

I couldn't think of any place to go. I had talked to our minister, but he just told me that a husband and wife belong together, and that if I was a good wife my husband would come around. I called the police once. They told my husband they thought I was exaggerating. The minute they left, my husband really let loose and knocked out some of my teeth. I locked myself in the bathroom all night.

Anyway, there I was wandering around, and I finally took a room in a boarding house. It's not much, but I've been here a year now. Even though I'm always worried he will find me, I'm glad that I am finally free. Being free, I have decided, is more important than my share of the house and our savings.

These case studies vividly demonstrate how retirement can either escalate or initiate battering. The husbands are bored, idle, and resentful, and they let out their frustrations by verbally abusing and physically beating their wives.

The skepticism that these women encounter when they attempt to confide in doctors, ministers, and the police is not uncommon. These officials express the typical belief that crimes of violence are usually perpetrated against young and attractive victims. People still think battering and rape are sexually motivated, despite overwhelming evidence that the cause is an expression of power and contempt for the victim.

Even though older women have no family to preserve, their tremendous sense of embarrassment and humiliation effectively silences them. Many are terrified of striking out on their own even though their home life may be intolerable. Most of them feel helpless because they are economically and socially dependent on their husbands. The world is a very cold and alien place for old women who run away.

5

To Be Old, a Woman, and Poor

The greatest fraud of all is the belief that as a society, we take collective responsibility to provide for our old. The two poorest groups of people in Canada are women and the old; the poorest of the poor are the old women.[1]

"Every woman is one man away from poverty" was a phrase coined by the women's movement in the early 1970s. This statement is especially true for older women, even those who have worked all their adult lives. There is a clear expectation that older women should have a variety of income sources to draw on in old age. These include: Old Age Security, Canada Pension, private pensions, earnings, savings and other assets, family contributions, and – only if these fail – public-assistance programs designed to supplement poverty-level incomes. Unfortunately, the grim reality is that the majority of older women rely on supplementary programs to bring their incomes up to something approximating a survival level.

Of women sixty-five and older who are single, widowed, separated, or divorced, two out of three suffer acute financial hardship.[2] In addition, women over the age of thirty-five who are homemakers and lose their means of support through the death of their husbands, through separation, or through divorce often have no income at all. They are too young to collect Old Age Security; they too frequently have little or no work experience; they do not qualify for Unemployment Insurance; and usually they cannot collect under their husbands' pension schemes.

In the United States, these women have organized politically under the name of Displaced Homemakers. This group represents between three and six million women.[3]

Displaced homemakers exist in similar circumstances in Canada, but they have not, as yet, organized politically. One can only conjecture how they survive. Presumably, many of them are forced to rely on the charity of their relatives and friends or to turn to public welfare for assistance. Even the traditional source of income for these women – demeaning means-tested welfare – is being increasingly restricted to women with preschool children.

There is an underlying assumption that women will be cared for in their old age by their husbands, children, or some other male relative. In fact, women outlive men by a growing margin that is currently about seven years.[4] In addition, women tend to spend an average of eighteen years alone at the end of their lives.[5] Yet most women are thoroughly socialized to be dependent. Very few women are prepared to live alone or to function independently at the end of their lives. Nobody tells us that we may face a bewildering set of financial and legal problems with which we have no experience. We are victims of a contradictory and confusing societal message that initially encourages us to be passive and dependent and then punishes us for these same qualities when we are old and alone.[6]

Demystifying Pensions

When the subject of pensions comes up, most women throw up their hands in frustration. There is an intimidating welter of material threaded with highly technical jargon. But it does not help to allow our eyes to glaze over in confusion and boredom. If we abdicate responsibility for understanding how the pension system operates, we forfeit our right to complain when the majority of us are doomed to a financially impoverished and demeaning old age. To accept that most women are inept at understanding math and economics is to succumb to the stereotype of women as inherently incompetent.

Policy-makers and politicians rely consciously and unconsciously on our ignorance of the pension system. The older female electorate is ill-prepared, uninformed, frustrated, and overwhelmed by the effort to survive. We have little energy to mount an effective fight for serious pension reform. And until very recently, younger women gave little thought to what seems, at twenty and thirty, a far-off and somehow unreal old age.

It is not my goal to shower you with an unmanageable mountain of facts and figures, but rather to discuss the clear premises upon which the Canadian pension structure is built. Those premises include an alarming number of preconceived notions about women, most of which bear little relation to reality. It is to our advantage to understand how these premises will ultimately affect our retirement income, and how they sentence many of us to an old age lacking in dignity and a reasonable standard of living.

It is equally important that we approach the issue of women and pensions with an appreciation that, as women, we have made an enormous contribution to Canada's prosperity. Whether we spend our lives as mothers, homemakers, and/or full or part-time wage earners, we are entitled to a dignified, financially secure old age. It is a national disgrace that a relatively rich country like Canada is as yet unwilling to consider old women's quality of life a priority.

The world of the old is increasingly a world of women. Today women older than sixty-five represent approximately 1.1 million votes,[7] a number that will grow dramatically as women born after 1945 reach retirement. We have great potential political clout with which to press for changes. First, however, we must start to grapple with the fundamental premises of our pension system.

The Public Pension System

The History of Universal Entitlement

Agitation for some form of old age pension began in Canada at the turn of the century. There was a public perception that a significant number of older people were unable to accumulate adequate savings to provide for their old age. The issue was first raised in the House of Commons in 1906. However, it was not until eighteen years later, in 1924, that the House of Commons took formal action by appointing a special committee, whose mandate was to investigate how a system of old age pensions could be administered and financed within the Canadian context.

A year later, the committee released its report, which recommended a non-contributory scheme of twenty dollars a month for persons seventy or older. Applicants were required to meet a residency provision and submit to a means test. The costs of the pension, the committee proposed, should be shared on a fifty-fifty basis by the provinces and the federal government. Therefore, the agreement of each province was required before the plan could become operative in its jurisdiction. This plan was designed to supplement personal savings, not as a viable pension in itself.

The recommendation that the plan be non-contributory was a socially advanced concept for its time. The rationale was that a contributory plan would be too difficult and expensive to administer and that it would not help the generation that was already old in the 1920s.

Two CCF members of Parliament from Winnipeg, J.S. Woodsworth and A.A. Heaps, ardently pursued the issue of an old age pension. They introduced the Old Age Pension Act in 1926 and again in 1927, when it became law. By 1936, all the provinces and the Northwest Territories had adopted the pension plan.

What is most significant about this pension plan is its departure from the traditional welfare approach to income assistance. Although an applicant was required to declare his or her total income when applying for the pension, he or she did not undergo the usual exhaustive examination of needs, means, and lifestyle.[8] From the beginning the old age pension was seen as a right, not a privilege.

The plan did not change between 1927 and 1951, aside from small increases to reflect the rising cost of living. However, after almost twenty-five years' experience with the plan, it was recognized that too many poor older people experienced difficulty in meeting the strict requirements.

In 1951 the Old Age Pension Act of 1927 was replaced by the Old Age Security Act. The plan was to be financed and administered solely by the federal government. Although the residency requirement remained, the means test was dropped. The concept of a universal, non-contributory plan had been fully accepted. This pension, known as Old Age Security, is a recognition that everyone – men, women, homemakers, and wage earners – is entitled to his or her own pension as a reward for a lifetime of contributing to Canadian society. Everyone's contribution is perceived to be equally meritorious; there are no distinctions made between wage earners and those who do not work outside the home.

Old Age Security
Today benefits are paid monthly and adjusted every three months to reflect the cost of living. In the first quarter of 1983, everyone sixty-five and older who met the residence requirements received $251 a month.[9] For 1983-84, it is estimated that Old Age Security will be received by 2.47 million Canadians.

Old Age Security recognizes that Canadian society accepts its collective responsibility to retired people. But debate continues as to how far this responsibility should extend. At the present time, Old Age Security alone does not come close to providing an adequate retirement income. It was never intended to do so, for the premise upon which it was built was that individuals should save to meet their own retirement needs. Old Age Security, it was assumed, would augment an individual's savings and assist low-income earners.

What the policy-makers never anticipated was that most retired women would depend almost exclusively on Old Age Security. This dependence keeps us well below the poverty line.

The Canada Pension Plan
When the Old Age Security became a universal plan in 1951, it was still viewed as a supplement. In the latter half of the 1950s, public debate began to focus on a pension that would be adequate in and of itself to meet retirement needs. It was recognized that many people could not accumulate sufficient private savings for their retirement. This debate culminated in the introduction of the Canada Pension Plan (CPP) in 1966.

The goal of the Canada Pension Plan was to cover full-time wage earners, especially those who did not have private pension plans at work. Quebec does not participate in the federal scheme, but provides a similar pension benefit known as the Quebec Pension Plan (QPP.) As well as providing retirement pensions, CPP and QPP also provide disability pensions, death benefits, and benefits for surviving spouses and children of contributors.

Both these government schemes were set up like private pension plans in that one's benefits were to be linked in some actuarially sound way to the amount one contributed. Currently, a wage earner pays 1.8 per cent of earnings, and this contribution is matched by the employer. The self-employed are required to contribute 3.6 per cent, both the employer's and the employee's share.

There is an upper limit to the amount an individual can contribute to the plan and, hence, to the pension one can receive. For an employed person, the maximum CPP/QPP contribution for 1983 was $300.60, which represents an earnings level of $18,500.[10] Any earnings above this were not covered by CPP/QPP. The maximum monthly pay-out to a retired person was $345.[11]

This immediately leads us to the most fundamental flaw in any work-related pension plan: as long as benefits depend on prior contributions and contributions are linked to earnings, women will suffer disproportionately until such time as there is full equality of participation in the workforce between men and women. (We shall return to this basic structural weakness later in the chapter when we consider recent attempts to change CPP.) There are also operational details of CPP/QPP that significantly disadvantage all women. Housewives, for example, are specifically excluded from participation in the plan, a fact which has caused considerable debate in the women's movement. (We shall expand upon this aspect later in this chapter.)

Since CPP/QPP is based on a percentage of earnings, low-wage earners pay in less and receive less in retirement benefits than do high-wage earners. Since women form a disproportionately large percentage of low-wage earners, the dollar value of our pensions will tend to be less than those of men.

Another serious problem with CPP/QPP is that there is an upper limit to the amount one can contribute. No one can pay in more than $300.60 for the year 1983. This means that high-wage earners, who tend to be men, will be paying in a very small percentage of their salaries in CPP/QPP contributions. Using 1983 statistics, the National Council of Welfare compared the CPP and QPP contribution rate for two workers, one earning $10,000 a year and the other earning $50,000 a year. The contribution rate for the $10,000 earner is 1.48 per cent of total income. For the $50,000 earner, however, it was only 0.33 per cent. The worker earning $10,000 a year would receive a pension credit of 54 per cent of the maximum retirement entitlement. The worker earning $50,000 a year would qualify for 100 per cent of the pension entitlement.[12]

So women suffer CPP/QPP inequities in two ways. One's *ability* to pay premiums has little to do with how the plan operates: the more one earns above the $18,500 1983 ceiling, the smaller the proportion of income you pay in premiums. Secondly, most women, who are below the ceiling, will receive small pensions.

And finally, the maximum monthly pension of $345 in 1983 cannot seriously be considered adequate retirement income even when combined with the universal Old Age Security. Therefore, although the original intent of CPP/QPP was to provide a retirement income sufficient in its own right, we are really still operating on the assumption that people have private resources over and above their government pensions.

Guaranteed Income Supplement and Provincial Supplements

In 1967, the federal government added another tier to pension income, the Guaranteed Income Supplement (GIS). This was designed as an interim supplement to Old Age Security, to cease when the first CPP matured. However, the GIS is still in place. Most older women rely upon it to keep themselves from abject poverty. But even with this supplement, too many old women remain well below the official poverty line.

Since 1973, GIS has been linked to the cost of living. Had it not been, the value of the payment would have been seriously eroded by inflation. The amount of benefit individuals receive from GIS depends upon what other income they receive. However, there is a maximum, set at $252 a

160

month for the 1983 first quarter, for an individual who has no income other than Old Age Security.[13]

Unlike OAS, GIS is means-tested. As well, for every two dollars of income from a source other than OAS, the GIS benefit is reduced by a dollar.[14] There is little incentive for retired people to attempt to raise the combined OAS – GIS benefit with outside earnings. The penalty of a reduced GIS payment too frequently outweighs the gain of supplementary earnings.

In six provinces in Canada, pensioners may apply for income-tested supplementary programs designed to augment the federal GIS. The largest supplements are provided by Alberta, Ontario, and British Columbia. (Saskatchewan, Manitoba, and Nova Scotia provide a supplement that is less than half that of those three provinces.) But even with these supplements, women pensioners usually remain below the poverty line.[15]

Relying Solely on Public Pensions
Today, women older than sixty-five can end up poor by many different avenues – through divorce, widowhood, and/ or low-wages. Most women were simply never in a position to accumulate savings or other assets. The majority of women over sixty-five were totally dependent on their husbands. Those who worked earned wages too paltry to allow for much more than basic living expenses.

Imagine you are a woman in your eighties, a widow, wholly dependent on Old Age Security and Guaranteed Income Supplement. You live alone and are trying to manage on little more than five hundred dollars a month. If you live in a city, you are likely living in a rooming house or run-down flat or apartment. Most of your income will be consumed by rent, even if you are lucky enough to live in subsidized senior-citizen housing.

Eighty-two-year-old Mabel describes this life.

My husband died fifteen years ago, without a pension. I live on about five hundred dollars a month. After I am finished paying for this shabby place, there is little left over for food, clothes, or any entertainment. I buy my clothes at rummage sales and I don't eat very much, a little cereal, some toast, and tea. Sometimes I buy some fresh vegetables and fruit, but then I am stuck and must cut back on Kleenex, toilet paper, shampoo, and the like.

My family and friends are all gone now. I do have a son, but he's off in the west and I rarely see him. He thinks I am managing and I guess I am, but it feels more like scrounging than really living.

This flat is badly located. There are so many robberies and assaults around here. I have two chains, a lock, and a device that would make a loud noise if anyone so much as touched the door. I even have an eight-inch butcher knife to wedge between the door and the jamb to make it secure if all else fails.

Mabel is part of a large group of almost invisible older women who are experiencing acute poverty. She belongs to a generation that rarely complains in a public forum. Like many of her generation, who lived through the Depression, she accepts hardship and suffering as an inevitable fact of life. She believes that things could be worse, but she had hoped that, in her old age, she would be enjoying a better life.

Besides, she is frightened that, if she complains, what little she has will be taken away from her and she will become a "charity case" in a nursing home. Mabel is proud of her self-reliance, but she is acutely frustrated and demeaned by living on the edge.

Margaret Birch, the former minister responsible for the social-development ministry of the Ontario Conservative government, publicly declared that elderly women living alone "are receiving their fair share at the moment....They are not living in luxury, but it is offensive to suggest they are disadvantaged."[16] If Mabel and those like her, who are subsisting on tea and toast, and living in wretched accommodations are not disadvantaged, then who is? It is small wonder that pension reform is a low priority, given the attitudes of too many of our elected representatives.

Low Salaries, Low Pensions
One would assume that a woman who worked all her life would fare considerably better than a dependent older

homemaker. But statistics show that older single women do not receive a significantly greater pension benefit than widows. Even CPP does not provide a hedge against poverty.

Rose worked steadily as a secretary from her teens until her retirement at age sixty-five. She never married. At seventy-two she is experiencing serious financial problems.

I never made a great deal of money, but it was enough to live on. I had my own apartment and I took the occasional trip. It would have been nice to own a car, but that was always beyond my means. I never thought much about my old age — it seems to sneak up on you. But I was happy to retire after so many years in the same office. I think it was fifty years altogether. They held a small party for me and gave me a gold watch. I thought I might receive a bonus when I retired for all my years of service, but my boss, the son of my original employer, just patted me on the back and wished me luck. Well, luck is what you need. The last seven years have not been a picnic. I had to give up my apartment and move into one room. I have my name in for senior-citizen housing, but there is a long waiting list. Besides, I am not sure it would be such a good idea. The building is far from downtown and I would always be waiting for buses to get into the city. All my old friends live near where I live now and we get together all the time to visit.

I haven't a dime to spare these days. Everything goes for rent, food, and the like. My total monthly income is less than four hundred dollars. With today's prices, it doesn't buy much. People are always asking me why I didn't save for my old age. To be honest, I never made enough to save. I guess I could have lived in a room like this all my life, but I'm glad that I had an apartment when I was younger — it was a great pleasure to have a home of my own, surrounded by my own things.

Now I live with other old people in this slum. I share a bathroom with five other people and I have access to the kitchen. But it's no use keeping food in the fridge: it gets stolen. I don't blame the other people in the house — they are all old and as poor as church mice. People get hungry and look in the fridge and take something. So I eat at cafeterias. The food is awful, but it fills you up and it's still cheap enough for me to afford. I worry about what I will do when they raise the prices. My monthly pension isn't keeping up with the cost of living.

Every time they raise the rent, I go into a panic, but so far I have managed by cutting back. It will reach a point where I won't have anything to cut back on. Then it's the old-folks' home, I guess. As long as I am able, I want to stay on my own. I know women at the homes: they have lost everything, they're like children. I don't want that to happen to me.

Rose is representative of another seriously disadvantaged group of older women, those who have worked full-time all their adult lives at poorly paid jobs. They have suffered a lifetime of discrimination in the workplace: low earnings and benefits, and limited job opportunities. In retirement, a disproportionate number of these older women are at or close to the poverty line, existing on a combination of CPP, OAS, and GIS, which barely covers the basic necessities.

Rose's predicament is more the norm than the exception for single women who have worked at low-paying jobs that did not provide private pensions. As she pointed out, women in her position rarely have substantial savings or assets to supplement their retirement incomes. Like two out of three women over sixty-five and living alone, Rose relies solely on public pension plans.

For single working women, old age is often a time of severe financial impoverishment precisely because they are the recipients of a lifetime of discrimination in employment. Exclusion from high-salary jobs has an enormous impact on the pension benefits women ultimately receive. Since we typically earn low wages, we end up with low benefits in retirement. The pension system is based on the amount of wages earned and does not compensate for the enormous difference between men's and women's lifetime earnings.

164

Private Pension Plans

One source of income that might have made Rose's retirement more tolerable and more secure is a private pension plan. Although private pension funds represent one of the largest accumulations of capital in Canada, older women receive little of that capital. In the private sector, approximately 51 per cent of men and 34 per cent of women are covered by employers' private pension plans. The discrepancy between men and women exists because the majority of these plans are only available to long-term, high-salary, or unionized workers.[17]

Basically, private pension plans are governed by stringent rules that make it difficult for a woman employee to accumulate substantial benefits. Many private pensions stipulate that the plan becomes locked in or "vested" only after ten years of service or when an employee reaches age forty-five. This means that an employee's contributions to a pension plan (if any), and the employer's contributions on that employee's behalf, belong to the employee only when the employee has worked for that employer for ten years, or when the employee turns forty-five, whichever comes first, or sometimes when both conditions are met. This provision works against women because women more than men often do not stay with the same employer for ten years. They leave the paid workforce to raise their children, to care for sick relatives, to follow their husband's careers, because they cannot stand the boring, repetitive, and dead-end jobs that characterize so much of women's work. A woman who does not stay at her job long enough for her pension to vest is entitled to the return of her own contributions (and not her employer's share) at a rate of interest frequently lower than the money would have earned had she been permitted to place her contribution in an ordinary bank account.

Unlike the Canada Pension Plan, private pension plans are not portable. An employee cannot transfer accumulated pension credits from one employer to another. So, even if a pension vests with one employer, it is often locked in, and the employee cannot get access to it until retirement age.

Because women change jobs more frequently than men do, and earn lower wages overall, one or even two private pension plans locked in until age sixty-five will provide a lower total pension pay-out than would a typical man's continuous employment with one employer and his higher overall earnings. Therefore, even if pensions were portable, and the final benefit were calculated on all earnings and all years worked, women would still fare worse than men.

There is another restrictive aspect of private pensions: most do not provide benefits for a surviving spouse of a contributor. If there is a survivor benefit, the spouse is usually entitled to only 50 per cent of the contributor's accrued pension.[18] (The Canada Pension Plan is almost as punitive: a surviving spouse receives only 60 per cent of a contributor's total benefit.)

In keeping with society's view of women as dependents, many private pension schemes stipulate that if the widow of a contributor remarries, she forfeits her pension. She becomes another man's dependent and is not entitled to the benefit in her own right.[19]

In the event of a divorce, private pensions make no provision for dividing pension credits. Some women are now taking issue with this inequitable situation in individual divorce actions.[20]

Some private pension schemes also practise sex discrimination in relation to life expectancies. Approximately 5 per cent of employees participating in private pension schemes receive retirement benefits from a source called "money-purchase pension plans." Under these plans, both employee and employer contribute a specified percentage of the employee's salary to a fund that accumulates until retirement. The money is then used to buy a pension, called a life annuity, from an insurance company.

On average, women live longer than men; hence they may be expected to receive their pension for a greater number of years. Some insurance companies respond to this situation by giving a woman a smaller monthly pay-out than they would give to a man earning the same salary, so that the total benefits paid to the man and woman would be the same. Other insurance companies charge women higher premiums in order to receive the same monthly payment as men.

But insurance companies are being inconsistent. If they want to charge women more because they live longer, they should also charge married contributors more (most of whom are men), to cover the extra pay-outs associated with survivor benefits. The companies argue that all pensioners should share the cost of benefits paid to survivors, as this is an act of collective social responsibility. Female pensioners do not, apparently, merit the same treatment.[21]

In the United States, the Supreme Court has judged that giving lower pension benefits to women is discriminatory. Their reasoning is that it attributes to an individual woman a characteristic — in this case, longevity — which is only true to women as a group. Since there is no way of knowing whether any particular woman will live longer than the average man, the Court decided that it should be mandatory to use the same mortality tables for pension and life insurance plans, whether they are for men or women.[22]

Divorcées and Widows
Divorcées and widows, especially those under the age of sixty-five, experience financial deprivation because of the inadequacy of private and public pension schemes. Divorcées are becoming an increasingly vulnerable group, as the numbers of mid- and late-life divorcées have soared during the past twenty years. On average, a man is most likely to initiate a divorce when he reaches middle age and is earning his highest lifetime income.[23]

Although I interviewed many mid- and late-life divorcées, one woman's experience graphically chronicles the transition from comfortable circumstances to poverty.

Holly had been married for eighteen years and had three children. She did not work outside the home. Her husband left her for a younger woman.

That was five years ago. We are divorced now and he has remarried. I have had a horrible time of it, both financially and emotionally. When I married, I thought I was settled for life. Our deal was that I stay at home and take care of the house and the children and he would earn our living.

The first thing that hit me when he left was that I had to find a way to support the family. I was so angry and hurt by his desertion that I very naively decided I wouldn't ask him for a penny. I had been a schoolteacher before I married, so I decided to see if I could do some supply teaching. There was absolutely nothing available and I found that I was competing with very young people, fresh out of school. Over and over again, I was told that my skills were out of date and that I was a bit old to be resuming a career in teaching. Old, I thought, at forty-nine.

My friends and relatives told me to go for alimony and get every cent I could out of my husband. When I became desperate enough, I contacted a lawyer to establish my husband's obligation to me and the children. He told me quite bluntly that times had changed and I had little chance of getting much. The modern approach was for a woman like myself to go out and get a job. I became so angry that I could hardly speak. For six months I had looked every day for a job; I was ready to take anything. Nobody wants a forty-nine-year-old who has been out of the workforce for eighteen years. The lawyer replied that I just hadn't tried hard enough and I was probably aiming too high. The whole experience was so upsetting that I decided to forget a court action, especially after the lawyer told me what his fees were.

I finally landed a job as a clerk in a department store. It didn't pay much, but it put food on the table. Then I contacted my husband and asked him to come over and discuss our finances. He cheerfully agreed and came over that night. Before I could explain to him how rough things were, he told me that he and his friend were quitting their jobs and taking off to Europe for a while. At that point, I lost my temper and asked him what he proposed to do about me and the children. His answer was that he had worked hard for eighteen years supporting us and now it was his last chance to have some fun. He said he didn't want to be unreasonable, so he was leaving me the house. I started to laugh hysterically, pointing out to him that the house was mortgaged to the hilt because of his business failures. He shrugged his shoulders and said he would send me what cash he could, but he couldn't promise me it would be much.

When he left, I almost collapsed I was so tense and angry. I felt totally defeated. There was nowhere I could turn.

I guess we all have strengths that we don't know about. In a few months I sold the house and most of our best things and moved into subsidized housing. I barely manage and I worry all the time about my youngest child. She is affected by this neighborhood, which is very tough. I can't give her the things the older ones had, like summers in camp, bicycles, and, most of all, a lot of my time. When I come home from the store, I am so exhausted that I can hardly move. The future doesn't look very good, either. I have no pension plan where I work and I am not entitled to any benefits when my husband retires from his job.

I tell my daughters that they should have their own career and not end up the way I did, alone, poor, and tied to a lousy job.

Holly is engaged in a daily struggle to survive. Her income is near or, perhaps, below the poverty line. Her economic prospects are not good – and they are getting worse. As the traditional family grows increasingly unstable, it is the homemaker who will pay the highest price. Too frequently, divorced older women are left stranded.[24]

Contrary to popular mythology about greedy women who fleece their husbands in their divorce settlements, in the United States, only 4 per cent of divorced women receive alimony. In single parent families such as Holly's, 89 per cent are headed by women and, of these, a mere 25 per cent receive child support from their husbands.[25]

As Holly's story demonstrates, divorced women with children frequently have limited employment opportunities and end up with low-paying jobs. Very few are eligible for or have access to private pension plans; they can build up only meager CPP or QPP retirement benefits.

A divorcée is now entitled to apply for half of the CPP credits accrued by her husband during the marriage. This entitlement does not become operative until the woman reaches sixty-five. Unfortunately, this provision has not been well publicized, and very few divorcées sixty-five and over are aware that they are eligible for benefits.

Even if a divorcée is able to apply for and receive her CPP benefit, when her ex-husband dies she loses her entitlement. For those divorcées collecting a CPP benefit, its sudden loss can have serious financial consequences.[26]

Another large group of women, those who become widows in their fifties and early sixties, face a desperate financial struggle. Most anticipate a secure and even comfortable old age shared with their husbands. An early widowhood leaves many of these women in acute financial straits. In effect, they are being punished with economic deprivation for having outlived their husbands.

One of these women, Amelia, found that becoming widowed at age sixty leaves one in financial and social limbo.

My husband died after a lengthy and costly illness. He needed around-the-clock care during his last year, and doctors with their extra billing also took their pound of flesh. The cost of his sickness wiped out most of our savings, but I thought I would be all right with his pension.

As it turns out, my husband's company pension has no survivor benefits. I'm too young to collect either Old Age Security or my portion of my husband's Canada Pension.

While I was recovering from the effects of my husband's long illness and death, I sat down and tried to work out my assets with our lawyer, who explained that I was flat broke and should start looking for work. I can't quite explain how I felt. I was simply terrified. I had no idea how I could maintain the apartment, since the rent was way beyond my means.

It was terribly humiliating, but I contacted my two sons and asked them to fly in for a talk. When I explained my situation, they were both speechless. Neither of them was in a position to help on a regular basis. They both had just begun families and recently bought their own homes. In the end, they loaned me enough to tide me over until I could find a cheaper apartment.

I muddled over my options. At sixty I did not hold out much hope of finding a job, especially since I hadn't worked since I was twenty-five. The only skill I had was typing and that was somewhat rusty after so many years out of the labor force. I eventually ended up babysitting at a dollar and a half an hour.

My life is now a struggle. I live in a two-room flat and I watch every penny. I deny myself very simple pleasures, which I used to take for granted. I almost never entertain or go out to a movie or a concert. My whole existence is bound up in survival. It is not much of a life. After a lifetime as a homemaker and wife, I feel like I have been cast on the junk heap. I feel old and used up.

Amelia is far from atypical. As the dependant of a company employee whose pension scheme has no provision for survivor benefits, she finds herself destitute, living well below the poverty line. Her prospects are extremely bleak: a woman of sixty is not a prime candidate for a well-paying job with generous benefits. Amelia is hard hit by agism and sexism; women like her end up with low-paying, often part-time jobs. She is further impoverished because she is ineligible for Old Age Security and CPP: she is less than sixty-five, is not disabled, is not caring for children younger than eighteen, and is not providing for full-time students up to the age of twenty-five. Even if she were eligible for CPP benefits payable to widows, the disabled or orphans, these benefits are significantly lower than the benefits paid to a contributor receiving a maximum retirement benefit.[27]

When Amelia does become eligible for Old Age Security and CPP, at age sixty-five, she will most likely need the Guaranteed Income Supplement as well. All of these benefits, however, will still leave her to manage, as best she can, below the poverty line.

Widows are sentenced to endure poverty at the very time when they are no longer raising children or able to find a job. There are no rewards for a lifetime contribution of unpaid homemaking and rearing of the next generation of workers. Our society views old women as expendable.

Widows and divorcées share the same fate as those women who have supported themselves all their lives. While a husband is alive and living with them, women receive higher Canada Pension Plan benefits and often share second pensions and supplemental earnings. Widowhood or divorce signals the end of these benefits for most women. As for single, self-supporting women, a lifetime of being discriminated against in the workplace locks them into low benefits in retirement. In short, a woman can "reach poverty by way of marriage or get there on her own."[28]

Professional Women and Discrimination

The relatively small number of women who work in high-profile jobs are not immune from the same insidious discriminatory practices that low-wage earners experience. Since eight out of ten women marry and have children, their careers are interrupted by childbirth and years of child rearing.[29]

While they are so engaged, they are prohibited from contributing to CPP or to a private pension; therefore, they do not accumulate future pension benefits. The actuarial assumptions that determine pension pay-out presumed an adult lifetime of participation in the workforce. For women, who often leave the workforce to raise children, many years of non-contribution were assigned zero values for pension purposes. As a result, the average pension pay-out was reduced significantly. It would have been a far more equitable approach not to count the years of non-participation and to base the pension on the years one is in the paid labor force.

Recognizing that women were unduly discriminated against, the federal government was prepared to enact a drop-out provision, whereby a suggested seven-year period spent raising preschool children would not be counted for pension purposes. The QPP was the only income-related pension scheme in Canada that had a seven-year drop-out provision for caring for children. But since the CPP exists by virtue of an amendment to the British North America Act, any change in its regulations requires two years' notice and the consent of two thirds of the provinces containing two thirds of the Canadian population. The only province large enough to block an amendment to CPP was Ontario. Since Ontario did not want more pension benefits paid to women, it chose to block this amendment until the summer of 1983.[30]

However skilled a woman may be, if she leaves the labor force to raise children and then attempts to work again in her thirties or forties, she faces an additional obstacle: negative age stereotyping. Employers are often extremely prejudiced against older women who are seeking work; they equate aging in women with illness, incompetence, and feebleness of mind and body.[31]

Many women, both professionals and nonprofessionals, also labor under a disadvantage because they work part-time. Part-time work has traditionally been a female pattern of employment, since it allows a woman to contribute to the family income without significantly affecting her role as child rearer and homemaker. A woman who works less than nineteen hours a week does not qualify for private or CPP pension coverage.

Lorraine is a classic example of a professional woman whose interrupted working patterns adversely affected her ultimate retirement income. She recently retired from teaching at a community college.

It is a tedious, frustrating story. My battles with the administration over my pension started in 1960, when I was hired on a year-by-year basis. It was the only way I could convince the administration to hire me, despite a Ph.D. from Oxford in English literature. I guess I am paying the price for having married and had children. It was never my intention to interrupt my career, but in the 1950s, when I was having my family, it was almost impossible to convince an employer that a woman with children was serious about

173

a career. When I finally returned to teaching I was forty-five years old. I was so grateful they agreed to hire me that I did not object to the low salary. In fact, my salary was half of that of men with comparable education and experience. I taught for five years before my marriage, but this was not taken into consideration, despite the fact that I had published many articles in scholarly journals during the years I was at home raising my children.

After five years of dealing with the hassle of having my contract renewed each year, my gratitude dried up and I began to realize that I was being unabashedly exploited. A permanent opening came up at about this time so I approached my department head and suggested that I be given serious consideration. I pointed out to him that I had published, done my quota of administrative work, and had received high evaluations on my teaching. His response was an unequivocal no. He pointed out that my husband had an excellent job and that I would be taking a job away from a serious male candidate.

His sexist attitudes kindled my anger and I decided to go over his head to the president of the college. It took another year and a half, but I finally was appointed to the permanent staff. Now I was eligible for the college pension scheme and salary raises. It took several more years to have my salary increased to a rate that was comparable with my peers in the department. What a bitter, tiring battle. It wore me out, but I persevered.

And now I am retired. A new battle begins. All those years that I was on a yearly contract are not included in the calculation of my pension. As a result I am receiving 15 per cent less than I feel I am entitled to. I believe that I was originally discriminated against in terms of my yearly contracts and my lower wages. The college is determined to fight me on this. They have indicated that they are not prepared to set a precedent. My situation is not unique. I am one of seven women currently in this position.

I regret now that I did not consider the effect on

my pension of the discrimination I suffered originally. It simply never occurred to me. I am particularly vulnerable since my husband died. His corporation only provides 50 per cent of his pension as survivor's benefits.

Of course, I appreciate that I am much better off than the majority of women. It is the injustice of the situation that rankles. I worked just as hard as my colleagues and I believe there should be equity in salaries and in pensions. With my full pension I would be able to live comfortably, with some dignity. Without it, I will experience financial difficulties.

Most of us can expect to confront poverty when we become old women. It's the inevitable outcome of the roles society demands we play during our lifetimes. As wives and mothers, we are dependent on our husbands, who may predecease us by an average of seven years. Those of us who work full-time generally end up being exploited, in low-paying jobs. The wives and mothers who work part time are not eligible for private pension plans or CPP. Even if we do work for most of our adult lives, many of us spend long periods as child rearers. These absences mean we receive reduced benefits.

The entire benefits structure is based on the premise that men are able and willing to support their wives and families. Families in which the husband earns low wages most often avoid poverty by the wife finding paid employment. If these women were not working, one report calculated, 51 per cent more two-spouse families would be included in Statistics Canada's definition of the poor.[32]

And the majority of women find themselves alone sometime in their adult lives, victims, in most cases, of marriage breakdown and widowhood.

Poverty is the root cause of the erosion of dignity in older women's lives: life becomes a grim battle for survival. Most of the women I interviewed had anticipated a reasonable old age, a decent place to live, enough food to eat, and a little left over to enjoy some minimal comforts. The death of a husband or retirement from a job generally precipitated a serious financial crisis. Life was pared down to the barest essentials. These women had trusted that Old Age Security, their husbands' pensions, and the years they had spent working would yield sufficient money to live with a measure of security. Very few had a basic understanding of how OAS and pensions operate. Among those who had been married, very few were aware of the family's financial status. Most had been assured by their husbands that they would be provided for in the event of their husbands' deaths. The details of how this would be accomplished were viewed as the husbands' responsibility.

Older women are being punished for surviving in our society. They are sentenced to living out the last quarter of their lives in desperate financial struggles. Seventy-six-year-old Mary is one of these women.

> If you're really interested, I'll tell you what it's like to be an old woman alone who's only got the government pension to live on. It's wearing out your second-hand shoes in going from one store to another trying to find the cheapest cuts of meat. It's hating having to buy toilet tissue or soap or toothpaste because you can't eat it. It's picking the marked-down fruits and vegetables from the half-rotting stuff in the back of the store – stuff that used to be given away to farmers to feed their animals. It's hunting the thrift shops and Salvation Army stores for half-decent clothes.
>
> Emergencies come up, grandchildren have birthdays, clothes wear out, cleaning products run out, bus rates go up. How do we manage? We pay our rent and utilities and eat less. We live in fear. Fear of the future, of more illness, less money, less pride. Fear that the check won't arrive and we won't be able to work our way through the red tape in time to pay our rent. Fear that we will run out of food before the next check comes in. Fear holds you in line. It is our punishment for getting old and sick.[33]

Confronting the National Action Committee on the Status of Women

In 1982 the federal government came out with a Green Paper on the future of the Canadian pension system. The

National Action Committee on the Status of Women known as NAC, Canada's largest feminist-lobby organization, prepared a detailed response entitled "Pension Reform — What Women Want." NAC is a national voluntary organization, whose members include more than two hundred and fifty groups purporting to represent the views of more than three million Canadian women. The bulk of its funding comes directly from the federal government. NAC considers itself to be an independent, nonpartisan, feminist lobby, although its critics accuse it of being too closely associated with the Liberal Party.

NAC's document created tremendous controversy among women. Some say it is the best we can hope for in these economic times; others dismiss it as middle-class and elitist — a cop-out. Since its document is the most widely circulated piece of literature dealing with women and pensions, it is extremely important to look at NAC's views.

My focus is not on actuarial details, but on the basic premises and the philosophical orientation that underlie NAC's approach. In its Green Paper on pension reform, the federal government quite clearly indicated that the major change for women is the expansion of the means-tested Guaranteed Income Supplement (GIS). This expansion will occur when the economy permits. In addition, the Green Paper focuses on the more flagrant inequities of private pension schemes. NAC accepted the concept of expanding the GIS, but advocated a number of changes in the Quebec and Canada pension plans, as well.

NAC is proposing that homemakers be included in these pension plans not as one deserving category, but as three distinct groups. The first group comprises homemakers with children younger than seven or with very disabled family members. NAC recommends that the cost of their benefits, set at half the average industrial wage (about ten thousand dollars), be subsidized by all other QPP and CPP participants.

The second group of homemakers that NAC recognizes is made up mainly of those whose children have left home. They, too, should be entitled to benefits equalling half the industrial wage, but their contributions should be mandatorily absorbed by their husbands or by the adult(s) who are the recipients of homemakers' services.

A third group of homemakers would be those whose children have left home or with children older than seven whose husbands cannot afford CPP or QPP contributions. This group, NAC recommends, should be given a subsidy, which presumably would be means-tested.

Let's look at these recommendations, taking them first within NAC's own frame of reference. For the purposes of calculating benefits, NAC values housework at half the industrial wage. Although NAC has never formally stated its reasons for choosing this figure, it is generally understood to be a recognition of present hard economic times. Such a compromise by NAC is fundamentally unacceptable. The issue is not one of the government's inability to pay, for the government can pay for anything it deems a priority. The issue is one of basic justice. If housework is to be treated as work for pension purposes, it must be acknowledged as work of worth and value. NAC's readiness to assess housework at such low value serves to reinforce the stereotype of housework as undemanding and trivial.

Another flaw in NAC's analysis is the division of women into three distinct groups. To so divide women presumes that women are not all equal, that some are more valuable than others. Women with children younger than seven would, under the NAC proposal, enjoy an automatic right to a pension; and women with older children would be split into two groups — those with husbands wealthy enough to pay their wives' pension benefits, and those who must submit to demoralizing means tests when applying for a government subsidy.

NAC's proposal would stigmatize low-income families. As with every other means-tested program in Canada, a significant number of low-income families will simply not apply for the subsidy. As a result, many women who will need QPP/CPP benefits most in old age will lose out. And those low-income families just above the subsidy cut-off level will not be able to afford the homemaker contribution.

NAC's approach to the federal pension plan perpetuates and aggravates homemakers' dependence on men. Entitlement on the basis of the husband's ability to contribute on his wife's behalf will unquestionably reinforce the male's dominant position.

In addition, the division of women into three separate groups buttresses the classical sexist argument that men and women should receive different treatment because of the different nature of our needs and contributions. To divide women by virtue of their husbands' wealth and the age of their children is similarly fallacious. Our goal is to achieve pension reform for women, not to divide them into artificial and potentially alienating categories.

Moreover, NAC never addresses the regressive aspect of the pension scheme: the ceiling imposed on contributions. A more equitable scheme of contributions would require all contributors to pay the same percentage of their incomes, with no upper limit. As things stand, those with high incomes receive the highest dollar benefit, although they contribute a smaller proportion of their income. The rich are able to take advantage of the system, but the poor cannot.

However, the real objections are not to these technical and operational details. They strike at the heart of NAC's approach to income security for women in old age. NAC's basic approach can only be described as middle-class, elitist, and indeed, touching upon chauvinism.

Any income-security scheme based on work contributions is fundamentally unacceptable, at least until such time as women have full and total equality in the workforce, and their contributions to a work-related pension scheme are treated as equal to those of men. Only then will pension benefits be comparable for men and women. Given society's continuing ambivalence about the merit of housework and raising children, it's unlikely that women's contributions will ever be valued adequately.

The fundamental issue is a question of values. Is adequate income in old age something to which we are entitled? Is it a universal and automatic right, a reward for a lifetime of contributions to society? Or should income security in old age depend on contributions to the paid workforce? If the latter, we penalize all those who do important but low-paid jobs or volunteer work, and reward high-income groups, who need pensions the least.

We must reject outright NAC's pension-plan proposal, and demand that CPP and QPP be de-emphasized. The federal plan, which is based on an earnings-related benefit, will never reward women fairly. Our goal should not be half the industrial wage, or reaching the poverty line. It should be guaranteeing a standard of living that allows older people to retain their dignity. The simplest, most equitable way to reach our goal is to fight for the expansion of the universal, non-contributory Old Age Security. Rather than means-test the poor to determine their eligibility for the federal pension plan or a guaranteed-income supplement, through GIS or QPP/CPP, give everyone an equal share of pension benefit. The plan would be financed by general tax revenues. Those who are rich would pay back their portion of OAS through the personal income tax system. Because of the nature of our personal income tax system, even the rich will pay back only a portion of Old Age Security through their taxes.

An important suggestion has recently been made by the National Anti-Poverty Organization (NAPO), a national, voluntary organization of low-income individuals and groups and others concerned about issues affecting the poor in Canada. NAPO advocates that an enriched Old Age Security continues to be paid monthly to everyone as a right. However, the many exemptions, deductions, and loopholes in the personal income tax system, which are of benefit only to the rich, should be reduced or eliminated entirely. This would make the personal income tax system more truly progressive and thereby, recover through taxes more of Old Age Security from the rich than is now the case. But as an important point of principle, every senior citizen in Canada should retain some portion of their universal entitlement.[34]

We must give our politicians a clear message that income security in old age is important to us. If we exercise our collective political strength, ultimately they will be forced to respond. We, the older women of today and the women pensioners of tomorrow, have a right to a dignified, secure old age. But we can only achieve this by voicing our discontent and fighting for *real* pension reform.

6

Magnificent Survivors:
Personal Responses to Aging

In this chapter, seventeen women discuss their personal responses to aging. None of these women has led a particularly unusual or spectacular life, but each has struggled against economic and social obstacles. The common goal that these women share is to create an old age that has meaning and dignity.

These brief glimpses of their lives portray their vitality, creativity, and courage in the face of societal indifference and neglect. Problems such as financial deprivation, diminished health, inadequate housing, loneliness, and boredom have not defeated them. They demonstrate that very ordinary women are magnificent survivors. Each woman has had the courage to do what is comfortable and right for her, not to follow the narrow lifestyle prescribed by society. By sharing their experiences, these women empower all of us.

Lettie is eighty years old. She works as a private nurse and babysitter.

I'm poor today because I never had a decent job. My husband left me with three small children right in the middle of the Depression. I had no mother to help with the kids, no car, and after the first year, I never received a penny from my ex-husband.

It is possible to do anything if you really have to. I sewed all our clothes and I took in boarders. It was a real struggle, especially while the children were small. At one point I tried to sell beauty products, but without a car and without any capital, I never made very much money. The thing I did best was raise my babies to be strong and healthy people. I remember feeding the four of us on a dollar a day.

Of course, I often thought it would be nice to remarry, but no one wanted a woman with three little children. There never really was a chance. In my day, a single woman was not a happy guest. You tended to become somewhat isolated.

I think my life really became much better from age fifty on. That's when I was most beautiful. I finally didn't have the heavy burden of my children wrapped around my throat. And I started to earn a decent salary for the first time. I moved to a new city and took up private nursing. I've been doing it for thirty years now, and I suspect I will for many years to come. My health is excellent and I take long walks for exercise.

My philosophy is to make the best of things. I get up every morning feeling good, looking forward to the day. I don't allow myself to brood or indulge in self-pity. I try never to leave my apartment without a smile on my face.

I work at looking good – I have to. If people knew that I was eighty, they wouldn't trust me to care for their children. It's a foolish, prejudicial attitude. Everyone is different. I have friends who are sixty and look a hundred. I make a point of moving quickly and I work at keeping slender. Maybe dyeing my hair at my age is a bit ridiculous, but people are terribly impressed with appearances.

My doctor has told me that I will probably live to be a hundred. He can't find anything wrong with me and keeps telling me that I am a medical wonder. I think part of the reason I am so healthy is that I read all the time and don't pollute my mind with television. I go to the symphony and to the theater when I can, but the public library is my greatest entertainment. Every week I take out three or four books on all kinds of subjects. And once a year I take a trip to a country I have never seen. At my age, I have to go on organized tours, partly for safety and partly for financial reasons.

But I would love to wander on my own, especially in the Orient, which fascinates me. My other greatest hope is to die while I am taking one of my daily walks.

The only thing really lacking in my life, aside from money, is a good man. I don't think of myself as elderly and most of my friends, male and female, are much younger than I am. I can't stand to be in a place with old, sick people. Everyone my age has given up. It's not their physical disabilities that disturb me — sickness is part of life — it's the fact that they're sitting back and taking it from people. I'm a fighter and I refuse to let anyone treat me like a little old lady. Just let them try.

To be honest, I don't know where I could meet a man I would find attractive. He would have to be at least ten years younger than I am — otherwise, how could I hope to have any fun with him? Men my own age are just too old for me. I do volunteer work in a nursing home and I find the place awfully depressing. I read, sew, and write letters for people much younger than myself. The home is such a waste of women. A lot of them are sick and need help, but I think they would be a lot happier living in their own homes.

I am very confident that I can continue as I am. I do all my own cooking and cleaning. This apartment is just filled with old things that I have collected over a lifetime. They are my old friends and give continuity to my life. The older you get, the more important it is to have a secure and familiar base.

It's too bad I was born when I was. The women's movement has made great changes that would have affected my life significantly. Better jobs, for one thing, are open to women like myself. And young women today are definitely more free than women of my generation were.

But I can't complain. I was born with a good mind and a strong constitution. I'm active and I seem to attract interesting people, who become part of my life. It's a two-way street: I find my friendships, particularly with younger women, very stimulating, but I know they find me stimulating, too. At my age, though, life shouldn't have to be such a financial struggle. I like to think that it will get better for other generations.

Seventy-two-year-old Hilary's aspiration is to have a house in the country with a few animals and a large vegetable garden.

Put it this way, I'm known as a loner and I like it. I am happiest when people just let me be, when they don't bother me. I'd like to spend some time on my own.

All my life I took care of other people. At fourteen I married the man my father chose for me. I was married for more than fifty years and I had six children. In my day you stuck to your marriage, no matter what. What a life I had! I worked very hard on the farm, but my husband was always nagging, smoking horrible cigars, or drinking too much. The worst part was being questioned all the time, as if I were a child. Now I have my own money and I can do what I like. I don't ever want to go through that rigmarole again – it's safer for women to be on their own.

I am in this convalescent home because of high blood pressure, swelling of my feet, and a whole lot of other things, which I don't really understand. I can't say that I like it, but I don't have much choice.

Two of my daughters have said I could live with them, but I will never do it. I have nothing against my children, but.... I don't know how to describe it. You feel out of place, as if they are watching you. Besides, I prefer not to be a burden to anyone. I get along fine with just me. I had my life and I want to let them have theirs. It's hard for people to understand that not all women like constant company. It's not that I don't want to see my children, my grandchildren, and my great-grandchildren, but I want some time to myself before it is too late.

When and if I ever get out of here, I would like to go back to the farm. I would get a couple of ducks and pigs and I would put a garden in. I'd say that is the life I would like best. Maybe I would have some hens and chickens. I would also love to have a little lamb. I think I could handle it just fine. It would be good for me in the country — it's where I feel most at home.

Melinda was stricken with polio when she was three years old.

I am a quadriplegic, so I have to have someone around at all times. Luckily my mother, who is over eighty, is still able to care for me, although I realize that I will need to hire someone when she isn't here any more.

I'm concerned about aging, especially now that I am fifty-two. But I don't think of aging in a bad way. When I assess things, I see aging as a form of maturity. Truthfully, I have no desire to go back to a younger age. I think that I was rather immature and perhaps too willing to accept people on their terms. Now I have much more confidence and self-awareness.

I'm a great believer in work and giving back to life what you get out of it. When I was twenty-six I went to college and earned a degree. This changed my whole life: it meant that I could earn my own money and be somewhat independent. It made it possible for me to become more integrated into life. A great many handicapped people are totally cut off from society; they feel very isolated and extremely cynical. At college I made friends, people I still keep in touch with. My work also puts me in contact with all kinds of people, though mostly on the telephone.

I am aware that, as I grow older, I will suffer a different kind of discrimination. North Americans tend to shun old people, to throw them aside. I can understand why a lot of today's young women are turned off motherhood. They see that old women have no place in our society. They recognize that old women are neglected even by their children.

I know that soon I will be both old and handicapped, but I hope the world will change. Right now we have created a society of young and beautiful people. Everyone is conditioned to feel that anything that is not perfect belongs in the glue factory. But I think that we are the sum of our lives. Admittedly, part of it is luck: you must be encouraged and come from a vital background if you hope to make a reasonable life for yourself.

The women's movement is a very positive force; it's a sign that there is progress in our thinking about women's roles in society. More than that, it is a sign that women are not prepared to be second-class. I'm sure it has affected my own thinking, even though I have never been a women's activist. The difference in me is that I am not a passive person any more; I am prepared to fight back and to stand up for my rights.

I would like to see the government provide more services to the old and to treat the old with respect. Our standards are very low. What good is a country that produces beautiful art and music alongside such staggering poverty and suffering? Old women have no choices in our society. It makes me very angry to think that I live in a country of hypocrites. We give lip service to the notion of respect to old women. Yet the last part of our lives is the worst part.

From what I can see, there are no rewards for most women. At least I have a skill. Most women in this country are either unskilled or poorly skilled; as a result, we are used as cheap labor.

And yet, despite all our disadvantages, I think we women are wonderfully strong. We are able to cope with problems, to laugh at ourselves. God knows most of us don't have a lot to laugh about, but we have a marvelous sense of humor. My life would have been very dreary, indeed, if I hadn't been able to see the humor of things.

Doreen became severely handicapped over a period of four years.

It all began in my mid fifties, when I developed both arthritis and cancer. Both are under control now, but I need a lot of services to maintain my independence.

I'm sixty now, and the word "aging" turns me off.

When you think of old age, you think of a wizened old lady. It's ironic that the young are worshipped, considering that most women don't develop any character until they are older than thirty.

I spend a lot of time at a community center and I see a lot of kids who are very mixed up. Without intending to, I have become a confidante to a lot of teenage girls. They come to me for advice, especially the handicapped ones. They like to talk to someone older, someone who has made a life for herself despite a handicap.

I think back on my life, and I see that I made a lot of mistakes. I married very young, but luckily I never had any children. When I became ill my husband left me – he just disappeared when the going got rough. But I've adapted and adjusted to my limitations. I need a walker to get around and I depend on special transportation services provided by the center. Luckily, I was able to get a subsidized apartment. It's small, but the privacy is marvelous, especially after all the time I spent in the hospital.

What bothers me most is that no one will employ me. This country has very stupid ideas about women and aging. I don't accept society's definition of aging or what it is to be handicapped. I was a bookkeeper for years until I became ill. There is no reason I couldn't still work in an office. It would take some organizing and a little bit of tolerance, but I am sure I could do the job just as well as I always have. But no one will hire me. They have all kinds of excuses and I haven't the energy to fight them in court.

But there's no sense crying about what you can't have. I have compensated by becoming a volunteer at the center. It helps me get out of myself, and I know that there are always people worse off. A few friends have stuck by me over the years. One friend in particular comes to visit me every week, no matter what. She does my shopping and picks up my dry-cleaning. Good friends are better than marriage. The good part of getting rid of a bad husband is that you can do as you please and you can enjoy some privacy. There is not much security in life for women and I know it gets worse as we age. If we want to change society's attitudes toward us, we must demand that we be respected for our maturity.

I have this image of myself at eighty-five on the back of a motorcycle, traveling around the country with a knapsack on my back. I want the freedom to see and do things I have never done before. Who knows? Maybe someone will come up with a cure and I will be able to realize my dream.

Nellie has tutored more than a hundred children over the years. At eighty, her fondest wish is to become a foster grandparent, but she is seen as too old to take on such a responsibility.

I never married and I don't have any children. Most of my adult life was spent working as a clerk at a very low wage. When I retired – or rather, when I was pushed out of my job – I had a very small retirement income. When you earn so little, you never put much by for your old age. I was saved by my mother, who hired me to help her when she was ill. Then my aunt needed me to care for her. Both women left me small inheritances, which have made it possible for me to own this house. It's a good thing I am very economical or I would be in a nursing home by now.

I have always loved children and plants. The neighborhood children are continually in and out of the house. Many of the children I cared for are now married and have children of their own. I seem to have a special affinity for children; they are so open and warm and very curious about things. The way I became involved with children was through coaching them in the schools. Many years ago I volunteered to help children who were behind in their studies because of illness or learning difficulties. Until about five years ago, my grandnieces and nephews used to come and visit me in the summer, but their parents now think I am too old to take care of them. That's a lot of rubbish, of course. I can do all that is necessary to care for a child.

I still bake my own bread and put up preserves every year. I love to garden and the housekeeping is still manageable.

When children come to visit me, I become very involved in their play. We often sing songs and make things together. What develops is a mutual respect. I especially like the very small ones, who climb up on my lap and ask all kinds of questions. I really wanted to become a foster parent after my aunt died, but I was told that I was too old. Then I considered becoming a foster grandparent, but I am considered too old for that, too.

I sometimes think the reason I like the company of children so much is that they accept you for yourself. When you are old, people won't be bothered with you. I still remember when my aunt became sick. None of the people from her church ever came to visit her. She was eager to hear what was going on, since she had been extremely active in the church.

I feel a bit cut off now because most of my immediate family has died off. I get tired of taking the initiative with people, telephoning and saying I would like to visit. I would love people to come here for dinner, but I don't think many couples like to visit a single woman. It's the way of the world, I suppose. It doesn't make much sense, since I like to cook and I would love to entertain. The women my own age are either dead or too sick to come by. It doesn't leave me with much of a social life, except for the children.

The radio is a great friend to me in the evening. I have never been much of a club person and I especially dislike meetings. What I would like to do is take courses at college, but I'm afraid to go out at night.

I hate this "old age" business. Your quality of life just goes down. I feel particularly sorry for a woman who has an old sick husband. That is probably the worst; it wears a woman out and shortens her own life. As a single woman, I learned to be independent and self-reliant very early on. I'm luckier than most because I have a home and I can manage well on my own. If I were a bit younger, I think I would get involved in changing things for old women. We all seem to end up poor and alone.

Sybil has been widowed twice, and is now trying to make a new life for herself.

I live close to my only daughter. For years I wandered all over the world, following my first husband's career. He died, after a long illness, at the age of sixty-two. I was just devastated at his death, but I returned home and took up with my old friends. Just before my sixty-fifth birthday I ran into an old suitor, a man I had known in my teens. His wife had just died and he was very lonely. The two of us started to go out together and within a year we decided to marry. The next five years were absolutely wonderful. We lived comfortably, traveled, entertained, and shared a warm companionship.

Without warning, my second husband had a heart attack and died. I think I was on the verge of a nervous breakdown after his death. I was all alone and I thought I couldn't go on. This was the second time I had lost a man I loved dearly. It was almost unbearable. I also had problems with my second husband's son regarding the will.

I am very fortunate to have a supportive and loving daughter. She came to me, packed my things, and took me home with her. After a couple of weeks, I decided to give her city a try. I rented this apartment and sent for my things. In just a couple of months I have met an amazing number of people, and they have started to include me in their activities. I am a very outgoing person and I think that helps. Of course, I recognize that, in our society, a woman without a husband is less included, less accepted. My daughter encourages me to go out and do things on my own.

I am seventy and I know that society sees me as old. But I don't feel old – I feel very young inside. I don't want to stagnate, so I am planning to go back to school and study philosophy and psychology. My life is quite peaceful now and I think I can settle here. My friends

190

back home tell me I should come back, that I am too old to start over. Actually I am very pleased with my adjustment to a new place; it has given me a new outlook on life. All my life I have been a very conventional woman. I find that being in a new place has encouraged me to change some of my old habits. I am more assertive; I call people spontaneously to invite them over. At social gatherings I don't wait to be introduced; I take the initiative and introduce myself. These are small things, but quite liberating for someone like me. There are a lot of good years left for me and I intend to live them as fully as I can.

At eighty-two, Vivian has become a public speaker, carrying on with the work she shared with her husband during his lifetime.

My husband's reputation as a scholar in Near Eastern Literature was quite widespread. During the fifty-six years we were married, I was always actively involved in helping him prepare articles, books, and speeches, although I was always somewhat in the background as a researcher and all-purpose assistant. My own education was quite modest, but I did manage to get my Master of Arts degree in my forties, specializing in one aspect of my husband's work.

Our time together was full, even though we never had any children. My husband's students and colleagues were very much part of our lives. There were always crowds of young people around, and when we grew older, they began to help out around the place, shoveling the walk, putting up the storm windows, and helping with the garden.

When my husband died I felt very lonely, and I was worried that no one would come to visit any more. Much to my surprise, many of his students and colleagues kept up the contact and included me in activities around the college. Shortly after my husband's death, one of the professors asked me to deliver a lecture to his students. At first I refused because I didn't think I could manage such a responsibility. I feared that, at eighty, my mind would be rusty and I would forget things.

But I finally decided that I would take a chance and see if I could do it. I wasn't half bad, and while I was speaking I felt more alive and stimulated than I had in a long time. It was very uplifting to be among young people with lively minds. They forced me to dredge up all the knowledge that I had stored inside my brain. I discovered that I know more than I ever gave myself credit for.

Now I have become something of a celebrity. I'm always in demand for the lecture circuit and I find that I am traveling quite a bit. I have stopped thinking of myself as a little old lady who was the wife of a famous scholar. For the first time I hold center stage and I like it. As long as my health holds -- and it should for quite a while -- I want to continue lecturing and learning. It's remarkable -- if you are treated with respect, you respond in kind. It does wonders for your self-confidence and self-esteem. I have been saved from a very lonely and limited old age by a skill that I didn't realize I had. There are probably many women like me who have lived in their husbands' shadows. Given the opportunity, they could contribute a great deal to society.

When Bertha retired from teaching, she started to take in student boarders in her home.

I married quite late in life and had my only child when I was forty-four. My son was away at college when my husband died ten years ago, and I found that I was desperately lonely.

I had retired early from teaching primary school to spend time with my son when he was in his teens. At sixty-six I didn't think anyone would hire me as a teacher. I was at loose ends and strapped for money. A friend suggested that I take in college students as boarders to supplement my income.

Well, that was the beginning of what has been a very satisfying period of my life. For the past ten years I have had two students living here at a time. They are usually between nineteen and twenty-three, far away from home, and quite lonely. The students are like a second family to me: we eat meals together, I help out with their studies, they take me shopping and help around the house. It's a mutually supportive thing. These have been very good years, because I have been busy and involved. There is lots of life around my place; there is always something happening. I have never been aware of my own aging during this time because I am accepted and I feel useful.

Of course, I realize that taking in students is not for everyone, but I think a lot of women in my position would benefit enormously from having young people around. Life is never boring or dull. These students respect me and ask my advice. I don't really feel like a grandmother figure; it's more like being an older friend. But it's not a one-way street. One winter I was very sick with bronchitis and could barely get out of bed. The students who were with me at the time took over the house. They cleaned, they cooked, they even took care of all the bills. Without their help I would have had to enter a nursing home. They kept encouraging me to get better and always made sure that I was entertained.

Last year my son suggested that I come live near his family back east. He asked me to try it for a year to see if I liked it. I wanted to be near my son and my three grandchildren, but I was very sad to leave my students. I only lasted five months. I was horribly lonely living in an apartment by myself without any friends. My son and his wife made great efforts to make me feel included in their family life, but no one would let me do anything. They treated me like a fragile, old lady. I started to feel awkward and physically weak. Everyone kept telling me to sit down and relax. At all the family dinners I was put off to the side while everyone bustled around. It made me feel old for the first time.

I think what finally made me decide to go back to my own house was my grandchildren's reaction to me. The oldest is six, the next is five, and the youngest is three. They are not used to old people. The subdivision they live in is filled with young couples and small children. The six-year-old was very outspoken. He kept pointing to my wrinkles and my pronounced veins, and yelling, "Gross!" He saw me as ugly and witchlike and refused to sit on my lap or come anywhere near me. The younger ones picked up his revulsion and refused to have anything to do with me. It was probably the lowest point in my life. I felt very depressed and lost a lot of my self-confidence. It was a shock and disappointment, especially since children have always responded well to me. My son and his wife were mortified, but I understood that it wasn't their fault.

Well, I packed my bags and came back home. Some of my former students came over and made a party for me. I now have two young women boarders studying law. It's like old times. There is lots of kidding around and warm feelings. I do miss my son and his family, and I intend to go for visits. But for now, at least, I want to live here with the students.

I have learned now how easily you can get cut off from life when you are an old woman. I never realized how awful life is for most women my age. When I was at my son's I used to take walks during the day and I would see all these old women wandering around aimlessly, looking bored and mumbling to themselves. The students make my life enjoyable, but they also force me to continue to learn and to grow.

For Polly, old age means keeping your pride and not pitying yourself.

I keep myself as active and as healthy as I can. I'm seventy-one years old, hard as that is for me to believe. But I am faced with a lot of problems, now that my husband is gone. I have the money from our house and a little from the government pension, but the cost of everything keeps going up and my money can't cover all the expenses.

A long time ago I said there was no reason to be poor in your old age if you worked hard. Well, I worked hard all my life, washing dishes in a restaurant, cleaning floors in office buildings at night, and doing piece-work in factories until I nearly went blind. What do I get for all of this? A kick in the teeth. I gave plenty to the government and I was happy to do it, but now I'm getting next to nothing in my old age.

I spend a lot of time helping out at an old-folks home near my apartment. The old ladies know I like them, so I do them some real good. Most of them are in better shape than I am and they have very clear minds. A lot of them have been dumped by their families.

I don't believe it does any good to feel sorry for yourself. Just a few years ago I had a husband and a home, and look where I am now. It isn't great, but it's okay. You can't live in the past. I've come through my bad time and I am trying to make the best of things.

My friends keep telling me to remarry, but who can you get at my age? Most of the men I know are boozers, and I don't need that. These old guys get drunk and go looking for women for sex. But I ask you, what kind of sex can you have with a drunk? Besides, I have made a lot of women friends in my building, some older and some younger. We enjoy each other's company; we shoot the bull and laugh a lot.

Ah, well, you just go on in spite of your troubles. A lot of people are worse off than I am, and I feel bad about that. That's why I help out at the old-folks' home. But the most important thing is keeping my pride; without it, you are nobody in this world.

Ada is a ninety-year-old woman who has come to the conclusion that most women would be better off if they never married.

I was married for thirty-eight years and that was quite enough. After that I did as I pleased. I had my own apartment; my health was good; I developed my own social life. I felt good. Until I ended up in this place, I was quite a theater- and concert-goer. I used to say to my children, leave me be, I have my own life now.

I regret never having had a job. My husband wouldn't

allow it. He was very authoritarian and I never felt strong enough to contradict him. When you marry at twenty-one, you don't know very much about life.

When I was widowed, more than thirty years ago, I finally started to do things I liked and to go places on my own. I am really pleased that so many women today are going out to work and that some have husbands who help out in the home.

I read in the paper that a lot of women are not marrying. I don't blame them. They look around and see the trouble it brings. If you marry, you are never free. Even if you have a good man, you find yourself attending to his needs rather than your own. I see it all the time, even in this hospital. Take these nurses here: they work all day and then go home and cook for their husbands. They are always tired and struggling to keep everything going. From what I can gather, few of their husbands lift a finger to help at home.

I think that women's lives are much harder than men's. Maybe that is why we live so much longer. We are strong because we bear children and we can cope with pain. Between you and me, men are big cowards.

If I had my life to live over, I don't think I would marry. There is so much I would have been free to do. As a young girl I had the ambition to be an architect, but all the men in my family discouraged me, and the women's opinions didn't count. I look at the world and I see what a mess it is and I think that if women were given the chance they could settle many of the problems. We are born mediators and we respect and cherish life in a way that men never do.

To live to ninety gives you a long view of life. I hope that my granddaughters and my great-granddaughter will have the freedom I missed.

For Louise, widowhood brought freedom from a stifling marriage.

I was a slave all the years I was married. I went directly from my mother's house to marriage. In my day, there were no options.

My husband died seven years ago, leaving me nothing but a pile of debts. I was a hairdresser in the early years of our marriage, so I was able to get a job and pay off what he owed. Although I don't have much money, I wouldn't trade my life for anything. I have my own place and I can come and go as I please. I go swimming twice a week, I bowl, and I paint. Every Saturday night I go to the dance at the church. My life really took off when my husband died.

My children keep asking me if I am lonely, but I tell them that life has never been better. The building I live in is full of widows and divorcées and we have a wonderful time together. My husband was a real nag. He was at me all the time, asking where I was going and who was I talking to. I see it happening to my daughters now, the same old abuse. But I know better than to interfere. I can't live their lives for them.

I now have the freedom I missed as a young girl. Next year, when I retire, I plan to take classes in pottery and jewelry-making. I am very good with my hands and I would like to do something besides painting. I have waited most of my adult life to have some time to myself, to have some fun.

Andrea considers herself a late bloomer. At fifty-eight, she is well established in her second career and is starting to make plans for her retirement.

I worked as a bookkeeper until I was forty-five, and in my spare time I worked as a volunteer at the Y. My volunteer work became increasingly important to me as time went on. I enjoyed setting up programs and working as a lay counselor.

I finally decided to go back to school and become a social worker because I was tired of not having a professional identity. Bookkeeping paid the rent, but it was never very satisfying. I decided that I needed a college degree to say that I was somebody, to legitimize me. It took me five years to get my B.A. and Master of Social Work and it was very difficult financially, but it was well worth the effort.

197

After graduation I became involved in a very innovative feminist-therapy program, and eventually I set up my own practice. My awareness was heightened by all the deserted wives I met during the years that I worked at the Y. I kept seeing women who had legitimate anger that they were forced to suppress. I now work with individual women to help them get some of this anger out and to sort out what to do with their futures. Most of the women I see are in their forties and older. They have raised their families and are now struggling to make a life for themselves. Money is what stops the majority from pursuing their goals. So many of them continue in terrible relationships, afraid to let go; but some eventually realize that they have been on their own within their relationships. It is less frightening to imagine a life on your own when you accept that you have little to lose emotionally, and perhaps a lot to gain in terms of self-respect.

Working with angry women for the past eight years has made me start to think more specifically about my own future. I am divorced and my two children are on their own. When I went back to school I made friends with women twenty years younger than I am. For a while I tried to find some friends my own age, but I found that they don't have the same life experience. At one point I looked up old friends from the time of my marriage, but I found I don't have much in common with them. So I have made my peace with the fact that I am happiest with the generation after me.

I do have some concerns and anxieties about aging. My health is good, but what if something goes wrong? What will I do? As I approach sixty, I realize that I am not in a very good financial situation. It looks like I will have to work beyond sixty-five and that I will never really be financially comfortable – I started a new career too late and my old one barely covered expenses. So I gave up my apartment and moved into some rooms at a friend's house. I had to go through some changes to cope with sharing. It had been a long time since I had to deal with anyone on a daily basis.

Aside from my financial concerns, which I think I

now have in hand, I am very excited about aging. It will be, I hope, a time when I will be freer and a time to do some traveling. I see myself continuing to work, but I would like to work with much older women. It takes a certain amount of energy, so I will have to guard against draining myself. But I love what I do. It is creative and I am never bored. Few people are that lucky! What you choose in mid life is often closer to what you really want and can effectively do. The problem is that most women never have this opportunity.

Joyce chose early retirement so she could pursue her interests.

Although a lot of people from the college talk about taking early retirement, very few actually do it. Several years ago I realized that I had been very careful with my finances and what I really lacked was time, not money. For twenty years I have shared a home with another woman; during that time we have paid off the mortgage. By retiring early, I have cut my salary in half and I find that I must be more careful about how I spend money. But it is worth it; I have cut my workload in half and I can spend the rest of my career doing research and exploring issues that interest me. I have worked hard to sort out how I would use my new-found time; I didn't leave it to chance.

I am sixty-one and not in the best of health. Luckily I am not responsible for other people – I never married and I don't have any children. A few years ago, I had a sense that I would have to limit my activities if I wanted to enjoy the remainder of my life.

Lily, with whom I share the house, is ten years older than I am, but she has never stopped working. Our relationship is very supportive; we are like sisters. It makes a big difference if you have someone with whom to share expenses and household tasks. I worry about Lily, though, because I know I may end up taking care of her if she becomes ill. I took care of my mother for many years. My brothers were very generous with money, but I was the one who gave my time and opened my home to her.

In my own old age I don't envisage any of my family caring for me, but I don't live in horror of spending my remaining days in a nursing home. I can afford good care and I have high standards for the home I will choose. Yet part of me can't imagine not caring for myself; most people have trouble imagining themselves helpless and too old to function. Unlike a lot of older women, though, I have the advantage of being well-educated and having been out in the world, on my own, most of my life. I am much better equipped than most to deal with systems and to get what I want and what I need. Passivity is not what I am known for.

Now that I work at what I want to, I find I am exploring subjects in depth. I don't have to rush around; I have the leisure to do things the way I want. I am working at a pace that is more appropriate to my physical capacities. It's wonderful to develop ideas and have the time to work on them. Also I have gone to more theater and concerts than I have in years. In addition, I sit on the boards of two organizations. For the first time in my career I have the time to give organizational work enough attention; I don't feel the usual strain of juggling more activities than I can comfortably handle. I seem to be developing every academic's fantasy, a nice balance between work and personal life.

I am lucky. Not very many women have a career that can go on indefinitely. I can pursue my academic interests until I drop. No one at the college will define for me when I must quit.

I see the future as very exciting. There will be time for me to get back to reading literature, and all my life I have fantasized about learning to fly. Maybe I will do that, too.

Several of my colleagues told me that retirement would be a horror story, that I would be lost. I seem to be proving them wrong. The single women of my generation have come to realize that we missed out on a lot of the problems that married women faced. We have our networks of support, our independence, and our highly developed careers and interests. Old age is not so frightening to us. We seem to have higher self-esteem and more confidence in ourselves.

As Lily and I grow older, I can envisage that we and our friends will organize our own retirement home. We would each have our own room and we would hire a staff to do the physical work. But we would actually run the place. We would work out the menus, make all the decisions about housekeeping, gardening, and house rules. It would be our place and we would not be at the mercy of any administrative whim. I see this home having an evolving population, the younger women caring for the older ones. Ideally, the population would remain small and intimate.

I'm quite optimistic about what future generations of women will experience. Many of the hang-ups that women have had in the past about personal fulfilment and sexual needs have changed dramatically. I credit the women's movement with having a profound effect on changing rigid and stultifying attitudes about women's roles in society. The women's movement won't die out, as some people predict. If anything, it is growing, but less dramatically than in the past. We can expect that there will be a real change in the way women will deal with their lives. What I see is a positive shift in perceptions of women's place in society. Women want more direct control over their lives; more power, more money, more creativity. What is exciting is that more and more people are stumbling on this idea that women want and need to open up their options.

Nettie has been a vegetarian for seventy years and has been actively involved in promoting vegetarianism as a way of prolonging life.

I'm eight-four years old, and there is absolutely nothing wrong with me. As a child I was always very interested in and fond of animals. By the time I was fourteen, I stopped eating meat. My mother was a very broad-minded woman, always open to new ideas. She accepted the fact that I did not want to eat meat, although the rest of the family ate meat every day. I had no idea about what it meant to be a vegetarian. At the time, it just meant going without meat, and eating dairy products and fruits and vegetables.

I married quite young to a man ten years older than I was. We had eight children, all of whom have accepted the vegetarian way of life. Although my children had all the usual childhood diseases, they never had them severely. In fact, we are all exceptionally healthy. My husband is ninety-four and a bit slowed down now, but he is still in good health.

About thirty years ago, I became involved with an organization for vegetarians. Most of the members are quite old now, like myself, and most of them are women. As a group I would say we are remarkably free from the diseases associated with old age: arthritis, high blood pressure, diabetes, and so on. I don't for a minute think that our good health is only a matter of diet; it has a lot to do with our inner lives. But good physical health is very important if you want to have a happy old age.

Our organization has experienced a rapid growth in the past five years. Young people are very interested in alternative lifestyles and a significant number are serious about our organization.

In all the years I have been active in the vegetarian movement we have never had a single inquiry from doctors. As a group they are not particularly interested in nutrition, and I understand they learn next to nothing about diet at medical school. We find that the older, more orthodox doctors consider nutrition a very minor part of health.

Old people have to take responsibility for their own health. It isn't necessary to spend the last part of your life plagued with disease. Our members don't smoke, or drink caffeine or alcohol. With today's prices, eating vegetables is far cheaper than depending on a meat diet. We would like to reach more old people, but we haven't the resources. At least, we would like them to know that there is life after eighty.

Mary Jane has found a new lease on life with a man she met in her late seventies.

My husband was not much good at anything but giving me children — I had nine all together, but two died. I had to go to work, too, to keep food on the table. There were only two things to do where I come from: pick and plant potatoes and do washing for the rich people. Digging and planting potatoes and washing clothes in big tubs — that's the way it was. Sometimes I just couldn't earn enough to keep us all. Then I went on welfare to tide us over a rough period.

I stopped work at seventy-two and came out here to live close to two of my sons. I had very little money and I didn't want to be a burden to my kids, so I became a housekeeper to this nice gentleman. I did what I was used to — washing, cooking, and cleaning. It was not very hard work after slaving over those big tubs and stooping all day picking potatoes.

This gentleman is eighty-one and I am eighty-two, so we're two old people. We are happy together. We go out for walks every day, and I paint pictures at the seniors' center. My man is very good to me — the best. I've taken a strong liking to him. He's very kind, not like my husband who was a cross and saucy man. But I'll never marry again. I can go where I want and so can my man. I would be sad if he were taken from me, but we are both strong and healthy, so I hope we will be together for a long time. I really love that man; I was lucky to meet him.

At the age of seventy-seven, Janette started a food co-op for seniors.

I was always a homemaker until my husband died. About three years ago I joined a community center and noticed that a lot of the women and men my age were pale and pasty-looking. I did a little investigating and found that most of them ate canned food — beans, stew, and the like. I'm quite a good cook and I am very nutrition-conscious, but I was finding it difficult to shop for one. They just won't sell you small enough quantities, so a lot goes to waste. When you live on a fixed income, you can't afford to waste a penny.

Well, anyway, I approached the director of the center and asked him to consider setting up a food co-op. To be honest, I got the idea from my teenage granddaughter who works at a food co-op. This whole thing has made us very close because I consulted with her about how one goes about ordering and all the other details of running such a venture. The director decided the co-op was a good idea and would probably pay for itself. I was given a small room on the main floor so that handicapped people could get to it easily. My granddaughter came with a bunch of her friends and they painted and put up shelves and signs for me. She took me to some junk shops and we found an old cash register and some wooden bins.

Then the hard part began. I had no idea what to order, or how much. My granddaughter took me to her co-op and introduced me to the members. They spent several days with me, introducing me to suppliers and teaching me about spoilage. I started quite small, just fruits and vegetables, but now I have branched out into grains, nuts, breads, fish, and chicken. You can buy as little as you like here and a lot of the other women have become involved in the work. It's a very relaxed atmosphere; there is no pressure to make a profit. The young kids at the center do the cleaning and the lugging for us. They love to be useful and we enjoy having them pop in and out.

We have also started cooking classes, so that people can learn how to cook cheap and healthy meals for one. I have all kinds of ideas for the future: holding a conference on nutrition for older people, sharing our ideas with other centers, writing a cookbook, and so on. This whole thing has been very good for my morale. Without it I might have died of sheer boredom.

I'm always busy, but not so much that I am tired out. It's a very social thing, this co-op. We have tea, take long breaks, and have a very relaxed attitude about money. Our prices are very low, so no one needs to be subsidized. People feel like equals here; there is no need to distinguish between the poor and those who are better off.

I have this dream that food co-ops for old people will spring up all over the country. It is not just the food, it is the social life it offers—a social life with a purpose. We old women need one another and this is a good way to help each other out. If you can't keep busy doing something worthwhile, you might as well curl up and die. Since I began here, I find my mind works better than ever. I used to think that sixty was old, but now, at seventy-seven, I feel very alive.

Margot was the oldest woman I interviewed. She looks back on the hundred and four years of her life and believes working kept her active and healthy.

In my day it was common to marry quite young. I married at eighteen to a man ten years my senior. We had thirty happy years together, mostly because we always worked side by side. I never once thought of remarrying in all these years—he was one of a kind. Good men were rare then and, I believe, even more rare now.

We lived in a small village where we had a shop filled with groceries, china, and baked goods. When my husband died I was forced to sell the building, but I hung onto the groceries and rented a store down the street. I stayed in that store for years and years, until I was seventy.

After that I thought I would get a rest, but I was asked to run the local library. I ran it for the next twelve years. When I began I didn't know very much, but I discovered that I had a real liking for books. They were lovely years.

At eighty-two I thought I would retire, but I was called upon to help out at the school. They needed someone to read to the children a couple of days a week, and since I now knew a lot about books, I was a likely candidate. I did this for eight years, until my ninetieth birthday.

Around this time my son and his family got after me to come live with them. They were worried about my rattling around alone at home. The house, in truth, was getting to be too much for me. For the next three years I lived with my son's family in the city, until they moved away; then I went to live with my niece for another seven years. I've been lucky because they both had lots of room and I never felt in the way. For the past four years I have been in this hospital because I need special help. My niece is only seventy-five, but she can't really look after me any more. But she comes to visit me every day. She's my closest friend. I would love to go home, but I have accepted that a person needs some help at a hundred and four.

The hardest part about living so long is having everyone die on you. I've outlived my husband, both my sons, and most of my friends.

I am happy, though, that things are changing for women. When I look back to my young days, when a woman was so limited, I realize how far we have advanced. Things are much better. It pleases me that my granddaughter chose to become a doctor and has a very secure and stimulating life. I think women today are more clever than they were in my day. Even though I had worked with him in the store, I knew nothing of our finances when my husband died. We should have talked things over and I should have learned to run my own affairs much earlier on. If I have any advice it is that women should plan ahead and not trust that the future will take care of itself.

There are hundreds of old women in this hospital, and I often forget that I am the oldest. I think it takes some courage to deal with being this old. I have to put up with deafness, blindness, and just plain oldness, but I'm still interested in life and I am happy to be alive.

The experiences presented here portray how intensely individual an experience aging is. Yet society tends to lump older women together and deny their uniqueness.

For the past four years I have met and talked with two hundred and fifty women, all of whom are angered by society's limited and stultifying definition of aging in women. They see themselves as having become increasingly individual as they age: the longer they live, the more clearly they know who they are and what they value.

The women represented in this chapter do share a number of characteristics. Although they differ in education, financial status, and social class, they are all seeking to live with dignity and self-respect. Their struggle involves overcoming poverty, loneliness, isolation, and purposelessness. ness.

Eighty-year-old Lettie lies about her age and works as a private nurse; Nellie opens her home to children; Vivian became a public speaker at eighty-two; Bertha takes in students as boarders; and Janette started a food co-op for seniors at seventy-seven. The coping strategies these women have evolved take courage and innovation. Yet none of the women I interviewed would describe herself as specially gifted or particularly outstanding. These are ordinary women who refuse to view life from the sidelines during the last quarter of their lives.

Two themes emerge from these case studies: intergenerational supports and self-help. I found that older women derived enormous pleasure and concrete benefits from developing intergenerational links and from evolving their own coping strategies.

All the women I interviewed were pleased and willing to relate both their personal experiences and their individual insights into how old age can be lived rather than endured. This chapter is merely a glimpse at our potential.

7

The Emerging Political Activists

One of the most exciting and positive responses to the issues beleaguering older women is the embryonic stirring of political activism. Women who are sixty and older today did not grow up in a feminist era. Nevertheless, a vocal and active minority have created a powerful political movement committed to fighting agism and sexism. They refuse to accept that poverty and decline are the inevitable lot of older women. If society refuses to acknowledge the gross inequalities and hardships that older women face, these activists claim, it will ultimately face the collective anger and discontent of older women in the political arena.

In this chapter I briefly look at the philosophy of Maggie Kuhn and the Gray Panthers, who pioneered the concept of militancy in old age. And I deal in greater detail with two older-women's political organizations, Displaced Homemakers and the Older Women's League, because I believe they are most representative of the philosophy and tactics of political activism among older women.

There are a number of other organizations that have emerged in the past decade dedicated to fighting for older women's rights. One of these, the National Action Forum for Older Women (NAFOU) publishes an excellent newsletter called *Forum*, that reports on issues which affect "mid-life" and "late-life" women. These issues – social injustice, poverty, isolation, and inadequate social supports – combine to erode older women's dignity and health. NAFOU defines its goal as "identifying, clarifying, and contributing to the resolution of these issues and encouraging women in the second half of their lives to appreciate their unique value and to explore their creative potential."[1] Founded in 1978 by two mid-life women, Jane Porcino and Nancy King, both affiliated with university gerontology programs, NAFOU is a non-profit national organization committed to increasing public awareness of the status of older women. Much of NAFOU's energies have been devoted to acting as a network and central resource exchange for individuals involved in issues of concern to older women.

The New York-based *Prime Time* was one of the first publications to address older women's issues. When it folded in the mid 1970s, two feminists, Polly Taylor and Mickey Spencer, began its successor, *Broomstick*. Operating out of San Francisco with a CETA grant, *Broomstick* is entirely about and by women older than forty. The paper discusses how they are at the mercy of such social institutions as medicine, housing, law, economics, and merchandising. Its analysis is feminist, but it also attempts to reach women who are less politicized. Taylor and Spencer define *Broomstick* as a forum to rescue the history of older women and as an opportunity for older women to learn that they can write and have something valuable to say. In effect, *Broomstick*'s authors are its subscribers, who for the most part have come to feminism late in life. In the long run, *Broomstick* hopes to help women share in evolving ways of living well in a society that ignores them.

In July 1978, a community-based organization, Options for Women Over Forty, opened its doors at the San Francisco Women's Center. It was set up to help local women with the practical aspects of mid-life trauma and dislocation. One of the four staff members, Pat Durham, described the clientele it serves as women who do not look at life practically.

> Some of the women who come here are in despair. They believe that there is no hope for them, that life will become worse and worse. Our philosophy is that older women have a lot to offer, that gray hair and wrinkles are natural, that life doesn't simply consist of putting all your energy into your husband and children.
>
> A lot of the women catch on that they are not alone. They start to realize that other women are struggling

with the same problems. One of the best things that happens here is that friendships flourish and networks are created. For many of the women, having women friends is a new experience.

Aside from providing support, we've started a number of projects. For women on their own in mid life, housing is a major concern, so we organized a shared-housing workshop. Although the idea of women setting up communal homes is still a dream, we are finding more and more women open to the possibility. You have to remember that, for women older than forty, communal living is a radical concept. They are not used to living with other women, and they are afraid of losing their privacy. But many, especially the professional women, recognize that shared housing could alleviate loneliness and significantly diminish each woman's financial burden.

The average woman we see is between fifty and fifty-five and on her own because of a marriage breakdown. Her most urgent need is to find a job. In response, we assess her skills and work on boosting her self-esteem. We also work with employers, to show them that older women are competent and reliable employees.

We hope to harness the energy of the older women we serve. Most of them have devoted most of their lives to being mothers, wives, and volunteers. When they find themselves alone through divorce, abandonment, or widowhood, they feel depressed and hopeless. Our goal is to help them pick up the pieces of their lives. They have a lot to offer society, and many good years left to live.

These older-women's organizations and publications share the view that older women must commit themselves to gaining power over their own lives. They also believe that older women must work collectively to make mid life and old age a time of growth and development. The fight, it is agreed, is to bring about major social change that will enable older women to live with dignity and participate actively in life.

The Gray Panthers

In 1972, a retired church-program executive named Maggie Kuhn founded the Gray Panthers. This organization is dedicated to eradicating agism by liberating older Americans from the "paternalism and oppression with which society keeps [them] powerless."[2] The Gray Panthers and Maggie Kuhn are the philosophical grandparents of the idea of political activism in old age. A highly articulate and dynamic advocate for social change, Maggie Kuhn has challenged the notion that old age is a time of decline and withdrawal from life. It is her contention that our society renders the old impotent through impoverishment, indifferent health care, premature institutionalization, and isolation. Her zest and enthusiasm for life stem from her belief that old age can be a time for self-discovery and personal growth. Unfortunately, the present generation of old Americans, she contends, has been "wrongly taught that old is a condition of loss, a time to quit, a mandate to withdraw."[3]

Maggie Kuhn admonishes the public that the old will use their brains, money, and voting power to fight back, to demand their rightful place in society as respected elders who have experience and wisdom to contribute. Using the political tactics of the 1960s, she has led the Gray Panthers on speak-outs, sit-ins, and demonstrations. Before large audiences, she passionately and intelligently exposes the shame of public policy toward the old. Her goal is to encourage old people to organize on their own behalf, and to wage war with a system that junks them as easily as it does old cars.

She reserves her greatest scorn for the gerontologists — professionals who research, write about, make policy for, and deliver programs designed for the old. The Gray Panthers, as an organization, publicly denounce the field of gerontology for "reinforcing societal attitudes which view old people as stuck in an inevitable chronological destiny of decay and deterioration."[4] The Panthers attribute to gerontologists the systematic devaluation of old people as resources, consultants, and experts in the field of gerontological teaching and research. What gerontologists do, according to the Gray Panthers, is present old people as problems to society, rather than acknowledge that the old are persons experiencing problems created by society. The situation is further exacerbated by a government-funded service-delivery system that serves the needs of practising gerontologists first and those of older people second. The Gray Panthers condemn gerontologists for maintaining the illusion that people become incapacitated by virtue of their age. It is their contention that gerontologists receive large grants to research and document their illusion, and that government money also flows to service providers who implement and sustain it.[5]

This powerful condemnation of the exploitation of the old by gerontologists is summarized with a witty prediction:

"Gerontologists who have a vested interest in the very system that fosters the oppression of the old will reap their just reward – as they grow older!"[6]

The message that Maggie Kuhn and the Gray Panthers are trying to disseminate is that the old must act, they must no longer depend on practising gerontologists. Old age, they maintain, will continue to be defined as a period of disease and decline unless old people themselves can assume a leadership role in the gerontological field.

Maggie Kuhn and the Gray Panthers have exposed the debilitating effects of assigning to old people a nonlife. By founding a national political organization, Maggie Kuhn has focused public attention on the negative stereotypes of and pervasive discrimination against old people. She has brought to the public's attention the fact that society suffers from "gerontophobia," an unreasonable fear and hatred of old people.

Claiming to have a membership of fifty thousand in the United States, the Gray Panthers believe that they can and will radically change society. In less than ten years, Maggie Kuhn and the Gray Panthers have succeeded in making the plight of old people a subject of continued debate and constant political and media interest.

However, neither the Gray Panthers nor Maggie Kuhn places a special emphasis on the bleak lot of older women. For that reason, I am more specifically interested in two political organizations, the Alliance of Displaced Home-

212

makers and the Older Women's League. Both groups are advocates solely for older women.

With women swelling the ranks of our aging population, vastly outnumbering men older than sixty-five, it is essential that their special interests be recognized. Old men, admittedly, experience some of the same problems, such as indifferent health care and limited housing options. As a group, however, men are less impoverished; they have more social options, and they have higher self-esteem.

Displaced Homemakers

In her excellent book, *Displaced Homemakers: Organizing for a New Life*, Laurie Shields recounts the founding of a political movement of older women. The group called Displaced Homemakers is the brainchild of Tish Sommers, a long-time feminist and champion of older women. Divorced at fifty-seven, Sommers experienced hardship and dislocation as an older woman pushed out of the traditional role of wife and homemaker by the breakdown of a marriage. She found that the feminist movement, academics, and existing political and social structures were not responding to women in mid life.

Many of these women, she discovered, had been divorced, abandoned, or widowed, and found themselves plunged into poverty. Some were too young to receive social-security benefits; some were disqualified from entitlement because their marriages had lasted less than twenty years. (In 1978, social-security entitlement was amended to ten years of marriage for divorced women.) The only mid-life women who were eligible for welfare assistance were those who were physically disabled and those who still had children younger than eighteen. Homemakers were ineligible for unemployment insurance because work in the home is unpaid labor. And, finally, they faced serious obstacles if they attempted to reenter the workplace. For the most part, employers dismissed them because they were "too old," but were often very willing to exploit them in poorly paid part-time jobs that did not offer pension or health plans.

Sommers coined the phrase "displaced homemaker" to describe women between the ages of forty and sixty-four who are abandoned, divorced, or widowed. A displaced homemaker is most often a woman who has recently suffered a traumatic and emotionally draining experience. Separation shakes a woman's self-esteem, at the very time when she must cope with myriad personal and financial problems. Sommers maintains that displaced homemakers also face acute agism: they are discriminated against because they are not considered particularly attractive or valuable. Isolated from the mainstream of life or herded into menial and unrewarding jobs, Sommers' constituency was overwhelmed with panic and hopelessness.

In 1973, Sommers drew on her long-time experience as an advocate and political activist to convince the National Organization for Women (NOW) to establish a national task force on older women. As the co-ordinator, she set about to make the task force's presence felt by holding press conferences and presenting briefs and position papers on discrimination against older women. She proposed that older women engage in both self-help and collective action to raise public consciousness about their problems. "Older women," she contended, "are denied the right to be old with options and choice of self-sufficiency." And, she argued, society has cut off "women who have talents and capacities to contribute." Sommers tried to rally older women around the slogan, "Organize, Don't Agonize."[7]

However, Sommers ultimately concluded that a separate organization of older women could more effectively promote those goals. She did some informal research in 1975, estimating that between three and six million women would qualify as displaced homemakers, and that an additional fifteen million women ran the risk of joining their ranks in the near future. Sommers put forth the idea of training programs that would prove that homemakers have a variety of skills that the labor market could utilize, and other skills that could lead to new careers.

Laurie Shields was a fifty-five-year-old widow experiencing difficulty reentering the labor market when Sommers convinced her to put her energies into founding a national organization of displaced homemakers. The organization, which became known as the Alliance of Displaced Homemakers, attracted widespread attention and

support from thousands of ordinary women who call themselves housewives.

Between 1975 and 1978, Laurie Shields acted as the
organization's national co-ordinator, crisscrossing the
country to build a strong grass-roots organization. She also
acted as a political strategist, working to bring the concerns
of displaced homemakers to the attention of federal
politicians.

The Alliance of Displaced Homemakers has succeeded
in crossing the usual boundaries of race, religion, and political affiliation. Its goal is to encourage and assist women
to move from dependency to self-sufficiency by pushing for
public recognition of homemaker skills as credible and
valuable for both sexes. To achieve this goal, the Alliance
of Displaced Homemakers proposed that homemaking be
designated a bona-fide occupation, with entitlement to unemployment insurance, social-security credits, and health
insurance. Another goal was to define homemaking as a
base from which an individual could create a future career,
if this proved necessary and desirable.

In 1975, Representative Yvonne Burke (Democrat, California) filed bill SB825, known as the Displaced Homemaker's Bill. Sommers prepared a comprehensive definition
of a displaced homemaker, "an individual who has, for a
substantial number of years, provided unpaid service to
her family, has been dependent on her spouse for her income but who loses that income through death, divorce,
separation, desertion or the disablement of her husband."[8]

Despite stiff opposition from California's Governor Jerry
Brown, who believed that displaced homemakers were the
responsibility of the church, relatives, and friends, the bill
was passed unanimously. Essentially, the bill established
a two-year, two-hundred-thousand-dollar pilot project to
assist displaced homemakers in finding and creating jobs.

A Displaced Homemaker's Center was set up in Alameda
County to administer the project. Very quickly, however,
the center found it had too little money and too few staff
to meet the enormous demand. Instead of devoting energy
to the actual job search, the center concentrated on what
it perceived to be the most pressing needs: building self-
esteem and self-awareness and developing job readiness.

By January 1977, legislators from twenty-eight states had proposed Displaced Homemakers' bills. The Alliance for Displaced Homemakers decided to concentrate its energies on the introduction of federal legislation. Their goal was to persuade congress that displaced homemakers were a special-interest group whose needs had been overlooked and ignored. But they found that politicians stubbornly resisted the notion that special legislation was needed to assist displaced homemakers. The politicians believed that adequate job training was available through the education acts, especially the Vocational Educational Amendments of 1976.

In an effort to consolidate their strength and to put pressure on the political system, the Alliance organized a conference in Baltimore in 1978. It was called the "Displaced Homemakers' Speak-Out." They received fifty thousand dollars from the federal government, and with this money they held their conference, which was attended by five hundred delegates. The conference spawned the Displaced Homemakers Network, whose role it was to establish a national clearing house, in Washington, "which would provide all [displaced-homemaker] programs and prospective program developers, data and resources, staff training, information on funding, legislative issues, further conferences or regional meetings, and, of course, a regular newsletter."[9] The network replaced the more loosely structured alliance and has, in the past few years, established a reputation as a national and regional expert on the issue of service to displaced homemakers.

Despite the three-and-a-half-year campaign by the alliance, the proposed federal displaced-homemaker bill never passed. Instead, in October of 1978, an amendment to the Comprehensive Employment and Training Act (CETA), Title III, included displaced homemakers as a hard-to-employ group requiring a special approach. Five million dollars were allotted, for fiscal year 1979, to the United States Department of Labor to set up multipurpose programs, including job training and placement, peer counseling, and the creation of new jobs for displaced homemakers. In 1980, the network was awarded the sole source contract by the

Department of Labor to provide technical assistance for the new CETA-funded displaced-homemakers program.

For Tish Sommers and Laurie Shields, the two principal organizers and founders of the Displaced-Homemakers movement, this represented a triumph of political consciousness-raising. Displaced homemakers, who less than ten years ago were perceived as individuals suffering a personal trauma, are now recognized as a substantial segment of society whose collected experience has been societal neglect and injustice. Even though the actual funding to sustain special programs to assist displaced homemakers is a mere pittance, Sommers and Shields are not discouraged. There are more than three hundred programs across the United States providing counseling, workshops, skills training, and job-placement assistance. Sommers and Shields believe that the first difficult, and important, step has been taken to arouse and mobilize older women to act in their own behalf.

The number of women forty-five and older will grow to an estimated thirty-six million by the year 2000; their political clout will be immense. This politicization process, begun by two dedicated women, has set in motion an irreversible and powerful push for social change.[10]

The Older Women's League

By the end of 1978, Tish Sommers felt she had accomplished her goal of building a strong movement of displaced homemakers. But she was not content to end the battle for women's rights at age sixty-four. As she entered her sixties, she addressed herself to the economic, social, and political problems of women who were sixty-five and older.

Her next move was to set up the Older Women's League Education Fund (OWLEF), which will "lay the foundation for the emergence of a significant advocacy organization for middle-aged and older women."[11] That organization is known as the Older Women's League (OWL). OWLEF is run out of an old, rambling house in Oakland, California. The group is devoted to researching and analyzing issues – social security, pensions, health care, and so on – all of which reinforce both dependency and inequity in the lives of older women. Always attuned to the need to attract media and public attention, Sommers and her colleagues published documents on these issues. The documents are called "Gray Papers."

In an interview, Tish Sommers pointed out how she had decided that this time she would reverse her plan of action, starting with an educational and consciousness-raising nonprofit organization that would lead to a national-advocacy movement. Although she was still looking at the total context of women's lives to trace their dependency, she particularly wanted to document how unprepared women are in old age, when they have outlived their economic and social-support systems.

> This is not a duplication of the Gray Panthers. Our only concern is older women, unlike the Gray Panthers, whose goal is age and youth united, acting together. We work closely with Maggie Kuhn, whose Gray Panthers fill a vacuum, providing society with an image of enthusiasm and vitality in old age. And Maggie Kuhn, especially, is a bona-fide charismatic leader who is asked to meet with all the biggies. Her approach is what I would call utopian; she tells us how life for older people ought to be and could be. We share her and the Gray Panther's long-range goal of eliminating the crippling effects of agism. But the Older Women's League Educational Fund has very carefully defined the specific and immediate issues affecting older women. These include poverty, isolation, poor physical and mental health, crime, affordable housing, adequate transportation, and premature institutionalization, all of which are disproportionately the problems of aging women.

> We are concerned that the current political climate is leading to the elimination of people programs. We fear that older women will lose out again. Our only course of action is to create a political organization that will keep older women's issues in the public's and politicians' consciousness.

> We are a shoestring operation, dependent upon honoraria, foundation grants, and individual dona-

tions. Our strategy is to operate independent of government funding so that we can remain free to needle and criticize.

I see the OWLEF as one step in a continuum that, I hope, will lead to a national-advocacy organization. I feel absolutely the need for a separate organization to focus on older women, to produce role models and leaders, and to empower older women. There are talented older women out there whom we must recruit to work within this movement. For now, OWLEF acts as the voice of older women, spearheaded by myself and four other full-time organizers. There are fifteen hundred subscribers to OWLEF, all of whom may potentially develop into advocates and political activists.

Older women as a group have a marvelous survival mechanism. We learn to make do with very little and we almost universally suffer in silence. To look for solutions we must examine our powerlessness. We tend to feel hopeless because we perceive our problems as a personal misfortune, the result of our own inadequacies. Our common response is to try to make the best of things. Unfortunately, those of us who appreciate that our situation is the product of injustice rarely believe that anything can be done. What we end up with is despair and paralysis.

It is my belief that older women must take control of their lives and collectively fight for social reform. We have laid the groundwork with the displaced-homemakers movement. There is now official recognition of older women as a disadvantaged group in need of special assistance. In a few short years we have mobilized thousands of older women as political activists working in their own self-interest. This victory is exciting because it has proven that older women have a latent potential for political activism and power. If we link our energies with the women's movement and aging activism, we become a powerful force.

As Tish Sommers so aptly points out, once an issue is raised, it can no longer be ignored. The idea that older women are a political force has been planted in the minds of our politicians and policy-makers. In October of 1980, the White House's Mini-Conference on Older Women, held in Des Moines, Iowa, provided an opportunity for Sommers and her colleagues to launch the Older Women's League as a national advocacy organization. It is hoped that OWL will grow rapidly; the founders' goals are large membership and active chapters in every state. The chapter members will learn the skills of policy-making, so that OWL can address issues at both state and national levels. In the long run, OWL is seeking to build a network of activists and advocates who recognize that their common interests will only be effectively served if they speak for themselves and unite to take action.[12]

Older persons have not traditionally been viewed as a force in North American political life. Older women, especially, have been viewed as uninterested in and incapable of political activity. Until quite recently, gerontologists have claimed that, as people age, they withdraw from life and turn inward. There is, in fact, no conclusive evidence to support this theory.

The older women's political movements discussed in this chapter demonstrate that older women are profoundly discontented with their assigned role in old age. The loss of status and the widespread poverty experienced by so many older women has turned a significant number of these women into activists. They are engaged in a serious struggle to reform society's attitudes and behavior toward older women because they are convinced that they must be the authors of their own liberation from the dual oppressions of agism and sexism.

In the past five years, the Displaced Homemakers and the Older Women's League, in particular, have worked hard to raise the political awareness of older women and to educate them about the politics of aging. Part of their success lies in the fact that their constituents have been able to cross political, racial, and social barriers because they share a common fate. Unquestionably, by promoting self-help and collective action, these organizations offer legitimate political tools. At the same time, they have started to communicate to legislators and other public officials that older women form a growing and potentially powerful political force. They point to the fact that older women are one of the fastest-growing segments of society, whose needs a responsible government cannot afford to ignore.

Although the older-women's movement is relatively small, with limited financial resources, it has begun an irreversible process of mobilizing older women. Equally important is that older women be seen as vital and valuable members of society.

When women who are now in their twenties and thirties, who are growing up with a feminist awareness, reach mid and late life, they will not be content to sit on the sidelines of life. Their self-esteem and expectations are higher than were the expectations of previous generations of older women; their potential for sophisticated political activism is immense. They will place far greater pressure on our social institutions to provide economic security and a wide range of social options. When they reach their sixties and seventies, they will not accept sexism or agism. They will expect and demand a major role in life.

Conclusions

Introduction

In "Magnificent Survivors," we saw the creative responses of individual women to the multiple problems of aging. These individual coping strategies are examples of personal courage by ordinary women. Although they are a source of inspiration and offer role models where few exist, they do not represent a long-term solution for all women. However much I admire individual women's struggles to live a dignified old age, I deplore the superhuman energy they are forced to expend to achieve this goal.

In the long run, society must undergo fundamental structural changes. There are three factors that are presently contributing to real change. First, the numbers of older women are increasing and will continue to increase as this century draws to a close. In the year 1900, there were only 132,000 women sixty-five years old or older in Canada. Society could afford to ignore us. We were not worth special consideration. But by the year 2000, there will be approximately two million older women.[1] This dramatic increase in the numbers of older women is the result of a declining birth rate and increased female longevity.

A second and equally significant factor that will fuel the drive for change is the breakdown of the traditional two-parent family. More and more women are assuming the role of the head of single-parent families (because of divorce and desertion). A smaller but significant number are actively choosing to raise children on their own. And increasing numbers are deciding to remain single. As more women become self-reliant and independent, either voluntarily or by force of circumstances, the traditional patterns of female dependence and passivity will cease to be the norm. These women will be less willing to tolerate an impoverished and demeaning old age.

These two factors, an increase in the aging female population and the decline of the traditional two-parent family, will undoubtedly have an enormous impact on the thinking of our politicians and policy-makers. However, the catalyst that will push the issues of women and aging into the political arena is the growing power of feminist thought and action. Although most women in the women's movement are between twenty and forty, the movement will be affected by its own aging. As these women turn forty, we see a preoccupation with mid-life issues. These women have gained experience through years of political activism; that experience will be an invaluable asset when these women turn their energies to the injustices and inequities of aging. They will have the support of large numbers of older women who are no longer constrained by divided loyalties to men and to families. These women will inevitably conclude that feminism and political activism represent their interests, their needs, and their goals. This grass-roots militancy is a necessary precondition to effect fundamental societal and structural change.

Our Collective Poverty

A central feature of older women's second-class status in our society is our collective poverty. Any political action by older women must involve an attack on the sexist and agist assumptions in the pension system. Applying Band-Aids to programs that are basically hostile to women's interests will not help. Instead, we must expand our universal, non-contributory, pension — Old Age Security. This is the only way we can assure that we will all enjoy an adequate standard of living in old age.

Having made this sweeping proposal, I think it is important to explain why I cannot support any other policy in the long run. Throughout this book I have attempted to demonstrate, issue by issue, that older women exercise little, if any, power over their lives. To understand this powerlessness, we must acknowledge that we live in a society where money is equated with power, power commands respect, and respect leads to self-esteem and dignity. I have presented enough data, illustrated by case studies, to show clearly that women as a group are poor, and that older women are especially poor. As a consequence, women neither exercise power nor command respect.

For some women this is because they are dumped by their husbands in their forties, when reentry into the workforce is difficult. Others lost husbands and discovered there was no survivor provision in the husband's pension: they receive reduced pension benefits. A few escape these situations and never experience low income. But the statistical likelihood of being poor is considerably higher for a woman than for a man. For older women, poverty leads to a profound sense of despair and futility.

Older women lack money for two reasons. First our public pension system is inequitable. Also, most women work at low-paying jobs. We must confront the inequities in the pension system as our first priority. Expanding Old Age Security is the only way we can ensure that older women will receive a reasonable and adequate income.

Obviously, the elimination of job discrimination and the creation of new jobs would help to reduce the enormous gap between the pension benefits men receive and those women receive. More specifically, men and women must enjoy equal status in the workplace. Then they may perform identical jobs for identical periods of time and make identical contributions to the Canada Pension Plan. Then they can receive identical benefits. At present, of course, women do not experience work patterns that are identical to those of men; as a result, they make smaller contributions and their benefits are considerably lower. One response would be to equalize women's access to the workforce. Training programs and job-creation programs could be established. To the extent that these programs work, they would ultimately narrow the gap in pension benefits. However, job training and job creation cannot be the sole or even primary course of action, for three important reasons.

First, the discrimination against women in the workforce is so entrenched that it will not vanish immediately.

(The low success rate of affirmative-action programs has demonstrated this.) To defer dealing with pension inequities until some glorious day in the future when job discrimination is eliminated means to defer action for a very long period of time. The income needs of older women are acute today. They cannot and should not be asked to wait until job opportunities are fully equalized, some time in the distant future.

The second compelling reason that job training and job creation are inadequate alone is that pension benefits are earnings-related. Too many women who enter the workforce in their forties or fifties will never be able to accumulate large enough benefits to afford a reasonable standard of living in retirement. Moreover, we have no reason to believe that social roles for men and women are likely to change completely. Many women will continue to spend much of their lives in the home as unpaid workers. Third, it is a fraud to ask women to undergo retraining programs at a time when jobs are not available to them.

Retraining and large-scale job-creation programs are therefore essentially long-term goals, dependent upon the health of the economy and the prevailing political climate with regard to affirmative-action programs. The more pressing need is to respond to the acute income problems of so many older women today.

What should be clear to the most casual observer is that the fundamental premises upon which the whole retirement system is based are inaccurate, and inequitable to women. In particular, there are three basic assumptions that are unacceptable and destructive. First, our society assumes a traditional nuclear family in which a woman will be cared for by a spouse. Evidence proves that the traditional two-parent family is not a reality for large numbers of women. Second, the system preaches the virtue of self-reliance. This translates into a benefits system that is earnings-related. Self-reliance may indeed be a virtue – for those who have the resources to practise it. Those who lack resources – namely women who are socialized to be dependent upon their spouses – cannot be self-reliant. And third, Old Age Security and the Guaranteed Income Supplement were never designed to be the sole source of income in old age. Nevertheless, as I have shown, a substantial number of women rely almost wholly on OAS and GIS, since they have neither savings nor pension benefits.

If public and private pension schemes are based on invalid and inequitable assumptions, then small changes are not a solution. Nearly all amendments to the pension system have been Band-Aids, applied on an ad-hoc basis in response to political pressures. It has often been said that the system is intentionally complex, that it suits government's convenience that the public in general is, and women in particular are, unable to understand what it's all about, to see the system for the sham that it is.

Since much of the system is structurally invalid and obviously does not work, we need radical alternatives. The premise upon which I would base a new pension system is that *every person has a right to an adequate standard of living in old age*. This right can be guaranteed only through our universal, non-contributory, government-run old age pension: Old Age Security. After a certain age everyone will receive a government cheque for an amount adequate to ensure a reasonable standard living. The payments must be fully indexed to the rate of inflation, to protect the purchasing power of the dollar. In addition, the payments must be taxable, to ensure that the money will be recovered based on one's ability to pay. (And, it goes without saying, the tax system must be made more truly progressive.)

My model has many advantages. Such a system will be simple and easily understood by everyone. It will eliminate bureaucratic confusion and complexity; it will eliminate the need for stigmatizing means-tested income supplements. Eligibility for a reasonable standard of living will become a right, not a privilege.

For women, the advantages would unquestionably be great. The program would narrow the huge gap between men's and women's retirement incomes. Men who have private pensions and substantial savings would pay back most or all of their government pensions through the tax system. And women, the majority of whom lack such private sources of income, would be entitled to most or all of the government pension. Old Age Security acknowledges every adult for his or her contribution, be it paid labor in the workforce or unpaid labor in the home, to society throughout his or her lifetime. Eligibility would not depend on the number of dollars an individual has earned.

To call for an enlarged universal government program in the 1980s may seem both preposterous and naive. Admittedly, the mood in Canada today is clearly not sympathetic to a massive expansion of Old Age Security. Yet this proposal is not essentially new; it is a form of guaranteed income for the old, with women as the primary beneficiaries. A guaranteed income has long been advocated by both the political right and left in this country. Universal programs are extremely cheap to administer and to deliver because they eliminate a variety of other programs. Such a program would result in a smaller administrative system than the one presently in place.

But the justification for the proposal does not rest on its administrative savings, the reduction of bureaucracy, or its relatively small cost. This proposal is fundamentally argued on the basis of equity, of justice, and of every person's right to enjoy an adequate standard of living in old age. That women will benefit more from this proposal is because women are disadvantaged under the present system. What this program will do is offset, to some extent, a lifetime of discrimination and disadvantage at home and in the workplace. And if the call for equity and justice is labeled "naive" or "preposterous," then so be it. An expanded universal non-contributory pension system for the old is the only humane answer. Any other course condemns far too many older women to lives of poverty and degradation.

Overcoming Negative Stereotyping

Overcoming poverty will allow older women to exercise some power over their lives. With this power, a woman's dignity and self-respect can flourish.

To guarantee a reasonable income level in old age, of course, will primarily help the poor. Most poor people are women, and most older women are poor. Nevertheless, money alone is not enough. Even financially comfortable and rich women suffer more as they age than do men. Rich women and poor women experience a diminished sense of self-esteem and dignity as a consequence of pervasive, negative stereotyping. Collectively, older women are portrayed as feeble, neurotic, difficult, incompetent, unreliable, and unattractive. Since our society measures people in terms of youth, beauty, and productivity, older women are viewed with distaste, and as lacking in value. This is clearly reflected in the media and in social policy, which virtually ignores our existence. It's not surprising, then, that so many older women feel invisible.

Too often our needs, our concerns, and our goals are defined for us by a whole army of professionals who base their analysis on sexist and agist assumptions. We are lumped together, with little or no consideration given to our individuality. What emerges is a general disdain for older women; this disdain is buttressed by the belief that we neither desire nor require much in the way of material comforts and social outlets.

These appallingly negative attitudes cause incalculable suffering for older women. So much of the unhappiness and depression I have documented stems directly from older women's relentless exposure to condescension, indifference, rejection, and hostility. The need to radically change our destructive way of looking at older women is an urgent priority.

Our Housing Needs

If an older woman had an adequate income, and were viewed differently by society, she would have more freedom in her choice of accommodation. Maintaining a home is, for most older women, the sole way to maintain some semblance of dignity. For many, a "home" is a walk-up flat or a room in a run-down and unsafe neighborhood. As she gets older and her health deteriorates, a woman might have to choose between a nursing home and a chronic-care hospital. Where home-care and volunteer services exist, they are frequently poorly run and inflexible. A small percentage of older women live with their families, but often find the arrangement stressful and filled with conflict. All these factors contribute to overwhelming feelings of insecurity and fear. For the majority of older women, the loss of a home represents an end to independence and the beginning of the humiliating process of infantilization.

There are, however, indications that attitudes toward the housing needs of retired people are starting to change. Although premature institutionalization is still an immense problem, older people are remaining in their communities longer than they did five years ago. Also, many professionals have begun to recognize that the old have social and intellectual needs. The theory that old age is a time of withdrawal from life is rapidly losing credibility.

Our feelings of fear and repugnance toward death and dying are changing, and we are beginning to treat the aged with compassion. One example of this is the hospice, a place that promotes the notion that a sick or dying person has a right to a compassionate and supportive environment. Those who stay in hospices come and go as they please, and are given access to pain medication on an unrestricted basis. The hospices are one sign that the old and the chronically ill are worthy people and can benefit from a rehabilitative approach. Other examples of changing attitudes are home-care services and day centers. All are indications of a growing recognition that the old want to remain in their own environment as long as possible.

No change of attitude has any meaning unless it is backed by funding, and by the transfer of control and decision-making to the old themselves. We can no longer plan in isolation, leaving our fate to architects, planners, medical personnel, and social workers. To present a fait accompli, be it a senior-citizen's building, a co-operative housing project, or a nursing home, effectively reduces the old to the status of children. Too many of the existing facilities attest to the fact that the potential residents were never consulted. Most buildings reflect the architects', the social workers', and the funding sources' particular biases about what the old need and want.

One exceptionally beautiful nursing home I visited was a striking example of this nonconsultive approach. Although the home was obviously designed with great care and attention to detail, the planners overlooked the fact that so many of the residents would be in wheelchairs or would be using canes and walkers. The foyer floor was built of cobblestones, to simulate the atmosphere of a European village square. I watched in amazement as handicapped residents stumbled and struggled painfully across the hall. (The administrators admitted their oversight and plan to remove the stones and replace them with something more appropriate.)

Institutions will only work if their residents are given control. Why, as many older women asked, is it not the residents who make the decisions? They do not want the token concessions they are given in some of the more enlightened institutions, but real power to direct their own lives. The residents should direct the running of a home. The staff would work for them, executing their decisions. One woman in her sixties made the following comments.

I would like to change the idea of a nursing home to a supportive community. I envisage a small group in need of support services. We would create our own environment, directing the staff about meals, housekeeping, and general maintenance. It would be our home and the younger and healthier members would help the older and more needy. We would contain it, never allowing it to grow into something large, unmanageable, and inhumane.

I know how to negotiate my way around bureaucrats — I'm one myself. I doubt very much if women like myself and those coming after us will allow ourselves to be treated like small children.

As we move from our sixties to our nineties, some form of assistance will be probably needed. One way to provide this is to offer different kinds of care. There could be independent housing units with nominal assistance (housekeeping, for example); there could be units with on-call medical staff, some with day care, and some with chronic care. People could age within a protected environment that responds to every stage of the aging process. The system could eliminate the common crisis faced by an individual who becomes too ill to remain on his or her own and is forced to move to a nursing home or a chronic-care hospital. The sudden thrust into an alien environment, usually with little preparation, is an experience from which few older people recover.

At present, continuums of care are few and far between. Where they do exist, there are more people who want to move in than space for them. And there is no guarantee that a place will be available at any point on the continuum as it is required. And the continuum of care provides the potential for abuse of power. Unless the participants have genuine decision-making power and exercise fundamental control over its management, the continuum might perpetuate the oppression of the old.

For the majority of older women, the most desired option is to remain on their own in a secure and supportive neighborhood. Studies have shown that older women, whether they are single, widowed, or divorced, would choose to live alone rather than with their families, provided they have enough money and are reasonably healthy.[2] Nevertheless, the myth persists that the solution to the housing problems of older women is that the women live with their families, usually a daughter, who would likely be thirty to fifty years old. But women of this age are often not full-time housekeepers with time left over to care for aging parents. Some may be widowed; many are separated or divorced. And many mid-life women are attempting to reenter the workforce or return to school. Or they may be coping with the demands of teenage children. The addition of a parent in the household can be a tremendous emotional and financial drain. Such a situation invites tension and conflict and has the potential to destroy relationships that were once supportive and happy.

Society expects a daughter will care for her aging parents. The daughter might be a single working woman, but she might feel pressure to accept primary responsibility for her parents. Sons, on the other hand, frequently are assumed to be too busy with their jobs or careers. Their contribution is generally merely financial. If a parent is lucky, the son may visit on a regular basis.

There are few supports or rewards for mid-life daughters who care for their parents. For many the burden becomes overwhelming: they are either consumed with guilt that they are not doing enough, or they are deeply resentful of the burden they feel forced to assume. Such guilt and resentment can affect a daughter's mental and physical health.[3] The myth that older women prefer to live with their mid-life daughters, and that mid-life daughters are able and happy to accept this obligation, is neither realistic nor desirable.

Another myth exists: that neighborhoods can provide companionship, a sense of community, and the necessary supports to sustain older women. If neighborhoods could be reconstituted and revitalized to reflect different attitudes toward older women, this would be an ideal solution. The younger residents of the neighborhood could help the older members. For example, they could take out the garbage, shovel the walks, do the heavy shopping, and intervene in a crisis. In exchange, older women could babysit, act as tutors, and supervise service people for working couples. This mutual assistance could lay the foundation for more social contacts in the form of visits, dinner parties, outings to movies and theater, and shared confidences. On a more restricted level, it could be nothing more than looking in on older neighbors on a regular basis. (In some communities the letter carrier checks to see if older people have collected their mail.)

Such a neighborhood could foster mutual respect and shared interests. An older woman might not feel superfluous and on the sidelines of life; she would feel needed. Her experience and her advice might command respect. And in a very real and practical way, she would participate as an equal to her neighbors.[4]

No doubt neighborhoods such as these exist. Most older women, however, live in cities, and many are congregated in deteriorating and high-crime neighborhoods. It is easy to become isolated from the existing community. For example, the type of accommodation available to them is usually public housing, highrise apartment buildings for the elderly, welfare hotels, and boarding houses. These places are unlikely to offer social supports or to build feelings of security.[5]

Clearly the lack of economic resources forces many older women into isolated and alienating living arrangements.

Even if an older woman had enough money to move to more satisfactory accommodation, her problem would only be partially solved. We cannot assume that the attitudes that cause people to shun and ostracize older women will disappear overnight. But, more importantly, older women should not be forced to rely solely on the goodwill of their neighbors.

A more practical approach might be to improve and to expand home-care and support services. But if these services are to meet the needs of older women, they must be fundamentally altered in their orientation. They cannot be viewed as essentially charitable. The present approach has proven, in too many instances, to be unreliable and open to abuse. The system can only operate successfully, and provide reliable, affordable, high-quality service, if the care-givers are well-trained and are paid good wages. The existing system is staffed principally by poorly paid, inadequately trained, often insensitive, staff, supplemented by volunteers who too frequently are unreliable or are meeting their own needs rather than those of the older women they are ostensibly helping.

Shut-ins and handicapped older women stressed how vulnerable and powerless they felt when a volunteer or paid care-giver behaved in a condescending or abusive manner. To complain, they found, might result in a further deterioration in the amount and quality of the service. Too many professionals, volunteers, and support staff think they know what's best for older women.

Virtually all the homecare and support services that older women receive are given in exchange for social control. Support services are considered to be privileges that are conditional on acceptable behavior. This attitude prevails because the care-giver has power. For example, the giving of meals on wheels carries with it the implied threat to withdraw the service. An older woman's program and activities, when she is in the community, can be defined with the implied threat to institutionalize her; a care-giver can and does define an institutionalized woman's program and activities with the implied threat to drug her senseless.

In every case, the older woman is not receiving a service as a right or as an entitlement earned by a lifetime's contribution to society. She is involved in an exchange with someone more powerful than she, and the terms of the exchange are clear: "Behave in an acceptable manner (and I, the professional or volunteer, shall define what is appropriate) or some privilege will be withdrawn." This power imbalance forces older women to be diffident, dependent, and to behave as a suppliant because the consequences of non-compliance are sanctions and reprisals.

It is inevitable that whoever holds power will attempt to use it and may eventually consciously or unconsciously abuse it. The only solution is to take away this power so that older women are not made to feel that they are the recipients of charity. Rather, they must become sovereign consumers who decide what services are needed and how they should be delivered.

Unless our society is both prepared to substantially expand and improve the quantity and quality of these services, and to give power over their lives to the old themselves, then the concept of the elderly living in the community as independently as possible is largely theoretical. We can expect, instead, that even larger numbers of older women will prematurely swell the ranks in nursing homes and chronic-care hospitals. Surely it would be better to prolong our independence in supportive and life-enhancing environments.

To take control over one's life does not necessarily entail marching in the streets, although the prospect of a million older women parading on Parliament Hill is a very compelling idea. Older women, particularly in small groups, can start seizing power on a much more modest level. One of the most exciting findings of my research was to discover a group of mid-life women who bought a street. These women are determined that what has happened to their mothers and to their grandmothers will not happen to them. They are actually taking control of their lives by preparing themselves for old age.

Within the group are several artists, an architect, a manager, and a number of college professors. Now in their forties and fifties, they have all accumulated some savings. The idea of creating their own supportive community evolved informally when one of their members bought a house on a small, dead-end street in a safe and central area. As each house on the block went up for sale, she alerted her friends of its availability.

Over a number of years, these women have bought most of the houses on the street. (The goal is to buy all eight.) The idea grew that they could create a community to sustain themselves in old age. Some of the women are living in the houses now; others have rented them out, with the intention of taking up residence at a later date. The group's architect organized the renovation and refurbishing of the houses to reflect an external uniformity and also cater to each woman's individual taste and needs. All this was accomplished at considerable savings because they all hired the same plumber, electrician, and carpenter.

Instead of facing the future with uncertainty or dread, these women feel confident and secure. They know they will live in a neighborhood they created themselves, not one that has been imposed by others. Moreover, they are looking forward to the prospect of living in a nurturing and sustaining community. Unlike many older women, these women will enjoy secure housing; they will not be subject to the whims of landlords or to inflated rents.

Such an undertaking, of course, requires substantial sums of money. However, women could pool their resources to buy a small apartment building or a house. The idea is to prepare for the future and to protect against premature institutionalization and a loss of power.

Taking Issue with Crime and Violence

One of the least explored areas affecting older women is that of crime and violence. As I described earlier, the problem is barely recognized, let alone understood. Although the full dimensions of the problem are unknown, there are four distinct kinds of violence — familial abuse, wife battering, institutional and social-service abuse, and crime. The issues associated with the problem are based on the fact that older women lack both money and power; as a result, they are the victims of negative attitudes.

Familial abuse (better known as "granny bashing") and wife battering are closely related to poverty. If older women in abusive family settings had enough financial resources, many would find better living arrangements. But adequate financial resources alone would not be enough to free most older women. They remain in frightening and dangerous situations because their confidence in their ability to live on their own has been badly damaged through a lifetime of dependence. As well, they may be paralyzed by feelings of guilt – that in some way they are responsible for their family's or spouse's behavior. And even those who have the courage to complain to the police, medical personnel, social workers, and so on may meet with skepticism or outright disbelief.

The problem is as serious as wife battering of younger women and child abuse, but it is not discussed. By making it a matter of public concern, we can put pressure on the police, medical personnel, and social agencies to recognize and treat abused older women with more compassion and sensitivity. Older women must be told that they are victims, and that they are not to blame for abusive or criminal behavior directed against them.

Older women must also recognize that they have a legitimate right to complain and to seek protection. None of these changes in attitudes will have any meaning unless they are supported with concrete measures, including setting up emergency shelters or adapting the existing ones; providing effective legal protection; training social workers and medical personnel to identify abused victims; developing a constructive police response; and providing funding for research.[6]

The problems of neglect and abuse in institutional settings and from social-service workers are more specifically associated with older women's powerlessness. As I have pointed out in the discusssion on housing, older women are too often reduced to the role of suppliant and are treated as if they were small children by care-givers and volunteers. Such treatment severely diminishes an older woman's self-esteem and sense of dignity. Clearly, what is needed is a radical righting of this power imbalance. The older woman must assume the role of a sovereign consumer who controls and directs her support environment. But the care-givers will only alter their behavior when they recognize that they are employees, not agents of social control — that is, when older women assume power over their own lives.

And finally, we must recognize how older women's special vulnerability and intense fear of crime have a devastating effect on the quality and enjoyment of their lives. As a group, they are fully aware that they are perceived as easy prey for crimes such as fraud, mugging, burglary, and assault.

Part of the problem is, again, attributable to their poverty, which traps them in declining and high-crime neighborhoods. If poor older women had the money to move out of these dangerous communities, much of their fear and victimization would be alleviated.

However, older women's restricted movements, especially in the evening, would still remain a critical problem. Regardless of the quality of the neighborhood, too many older women spend their evenings behind multiple-locked doors, afraid to venture out. For one thing, they do not believe that their fears and actual victimization are taken seriously by the police and the criminal-justice system. Both tend to view older women as not particularly creditable. Especially in crimes of sexual assault and rape, an older woman "may believe that her story will not be taken seriously and she will be denied her rightful redress under the law."[7]

Older women will not feel safe in their homes and in the streets until society stops ignoring their paralyzing fears about or particular vulnerability to crime. They do not receive adequate legal protection or a sympathetic and constructive response from the police. Older women must take positive steps on their own behalf. As one woman of eighty aptly put it: "I refuse to hide in my apartment at night. I go out to concerts, I take evening courses, and I often have dinner in restaurants. The solution, for me, is to go out in a group with other women. We range in age from sixty to eighty. In the streets, we link arms. We stride with confidence; we don't creep in fear."

Overhauling Health Care

In the area of health, the dilemmas are even more complex and the struggle will be especially bitter. Here the key issues for older women are a lack of money (which leads to powerlessness) and the subsequent negative stereotyping. Nowhere are these issues more pronounced than in health care.

Older women, as I have documented, are subject to unnecessary surgery, overmedication, adjustive psychotherapy, and premature institutionalization. From menopause on, we receive increasingly indifferent and fragmented care. As one study found, major barriers to medical care for older people were the fragmentation and depersonalization of the health-care system. These barriers include: "having to wait too long, inconvenient hours, the confusing atmosphere of clinics, and the insensitivity of doctors and nurses toward older people."[8]

The chronic diseases to which we are potentially at risk, such as osteoporosis (brittle bones), arthritis, and breast cancer, receive relatively little funding and attention from the medical-research establishment. For example, although breast cancer is the most prevalent form of malignancy in mid-life and older women, accounting for thirty thousand deaths a year in the United States, only 4.1 per cent of cancer research funds are devoted to research in breast cancer.[9] And even though there are a number of major studies pointing to the aggravated risk of cancer in women who routinely take estrogen, a large number of doctors still prescribe the drugs. Quite clearly, our health concerns are an especially low priority among health professionals. In fact, we can expect progressively poor treatment as we pass from forty to fifty and beyond.

Medicine as it relates to women is focused on fertility and birthing; this orientation is destructive toward our interests. While younger women of child-bearing years must confront the medical profession's overt sexism, older women face the double impact of sexist and agist assumptions. To treat older women's complex chronic illnesses requires knowledge, patience, and skill. Doctors tend to focus on the acute illnesses of younger people because young people generate more income and respond relatively quickly to treatment. In addition, too many doctors exhibit extremely negative attitudes toward older women, reacting to their complaints with condescension, paternalism, repugnance, and distaste.[10]

In large part, the shabby treatment of older women is an expression of the medical profession's power and arrogance. At the same time, older women have been socialized to defer to doctors as all-knowing gods in whom they must place absolute and unquestioning faith. Doctors obviously want to retain their power by encouraging older women's ignorance and dependence. Nothing can change until older women challenge this power imbalance.

The Older Women's League, in keeping with its philosophy that older women must take direct political action on their own behalf, has prepared an excellent discussion paper that presents a whole range of essential strategies. It is their contention that the existing women's health movement does not extend its focus beyond menopause, but does offer a powerful model from which older women could greatly benefit. The younger women's health movement encourages women to adopt a more assertive and less accepting attitude toward doctors and to insist that doctors supply sufficient information about a treatment or medicine so that women can make truly informed decisions about their own health. This questioning has contributed to the demystification of doctors' presumed omnipotence. Many women have begun to appreciate that doctors are not gods, but rather self-interested business people from whom they are purchasing a service. Women are beginning to recognize that their best interests lie in doctor-shopping and seeking second and even third opinions when a dangerous or controversial treatment is proposed.

Although the Older Women's League believes that it is crucial to address the issues of passivity and dependence, they are particularly concerned that older women define for themselves their own special health concerns. Since, for example, older women are more prone to chronic and debilitating diseases than younger women, it is essential to promote the concepts of self-help and self-management. What this means is that individuals could learn about and take more responsibility for their own health. The emphasis should rightly be placed on prevention of disease by such strategies as good diet, regular exercise, and sufficient rest. It is also important to monitor one's own health to try to prevent one illness from deteriorating into another, more serious and potentially life-threatening one. Those older women who suffer from chronic and life-threatening diseases could be helped enormously by support groups and by sensitive and responsive medical care.

The Older Women's League also advises older women to explore alternative therapies that offer a holistic approach to health care. This might help to circumvent our total reliance on the medical model.

Within the context of older people's organizations, older women could draw attention to the appalling neglect their special health concerns elicit from politicians, medical personnel, researchers, and health organizations. To ensure that future generations of doctors do not perpetuate a sexist and agist approach to women's health care, older women could join with the younger women's alternative health movement to fight stereotyping in teaching institutions. Moreover, if younger and older women combined their efforts, they could launch very effective public-education programs about the concerns in women's health throughout life. They could promote, for example, prevention programs, self-help groups, chronic disease control, menopause workshops, and so on.[11]

The ideas presented here represent merely a sampling drawn from a comprehensive document prepared by the Older Women's League — Gray Paper Number 3, "Older Women and Health Care: Strategy for Survival." This should be read by any woman interested in the problems of health care and aging.

There is also an economic dimension to the problem of ensuring access to quality medical care: growing numbers of older women lack the financial resources to purchase medical care. In many health-care systems, per-diem charges are levied in hospitals; extra charges often are demanded in advance by doctors who are not content with their medicare payments; and charges for a growing range of health-related services are placed directly on the consumer.

What was intended as a comprehensive and humane public medical-insurance program in Canada is slowly being eroded. For older women, this has serious implications: they lack the financial resources to pay for extra billing, yet they need a disproportionate amount of medical services.

We are in the process of moving backwards, back to a time when access to health care was the prerogative of the rich. Canadian doctors who extra bill claim that they personally assess their patients' ability to pay and that they do not turn anyone away. Even if this were entirely true (and newspaper stories show increasingly that it is not), the health-care system is reducing the old and the poor to the status of charity cases. Health care may soon no longer be a right, but rather a privilege accorded to the rich and to those whom doctors deem to be worthy and deserving. Our goal must be to ensure access to quality medical care for every older woman, and for that matter for every citizen, as a right, without financial obstacles and without the stigma of means tests.

The Present and the Future

My goal in this concluding chapter is not to present a detailed blueprint for some future utopia. To do so would be to assign to myself the power held by gerontologists, other professionals, and the rest of society, namely, the right to define life for older women. Most of the options I have explored here evolved from my discussions with older women over the past four years. Their insights, experience, and collective wisdom provide the basis for my analysis.

But to identify options is a meaningless exercise unless those options are available to all of us. If there is one clear and unequivocal theme that emerges, it is that older women lack the power to make these choices about their own lives.

For many women powerlessness begins with a desperate and grinding poverty that effectively narrows their lives. In response, I have strongly advocated an expanded universal old-age pension and the restoration of our universal medical-care plan. I have not tried to cost these programs; I am arguing my case on the basis of equity and justice. But I have pointed out that universal plans of any sort are cheap to administer because they eliminate the need for a massive and demeaning welfare bureaucracy.

At the same time, I can hear the actuaries tapping away on their pocket computers, calculating the cost at so many dollars. But the issue is not really one of cost; it is rather one of priorities. If we, as a society, consider a large defence budget, an additional farm subsidy, or tax concessions to large corporations to be necessary or desirable, the money exists. My challenge is whether our society is prepared to consider older women to be important in the same way.

I have also shown that, while poverty is a substantial part of the problem, it is by no means the total issue. All women, regardless of their income level or educational attainment, experience aging as a social judgment. Older women lack the freedom to exercise control over their own lives. As we age, we are progressively infantilized by doctors, gerontologists, drug companies, the media, and volunteers. The power of each of these groups is reinforced by older women's traditional socialized passivity. Often older women find they have little or no power to define their own goals in life. This realization has a profoundly negative effect on their self-esteem and leads irrevocably to a diminished sense of dignity.

The only plausible answer is to reverse the power imbalance by demanding control over our own lives and by defining for ourselves our goals and our needs. We must fight society's restrictive and narrow definition of female beauty and female worth. We must fight any individual or group who tries to treat us as children; who defines us as unattractive and undesirable; who tells us how to act; who expects our gratitude for meager handouts. The call to arms has already been sounded and the first steps have been taken individually and collectively, challenging society's notions of what it is to be an older woman. Older women are developing their own ideas and their own strategies for change and they are starting to demand that they be heard.

Epilogue

When I first began to research this book, I had a dream that has recurred frequently during the past four years. In my dream, a million older women march together chanting in chorus, demanding their rights. At times the women are angry; on other occasions the mood is more like a party; but always there is determination and very great pride. When I first had this dream there were only older women in the march, but after a while a few younger and mid-life women began to join them. More recently, there are scores of women of every age – from ninety-year-olds in wheelchairs to toddlers in prams and backpacks. As one, they link arms and march together.

My dreams, I believe, are a response to all the pain and neglect I have seen during the past four years. I cannot accept that this suffering is rare and represents regrettable exceptions. My own research included interviews with a broad spectrum of older women, cutting across class, education, race, and income levels. I am still reeling from the shock of meeting women whose lives more closely reflect nineteenth-century poverty than the supposedly enlightened 1980s. When women of seventy, eighty, and ninety do not have enough to eat, a safe, decent place to live, and can anticipate spending the end of their lives in nursing homes, either pacified with drugs or reduced to the status of children, I can only conclude that our society must have an amazing capacity for indifference and cruelty.

I have often felt overwhelmed with anger and despair because I realized that the neglect and abuse of older women is deeply entrenched in every aspect of our culture. Yet I also felt inspired and uplifted by all the women who face one crisis after another and endure disappointments and losses with tremendous humor and courage.

I was forced, in a way few women in their thirties are, to come to terms with my own aging. During these four years, I began to understand that unless I faced several issues — how much money I could expect to have in old age, where I would live, and what I should do about maintaining my own health — I would, at age sixty-five, be totally unprepared and as bewildered and victimized as were many of the women I met. I realized, too, that as an individual I must take some personal responsibility, but that my dignity would become increasingly fragile, assaulted on all sides by an insidious system that accords less value to women as they age.

Over and over again I was struck by how vulnerable older women are. They command little power or respect. I saw many blighted lives: women who are prematurely institutionalized, cut off from life; women who are trapped in abusive family situations; women who live in squalid, dangerous housing; women who are demeaned and humiliated by doctors, social-service workers, or the welfare bureaucracy. Yet in the midst of this cruel and humiliating treatment, I found women who, through heroic efforts and with enormous resourcefulness, carved out dignified and fulfilling lives. They employed a lifetime's experience and wisdom to circumvent oppressive situations.

Much of my research involved interviews, primarily with women between the ages of sixty to one hundred and four. For many, the interview was an occasion to entertain, to offer hospitality, to engage in conversation. I remember, in particular, one woman in her late seventies who met me at the door in a flowing red gown. She told me that I was her first guest in more than two months because in cold, icy weather neither she nor her friends budge from their apartments. I was moved by the obvious efforts she took to prepare a special lunch. On a small bridge table, which she had covered with a white tablecloth, she had laid out her best china. She served me chilled white wine, a fresh green salad, a perfect mushroom omelet, French cheese, and some of her own preserves. I looked around her tiny apartment, which was really only one room, and as we talked I realized she was barely making ends meet. She had apparently saved for some time before our meeting, cutting corners, so that she could offer me a good meal. I felt utterly miserable that she had deprived herself, but she made it clear that it was very important to her to extend hospitality – it made her feel like she was still someone significant and not, as she put it, "a pathetic old lady." In the past five years, she told me, I was the only person who had asked her what she thought and had listened to her opinions aside from the few friends she had who were well enough to visit.

I have made friends with women whom otherwise I might never have had the opportunity to know. They have sent me articles, suggested people for me to interview, shared ideas and experiences, written me letters of encouragement, opened up their homes, and offered me a special kind of warmth and friendship. I have personally been immensely enriched by meeting and getting to know them.

I was told by experts in the field that older women ramble and have trouble focusing their thoughts. When I talked to women in hospitals and nursing homes, I was repeatedly warned by the staff that I should expect difficulty in conducting a rational interview; that the women were either senile, unstable, or prone to exaggeration. This was not my experience. Instead, I was privileged to listen to observations and insights based on a wealth of experience and a lifetime's accumulation of wisdom. For many, too, this was a chance to vent an enormous well of anger about the injustice of their situations. Few engaged in self-pity; instead they passionately expressed their frustrations at the narrow confines of their lives.

Over time, I came to loathe the word "old," which carries with it such profoundly negative connotations. I found that many women studiously avoided referring to themselves as "old," "aging," "elderly," or "senior" and used instead more positive words, such as "maturity," "growth," or "the attaining of wisdom."

In my efforts to substantiate my own findings with other studies, I found that very little of the gerontological literature specifically focused on older women, even though women are the largest segment of the older population.

What literature did exist was mostly riddled with sexism

and agism. It appeared that older women were not deemed worthy subjects of research, especially in the critical areas of health and poverty. I did, however, find the beginnings of a small body of work, researched and written by women with a feminist consciousness.

In discussing the ideas in this book, I was surprised that the initial response of a number of supposedly informed commentators on social policy was to challenge the premise that older women are poor. On more than one occasion I was told that there are a large number of rich old women who own much of the expensive property in Canada and spend their time clipping coupons from their blue-chip bonds. Poverty among older women, these commentators contended, was an exception because women were nearly all well provided for by their husbands' pensions.

But the denial of poverty that surprised me most came from an audience made up of mid-life and older women. I had been asked to participate in a noon-hour lecture series sponsored by the Department of Continuing Education at the University of Toronto. After I had finished outlining why so many older women suffer acute financial deprivation, a substantial number of people in the audience were livid and simply denied that my analysis was rooted in reality. Their attitude was that they were doing just fine, and that if older women end up poor "it's their own goddamn fault" – they should have acquainted themselves with their husbands' financial situations, and they should have somehow saved up some money of their own. I was stunned by this lack of compassion and disturbed by their anger. But I recognized that I had struck a nerve. They were expressing raw fear. A small number of women in the audience, most of whom were older than sixty-five, stood up and talked with great emotion about their sisters and friends who had been comfortable and secure until their husbands died. These women, they explained, were now destitute and lived in appalling circumstances. A rather bitter and acrimonious debate evolved between these two camps; it continued well beyond the allotted time.

This audience was made up almost exclusively of middle-class women. (Poor older women are admittedly less likely to attend a paid lecture series at a university.) What I found upsetting was the fact that the majority of the audience was denying that a problem existed, despite the fact that I had presented unrefutable statistical data supplied by the federal government that demonstrated unequivocally that older women suffer disproportionately from poverty. I also pointed out that the discrimination and low wages women receive are unlikely to change in the foreseeable future.

The more data I presented, the angrier they became. What they were practising was denial; they were blaming the victim. Feminism and sisterhood were obviously alien concepts. They could not cope with the notion that the majority of women may never have the resources to plan for old age.

Through the course of my interviews I also observed that there was a pronounced difference in the way poor and rich women come to terms with their own aging. Since poor women undergo the least change in life status, they seem to cope best with aging. Most have neither the money nor the time to wage more than a token battle with the physical effects of aging. And their financial situation is unlikely to alter dramatically. They have managed on very little all their adult lives.

Middle-class and rich women, in contrast, are apt to be anxious about their changing physical appearance and have difficulty adapting to drastically reduced financial circumstances. They talked almost obsessively about the importance of looking as young as possible by preserving their figures, dyeing their hair, and using makeup skillfully. Aging, for so many of these women, was clearly experienced as defeat, not as a natural part of life. They were keenly aware that their value as desirable and attractive women took an enormous plunge when they turned forty and declined steadily thereafter.

Certainly there are enough influences and pressures on all women to approach aging with anxiety and fear. What I had not anticipated was how differently poor women experience this process. For them, aging is not quite so traumatic and does not involve nearly as much change. A married middle-class or rich woman is more likely to be devastated if she is left manless and poor. These women tend to describe their change in status as a personal failure. Poor women are not generally as tightly tied to their physical appearance, because for them aging is a biological event that deserves to be treated with humor and a comfortable acceptance.

I found, too, that older, single women went through considerably less change as they moved from mid to late life. Their identities were not especially linked to male approval, and they were less likely to experience the trauma of losing a male partner. Many appreciated their friendships with other women, which were sustaining and nurturing. Unlike widows and divorced women, who often find themselves cut off from married friends and suddenly isolated, single women tend to enjoy more continuity from mid life on. Many have established a strong personal network of friends whose continuing support and comfort are assured into old age.

Despite these differences in the way women cope with aging, nearly all the women I interviewed felt that the public image of older women was confined to two derogatory and restrictive stereotypes. The most evocative description of these two images was related to me by a sixty-five-year-old actress who is constantly in demand for TV commercials.

When I am asked to portray an older woman, invariably the producer suggests that I wear a dress with a lace collar, and talk in a high-pitched voice; all of which suggests a somewhat comical and slightly absurd figure. The whole image is an absolute caricature of what they think a typical matron is like. The only other portrayal of an older woman that I have ever been asked to do is the classic sweet, kindly grandmother in a family situation. Not once has anyone considered the possibility of an older woman who is fiery and powerful.

These confining and restrictive images of older women are not only limited to the media. They are so pervasive and negative that the fashion industry does not devote much time or energy to offering us interesting clothing. There is little that is attractive and colorful for a woman who is older than fifty or larger than size twelve. High style has been deemed the prerogative of young, thin women and a few affluent, svelte, older women.

Whereas the fashion industry virtually ignores our existence, the beauty industry has defined us as a highly lucrative and easily manipulated market. The message we receive is clearly that there is no such thing as a beautiful older woman. Our culture exhibits a repugnance to the most obvious and natural signs of age. There appears to be no place in our imagination for the concept of beauty beyond a woman's youth.

A woman of fifty whom I interviewed has lovely, thick, straight steel-gray hair framing a totally un-made-up face. She is literally bursting with vitality and exudes a strong self-confidence. I had thought that someone like her, so obviously comfortable with her appearance, would experience considerably less pressure to conform to the society's rigid idea of the appropriate image for a mid-life woman.

> Every time I enter a beauty salon for a hair cut, I
> am told that my gray hair is ugly and that it makes
> me look old. The hairdressers and beauticians simply
> assume that I should be ashamed of my gray hair. They
> think they have a right to define for me what beauty
> is. They can't conceive of a woman who is proud of her
> mature appearance and takes pleasure in her own aging.
> Every time I go through the ritual of a hair cut, my
> self-esteem takes a beating. It has had, over a time, a
> significant influence over how I feel about myself. This
> is reinforced by the piles of fashion magazines that I
> flip through at the salon. I have never seen a single
> magazine photo of an older woman with lines, gray
> hair, and a less-than-perfect figure. What older models
> I see are made up to ape younger women and they often
> succeed only in looking grotesque.

However much the media, beauty, and fashion industries denigrate mid-life women, women older than seventy-five receive virtually no attention at all. It's almost as if extreme age is so incomprehensible and unacceptable to our notions of appropriate appearance that we deny this stage of life.

I met a woman in her early eighties who explained that she was so angry at fashion's dictates that she has created her own style.

It infuriates my daughters to see their mother wearing cast-off army fatigues with leather boots, a colorful blouse, and a fleece-lined vest. I refuse to wear the shapeless smocks and hideous housedresses that one of my daughters insists on buying me. This outfit I pulled together at rummage sales is comfortable, cheerful, and lively. It's the only way I can say to the world — yes, I'm old — yes, but I'm still alive. I have this feeling when people stare at me on the streets that they are affronted by my boldness and flamboyance. It flies in the face of their preconceived ideas about old grannies. In their minds, a very old woman like myself is more properly tucked away in a nursing home, bundled up in a hospital gown, padding around in wooly slippers.

Another theme that ran through all my research was the growing importance of friendships and networking as we move through the various stages of our aging. As husbands died or left and children moved far away or became caught up in their own lives, friendships with other women often became the only real source of support. These friendships were based on mutual respect and a shared empathy, and were particularly characterized by their intensity and loyalty. For many women these relationships were far more important than families. As much as older women might genuinely love their children and other relatives, they prefer to seek out the companionship of their friends. A large number of older women maintained that, however well-meaning their families were, there was an underlying mixture of tension, conflict, and guilt — which presented a serious barrier to happy and mutually satisfying relationships.

Women who had never uttered a feminist word or idea in their lives seemed to appreciate that female friendship was perhaps the most sustaining aspect of their lives. As many said, it was only with other women that they felt valued and taken seriously.

Although I came across countless friendships I admired, I was especially moved by the friendship of two older women who live in my own neighborhood. They shared an old run-down house with two male boarders in their mid thirties. These men, I learned, who had severe learning disabilities, had been taken in as foster children and continued to live with these women as adults.

For several years I saw these two women, who were perhaps in their late seventies or early eighties, walking up and down my street, holding hands, and engaged in animated conversation in Yiddish.

Not long ago, I was picking up my dry-cleaning at the corner store when one of the women came in alone, obviously in great distress and on the verge of tears. In heavily accented English, she told the woman who ran the store that her friend had been taken away to a hospital by her son.

> I am a lost soul without her. She's like a sister to me; we're that close. I never did anything without her for the last twenty years. I go to the hospital every day and bring her food from home and I read the papers to her. She keeps begging me to take her home. What can I do? When I tell the doctors and her son that I can take care of her and that she is better off with me in her own home, they just ignore me or tell me it's impossible. I wander around feeling so lonely.

Whenever I see her now, walking alone in the neighborhood, she always seems depressed and utterly forlorn. She does not smile much any more and often mumbles angrily to herself. Her acute frustration and despair have made me realize how a friendship between women in old age may be a woman's only life-affirming relationship.

For some women these friendships expanded to include an informal system of networking, which provided mutual protection and a variety of information and exchanged services. In a sense, these women were pooling their time and resources to assist each other in coping with a largely indifferent and at times hostile environment. The network is often simple: older women who are alone and in poor health call each other daily, partly to check up on each other and partly to help ward off total isolation.

On a more sophisticated level, I discovered a number of older women, living on their own, who had organized a self-help group. They met weekly to share a meal and to help each other with the special concerns and problems they are facing as late-life women.

When I spoke with women in their eighties and nineties, they frequently pointed out that too many women limit their friendships exclusively to their own age group. I saw many women, eighty and older, extremely isolated because all their friends had died. On a practical level, especially since a sizeable number of women can expect to enjoy a long life, we are extremely vulnerable if we limit our friendships to people of our own age. Having inter-generational friends provides us with a wedge against loneliness and can significantly enrich our lives. I found that older women who made special efforts to cultivate friendships with younger women enjoyed the stimulation and vitality that these relationships afforded. And younger women who developed special friendships with older women cherished support, comfort, and wisdom they would not otherwise experience.

Unfortunately there are few opportunities and little encouragement for these kinds of relationships to flourish. The present generation of older women is socialized to believe that it is more appropriate for their friends to be their own age. I am not suggesting that these friendships are not extremely valuable, and perhaps the most intimate ones that we can expect to have. However, I have come to the conclusion that such exclusivity can lead to a very lonely old age.

At the same time, I discovered that older women are not resistant to the notion of developing friendships with younger women. It is often the attitudes of younger women that are the real barrier. At a very early age, women receive the societal message that old age is horrific, depressing, and the end of everything. Unless we can take the fear and dread out of old age, we can expect large numbers of younger women to continue to avoid older women and to respond to them with fear and repugnance.

I found, though, that women who had a supportive and loving relationship with their grandmothers, aunts, or a family friend tended to be less obsessed with the negative aspects of aging. And if the older woman in their lives was a particularly powerful woman who was accorded respect for her intelligence, they were more likely to see life as a continuum, with each stage offering interesting and different possibilities. Old age became a natural part of the life cycle and held out the promise of creativity and fulfillment.

I will always remember one woman in her mid thirties who was fortunate enough to have five great-aunts, who have provided her with very positive role models of old age.

> My aunts have always struck me as being free and independent. They're all quite old now, but I find them even more outspoken, irascible, and eccentric than when they were middle-aged. When I go home and visit them, I always come away feeling hopeful about the future and excited about the possibility of reaching an age where I too can defy social conventions and do as I please. Old age, for me, represents a time when I will be more free, less dominated by what other people think. I don't believe that I would feel this way if I hadn't grown up surrounded by my very wonderful and dynamic aunts.

When I look back on the past four years' work, I see that the key to real change is political action. Today in Canada older women are suffering from powerlessness. Few older women can extract themselves entirely from the obstacles that frustrate older women's efforts to retain their dignity and find fulfillment in old age. If we are fortunate enough to escape poverty, we still must cope with the debilitating effects of society's rigid youth tradition. Our society admires and indeed almost worships strength and vigor.

The 1980s are not particularly responsive to the needs of older women. Public policy is slowly grinding away at those programs that provide us with the barest essentials — a basic income, health care, and social services.

253

Women like Maggie Kuhn of the Gray Panthers and Tish Sommers of the Older Women's League have mobilized a vocal group of older women to fight these regressive and destructive trends. I find it exciting to see women in their sixties and seventies preparing briefs, addressing congressional committees, delivering powerful speeches, and appearing on television and radio. Admittedly, this political activism is confined to a small group of older women who have highly developed political consciousnesses. I was privileged to catch a glimpse of their enormous enthusiasm and commitment. They have defined the issues with great clarity and have applied their collective life experience to develop excellent strategies, which they plan to employ in their quest for fundamental social change.

Perhaps the most encouraging sign of all is that large numbers of women in their thirties have grown up with exposure to feminist thinking. We are a generation that has had easier access to contraception and public education. As a result, we have exercised greater control over our lives than did our mothers before us. We are, too, a generation that has a better understanding of finances and the workings of bureaucracies, at least in part because so many of us were not raised in and do not live in traditional two-parent family units with a man who orders our lives. Society will not be able to convince us that we are entitled to only subsistence at the poverty line, that we must endure neglect, exploitation, and abuse. We are unquestionably a generation of women who are more angry at injustice and less easily manipulated. I am confident that it will be very difficult to shunt us aside. Politicians and professionals will find that we are far less willing than the women that precede us to be led, guided, and condescended to.

Not so very long ago, thirty was the beginning of middle age. Enough women today are rejecting the culturally induced notion that we are finished at menopause. Many of us adamantly refuse to accept that life for women is confined to a brief blaze of glory in our teens and twenties when society defines us as attractive and sexy.

It is, I believe, the influence of the women's movement that has so radically altered both our expectations and our self-image. Our collective consciousness has been raised to the point where a significant number of us appreciate that it is our right to pursue our own goals and seek personal fulfillment. We are in the midst of a process that will revolutionize our ideas about older women. We are starting to challenge the antiquated and destructive images of mid- to late-life women. Rather than passively accept the last forty years of our lives as a time of depression and decline, many of us are insisting those years are a time of growth and maturity. We may witness the emergence of the older woman as a healthy, attractive, and valuable member of society.

Although I am extremely optimistic about the change that will take place for women in their thirties, I am filled with shame and anger at the plight of today's older women. Throughout this book I have attempted to expose our society's shallow and brutal attitudes, which I believe stem from our hatred of aging and our fear of decline. Older women are victims of sexism and agism, which makes their predicament doubly oppressive.

Neither older nor younger women can afford to trust that society's attitudes and practices will change quickly or easily. Our battles must be fought by marshalling a grass-roots militancy that will let our legislators know that our interests can no longer be put aside. We must demand a future where we receive our fair share, and where our dignity is assured. The prospect of a million angry women of all ages marching arm in arm on Parliament Hill may yet come to pass. . . .

Appendix

Defining Poverty

In Canada there have developed several different definitions of a "poverty line," the line below which an individual or family is deemed to be "poor." There is considerable disagreement about what is an acceptable minimum income for a family or an individual.[1]

Most of the attempts to define poverty focus on whether an individual or family suffers deprivation in relation to the rest of the community. More precisely, a poor person or family has "insufficient access to certain goods and services which are available to most other people and which have come to be accepted as a basic standard of living."[2] These goods and services generally refer to "the diet, living conditions and amenities customary in the society to which they belong."[3]

There are two frequently used measures of poverty. One relates to income "inadequacy" – does the income insure physical survival? The other relates to income "inequality" – is the income equitable in relation to community living standards?[4]

Statistics Canada, the Canadian Council on Social Development, and the Social Planning Council of Metropolitan Toronto have developed the most commonly used "poverty lines" in Canada. (Statistics Canada officially uses the term "low income cut-off," rather than "poverty line.")

The poverty line developed by Statistics Canada is the closest we have to an "official" national definition.[5] Using the concept of income "adequacy" for 1983, Statistics Canada drew the poverty line for an individual living in an urban center (500,000 or more) at $9,538; the figure for an individual in a rural area is $7,052.[6]

To develop its poverty line, Statistics Canada used historical survey data, which showed that, in 1978, the average family spent 38.5 per cent of its income on what Statistics Canada called the basic necessities of life. According to Statistics Canada any family that spent 58.5 per cent of its income on basic necessities (that is, an additional 20 per cent of its income) was defined as being in "straitened circumstances."[7] The figures are arbitrary. But Statistics Canada does not explain why it selected the 20 per cent increment as the poverty line. It could just as easily have selected 10 per cent or 30 per cent, thus either raising the poverty line to include larger numbers of poor individuals and families, or lowering the poverty line and significantly shrinking the ranks of the "officially" poor.

Another poverty line that is frequently quoted is that developed by the Canada Council on Social Development. Based on a measure of income "inequality," an individual or a family falls below the poverty line if its living income is less than half the average individual or family income of the community. The poverty line for an individual for 1983, according to the Canadian Council on Social Development, was $8,562.[8]

The least restrictive poverty line, which defines basic needs by the most comprehensive categories, was devised by the Social Planning Council of Metropolitan Toronto. These categories include: food, clothing, shelter, health care, personal care, transportation, recreation, and household items. When calculating its poverty line, the Social Planning Council also considers family size, age, and sex of family members, and the activity level (this is a measure of quality of life) and employment status of adults. Although this poverty line is based on income "adequacy," it moves far beyond mere physical survival by raising the poverty line sufficiently above subsistence to ensure good health and self-respect. Nevertheless, at $11,530 for an individual, the 1983 poverty line is still substantially below community living standards.[9]

None of these poverty lines provides for a standard of living that will necessarily mean a comfortable old age. What they indicate is a minimum income needed to cover the basic necessities of life. Admittedly, the Social Planning Council's definition of necessities is considerably more humane than the others, taking into account some of the amenities that contribute to an enhanced quality of life. However, Statistics Canada's less generous definition is the more common standard used in this country.

When Statistics Canada's poverty line is used to determine poverty among older women, a grim picture emerges. According to the latest published census figures (1981), there are 1.3 million Canadian women who are sixty-five or older — 1 in 11 persons in the total population. The approximate life expectancy of these women is eighty years. In addition, 60 per cent of these women are single, widowed, or divorced.

In Table 1, 1981 data from Statistics Canada show 34.6 per cent of all women under sixty-five fell below Statistics Canada's low income cut-off (i.e., their poverty line). The figure nearly doubles to 62.2 per cent for women over sixty-five, almost two out of every three women in this age group. In comparison, men fare much better. Only 24.5 per cent under sixty-five have incomes below the poverty line. This figure doubles to 48.4 per cent when men reach sixty-five, i.e., one out of every two men over sixty-five fall below Statistics Canada's poverty line.

Even allowing for inflationary adjustments since 1981, poverty, particularly among older women, remains common. Older women are still the poorest of the poor in Canada.

How poor are older women in relation to the poverty line? Table 2, also based on Statistics Canada data, shows that 40 per cent of single women sixty-five and older had incomes below $6,000 in 1981. (This is two out of every five.) Surely this figure of $6,000 should be far below any reasonable poverty line.

The figure jumps to 60 per cent when we include all single older women with incomes under $7,000. And if we consider women with incomes below $10,000, we include about 77 per cent of all single women age sixty-five and older. This is and should be considered a national disgrace.

Statistics Canada's rather arbitrary poverty line does not give a complete picture of older women's income status.

Table 1

Incidence of Low Income in Canada, 1981
(Statistics Canada Low Income Cut-Offs)

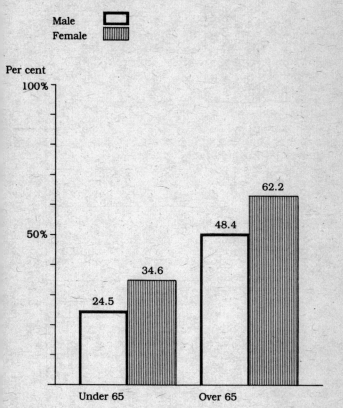

Source: Statistics Canada,
Income Distribution by Size, 1981,
Table 85, p. 163 (Ottawa: 1983).

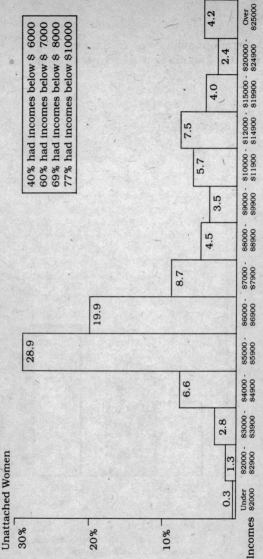

Table 2

Per cent Distribution of Incomes of
Unattached Women in Canada, 1981

Per cent of
Unattached Women

40% had incomes below $ 6000
60% had incomes below $ 7000
69% had incomes below $ 8000
77% had incomes below $10000

30% — 20% — 10%

| 0.3 | 1.3 | 2.8 | 6.6 | 28.9 | 19.9 | 8.7 | 4.5 | 3.5 | 5.7 | 7.5 | 4.0 | 2.4 | 4.2 |

Incomes: Under $2000 | $2000-$2900 | $3000-$3900 | $4000-$4900 | $5000-$5900 | $6000-$6900 | $7000-$7900 | $8000-$8900 | $9000-$9900 | $10000-$11900 | $12000-$14900 | $15000-$19900 | $20000-$24900 | Over $25000

Source: Statistics Canada, *Income Distribution by Size, 1981*, Table 32, p. 80 (Ottawa: 1983)

There are many who are not officially classed as poor, but whose total incomes place them close to the poverty line. They have been described as the "near poor." If the poverty line were raised so that "poor" included those individuals whose income is 10 per cent above the present low-income cut-off point, there would be an 11 per cent rise in the numbers of poor individuals. A 20 per cent increase would add 20.5 per cent to the ranks of the poor.[10]

If we include the "near poor" in the calculation of poverty among old women, it becomes clear that only a tiny minority can honestly be described as enjoying a financially comfortable old age.

All the poverty lines are somebody's subjective assessment of an income level below which people are defined as poor. But rarely are people themselves asked what they think a person needs to live on. In 1981, Health and Welfare Canada conducted a postal survey of 16,950 Old Age Security recipients, with a response rate of over 70 per cent. Respondents were asked what they thought would be an "adequate income" for 1981; the replies averaged out to $10,600. They were also asked at what income they could live comfortably, without worrying about money; the average reply was $12,690.

Respondents were then asked about their own incomes. For men, the average income was $10,535 or almost exactly at the adequacy line. For women, however, the average income was only $6,785, approximately two thirds of both the male figure and the adequacy line.[11]

Notes: Self-Image and
the Cult of Sexuality

1. Charlotte Gray, "How Growing Older Affects Your Body," *Chatelaine* (February 1983): 51 – 56.
2. *Toronto Globe and Mail*, 28 July 1983, p. 16.
3. *Globe*, p. 16.
4. *Globe*, p. 16.
5. Nora Scott Kinzer, *Put Down and Ripped Off: The American Woman and the Beauty Cult* (New York: Thomas Crowell and Company, 1977), p. 110.
6. "Muscles In," *New Society* (7 July 1983): 4.
7. Kathrin Perutz, *Beyond the Looking Glass* (Harmondsworth: Penguin Books, 1972), pp. 25 – 28.
8. Beth Stillborn, "Sexploitation in Advertising," Institute for Saskatchewan Studies (March 1979): 5.
9. Gloria Heidi, *Winning the Age Game* (New York: Doubleday, 1976).
10. Sandra Gorney and Claire Cox, *How Women Can Achieve Fulfillment After 40* (New York: Dial Press, 1973).
11. Susan Sontag, "The Double Standard of Aging," *Saturday Review of the Society* (23 September 1972): 35 – 37.
12. Toronto *Globe and Mail*, 19 March 1979, p. 4.
13. Domeena Renshaw, "Sexuality in Nursing Homes," *Symposium on Aging and Dying* (Ottawa, 1979), p. 44.
14. Margaret Hellie Huyak, "Sex and the Older Woman," in *Looking Ahead: A Woman's Guide to the Problems*

and Joys of Growing Older, ed. Lillian E. Troll, Joan
Israel, and Kenneth Israel (New Jersey: Prentice-Hall,
1977).

15. Toronto Globe and Mail, 23 April 1980, p. 10
16. Sontag, p. 37.
17. Judith Posner, "Sex and Older Women," Homemaker's
    (July/August 1980): 32 – 37.
18. Sontag, p. 38.
19. "How to Be Happy Through Middle-Age," Psychology
    Today (June 1980): 30.

Notes: Older Women and Health:
The Hazards We Face

1. Mary Daly, Gyn/Ecology – The Metaethics of Radical
   Feminism (Boston: Beacon Press, 1978), p. 230.
2. The Boston Women's Health Book Collective, Our
   Bodies, Ourselves – A Book By and For Women (New
   York: Simon and Schuster, 1976), pp. 124 – 125.
3. Ibid., p. 133.
4. Ibid., pp. 125 – 126. This is a chronic swelling and
   lumpiness in the breast, an inability of our system to
   deal with the buildup of fluid and congestion each
   month.
5. Gena Corea, The Hidden Malpractice: How American
   Medicine Treats Women as Patients and Professionals (New York: William Morrow and Company, 1977),
   pp. 241 – 242.
6. Ibid.
7. Ibid.
8. Ibid., p. 7.
9. Rose Kushner, "Unnecessary Mastectomies," National
   Women's Health Network News (April/May, 1979), p. 5.
10. Corea, p. 236.
11. Ruth Weg, "More Wrinkles," in Looking Ahead: A
    Woman's Guide to the Problems and Joys of Growing
    Older, ed. Lillian E. Troll, Joan Israel and Kenneth
    Israel (New Jersey: Prentice-Hall, 1977), p. 22.
12. Barbara Ehrenreich and Deirdre English, Complaints

and Disorders: The Sexual Politics of Sickness (London: Writers and Readers Publishing Cooperative, 1973), p. 80.

13. Leah Cohen and Constance Backhouse, "Women and Health: The Growing Controversy," *Canadian Women's Studies* (Summer 1979): 7.
14. Ibid., p. 7.
15. Ibid., p. 7.
16. Paula Weideger, *Female Cycles* (London: The Women's Press, 1979), p. 206.
17. Ibid., p. 213.
18. *Our Bodies, Ourselves*, p. 329.
19. Beverley Rutziek and Verna Pedrin, "Menopause, Myths and Realities," in *Health in the Middle Years: A Symposium About Women* (Mountain View, California: Arachne Publishing, 1976), pp. 11 – 15.
20. Barbara Joans, "The Anthropological Aspects of Menopause," in *Health in the Middle Years*, pp. 3 – 8.
21. Barbara Seaman and Gideon Seaman, *Women and the Crisis in Sex Hormones* (New York: Bantam, 1977), p. 338.
22. Ann Pappert, "Menopause: The Myth," *Homemaker's* (October 1979): 84.
23. Cohen and Backhouse, p. 7.
24. Ibid., p. 7.
25. Pappert, p. 83.
26. Lisa Snow and Leona Bayer, "Menopausal Symptoms and Estrogen Replacement Therapy," in *Health in the Middle Years*, p. 38.
27. This advertisement was printed in *Whistlestop* (Published by The Creamery Educational Foundation: Winter, 1980, Vol. 2, No. 1), p. 3.
28. Pappert, p. 80.
29. Seaman and Seaman, p. 373.
30. Cohen and Backhouse, pp. 5-6.
31. Deborah Larned, "The Greening of the Womb," *New Times* (27 December 1974): 36.
32. Ibid., p. 37.
33. Seaman and Seaman, pp. 373 – 374.
34. Larned, p. 38.
35. Cohen and Backhouse, p. 6.

36. Ibid., p. 6.
37. Ibid., p. 6.
38. Larned, p. 36.
39. Cohen and Backhouse, p. 7.
40. Erenreich and English, pp. 80 – 83.
41. R. Cooperstock, "Psychotropic Drug Use Among Women," *CMA Journal* 115 (23 October 1976): 760.
42. Linda Fidell, "Put Her Down on Drugs: Prescribed Drug Usage in Women," an address to the Western Association of Women Psychologists, Anaheim, California, 12 April 1973.
43. Phyllis Chesler, "Patients and Patriarch: Women in the Psychotherapeutic Relationship," in *Women in Sexist Society: Studies in Power and Powerlessness*, ed. Vivian Gornick and Barbara K. Moran (New York: Basic Books, 1971), pp. 382 – 385.
44. Cohen and Backhouse, p. 5.
45. Ibid., p. 5.
46. Ruth Cooperstock, "Women and Psychotropic Drug Use," in *The Chemically Dependent Woman*, ed. Janet Downsling and Anne MacLennan (Toronto: The Donwood Institute, 4 June 1977), pp. 40 – 41.
47. Janet S. Downsling, "The Chemical Trap: A Physician's Perspective," in *The Chemically Dependent Woman*, p. 58.
48. Patricia Badiet, "Women and Legal Drugs: A Review," in *Women: Their Use of Alcohol and Other Legal Drugs*, ed. Anne MacLennan (Toronto: Addiction Research Foundation of Ontario, 1976), pp. 72 – 75.
49. Judy Dobbie, "One for the End of the Road: Alcoholism and Drug Abuse Among the Elderly," *Maclean's* (19 September 1977): 69 – 70.
50. R. B. Palmer, "Use and Abuse of Drugs in the Difficult Psychogeriatric Patient," a paper presented at the annual meeting of the Ontario Psychogeriatric Association (in Stratford, Ontario in September, 1975), pp. 17 – 18.
51. Ibid., p. 19.
52. Ibid., p. 25.
53. "More Wrinkles," p. 25.
54. Ibid., pp. 26 – 27.
55. Cohen and Backhouse, p. 5.

56. Brian L. Mishara and Robert Kastenbaum, *Alcohol and Old Age* (New York: Grune & Stratton, 1980), p. 81.
57. Judy Dobbie, *Substance Abuse Among the Elderly* (Toronto: the Addiction Research Foundation of Ontario, 1978), pp. 4 – 8.
58. Sarah Saunders (Medical Consultant), Addiction Research Foundation, Toronto, in conversation with the author.

Notes: Living at the Edge: Older Women and Housing

1. Robert M. Press, "The Hidden Problems of Elderly Runaways," in *The Christian Science Monitor*, 26 August 1980, p. 4.
2. Bert Kruger Smith, *New Living Alternatives for the Elderly* (Boston: Beacon Press, 1977), pp. 21 – 22.
3. Ibid., p. 22.
4. Elaine M. Brody, "A Million Procustean Beds," in *The Gerontologist* (No. 13, Winter 1973): 430 – 35 (original). The article was reprinted by the National Conference of Jewish Communal Service (Philadelphia: 29 May 1973): 266.
5. Ibid., p. 269.
6. Diane DeGraves, "Women Caring for Women," in *Resources for Feminist Research*, ed. Emily M. Nett, II, 2 (Toronto: O.I.S.E., July 1982): 212.
7. Belinda H. Morin and Joan Christensen, *Adult Residential Facilities: Boarding Homes and Lodging Houses* (First Report to the Metropolitan Toronto Social Services and Housing Subcommittee on Boarding Homes and Lodging Houses, October 1979).
8. Vivian Gornick, "A Splendid and Bitter Isolation," in *Voice* (16 – 22 July 1980): 21.

Notes: Violence Against Older Women

1. A letter I received from *Aegis* – a magazine about violence against women – in response to my inquiry about

information on older women and violence. (*Aegis*, P. O. Box 21033, Washington, D.C.).

2. Kathryn Painter, *Granny Battering*. (An unpublished dissertation, Lanchester Polytechnic, Coventry, England, 1980), p. 1.

3. Suzanne K. Steinmetz, "Battered Parents," *Society*, Vol. 15, No. 5 (July/August 1978): 54 – 55.

4. G. R. Burston, "Granny-Battering," *British Medical Journal* 3 (6 September 1975): 592.

5. Jean Renvoize, *Web of Violence* (London: Routledge and Kegan Paul, 1978), pp. 113 – 127.

6. "Manitoba Study on Elder Abuse," *Vis-a-Vis*, Vol. 1, No. 2 (Autumn 1983): 3.

7. Lois A. West, "Family Violence and Aging," a fact sheet from the George Washington University Women's Studies Program and Policy Center, 1980, pp. 1 – 2.

8. "Resources: Abuse of the Elderly," *Response*, Vol. 4, No. 2 (November/December 1980): 3.

9. "Granny Bashing," in *Human Behavior* (April 1979):48.

10. Karen Warmkessel, "Beating of Elderly Cloaked in Secrecy," *Toronto Star*, 6 December 1979, p. C-6.

11. Nancy R. Hooyman, "Older Women as Victims of Family Violence," a paper presented at the Annual Meeting of the Western Gerontological Association, March 1980.

12. Steinmetz, pp. 54 – 55.

13. Ibid., pp. 54 – 55.

14. Painter, pp. 1 – 28.

15. Charles I. Stannard, "Old Folks and Dirty Work: The Social Condition for Patient Abuse in a Nursing Home," *Social Problems*, Vol. 20, No. 3 (Winter 1973): 329 – 342.

16. Ibid., pp. 329 – 342.

17. Linda J. Davis and Elaine M. Brody, *Rape and Older Women: A Guide to Prevention and Protection*, (Washington, D.C.: U.S. Department of Health, Education, and Welfare, 1979), p. 9.

18. Ibid., p. 30.

19. Leah Cohen, Violence Against Older Women: An International Survey (Ottawa: Canadian Advisory Council on the Status of Women, October 1982), p. 7.

20. Ibid., pp. 7 – 8.

21. Ibid., p. 22.
22. Ibid., pp. 23 – 24.

Notes: To Be Old, a Woman, and Poor

1. *Women and Poverty*, a Report by the National Council of Welfare (Ottawa, 1979), p. 48.
2. *Pension Reform – What Women Want*, a report by the National Action Committee on the Status of Women (Toronto, 1983), p. 1.
3. Laurie Shields, *Displaced Homemakers: Organizing for a New Life* (New York: McGraw-Hill, 1981), p. x.
4. *Women and Aging*, a draft report of the Ontario Status of Women Council (Toronto, 1981), p. 1.
5. *Older Women: The Economics of Aging*, a report by The Women's Studies Program and Policy Center at George Washington University in conjunction with The Women's Research and Educational Institute of the Congresswomen's Caucus (Washington, D.C., 1980), p. 5.
6. Ibid., p. 13.
7. *Women and Aging*, p. 1.
8. Denis Guest, *The Emergence of Social Security in Canada* (Vancouver: University of British Columbia Press, 1980), pp. 74 – 79.
9. *Pension Reform*, p. 3.
10. *Pensions and the Poor*, a brief submitted to the Parliamentary Task Force on Pension Reform by the National Anti-Poverty Organization (Ottawa: September 20, 1983), p. 10.
11. *Pension Reform*, p. 4.
12. *Pensions and the Poor*, p. 11.
13. *Pension Reform*, p. 4.
14. Ibid., p. 4.
15. *Women and Pensions – An Overview of Issues and Solutions*, a report by the National Action Committee on the Status of Women (Toronto, 1981) p. 5.

16. Rosemary Speirs, "Make Do, Birch Tells Elderly Single Women," *Globe and Mail*, 4 December 1982, p. 1.
17. *Women and Pensions*, p. 5.
18. Elizabeth Pickett, *Women and Pensions in Ontario* (Toronto: Osgoode Hall, 1980), p. 24.
19. Ibid., p. 24.
20. *Women and Pensions*, p. 5.
21. Pickett, p. 24.
22. *Women and Aging*, p. 15.
23. *Older Women*, p. 13.
24. Tish Sommers and Laurie Shields, "Social Security: Adequacy and Equity for Older Women," *Gray Paper No. 2: Issues for Action* (Oakland, California: Older Women's League Educational Fund, 1979), p. 2.
25. *Older Women: The Economics of Aging*, p. 13.
26. Andrea J. Seale, *Can the Canada Pension Plan Survive The Charter?* (Toronto: Osgoode Hall, 1983), p. 10.
27. Ibid., p. 10.
28. Sommers and Shields, p. 4.
29. Penney Kome, "Women and Pensions," *Homemaker's* (Toronto: August 1979): 68J.
30. Pickett, p. 37.
31. Andrew Allentuck, *The Cost of Age* (Toronto: Fitzhenry and Whiteside, 1977), p. 28.
32. *Women and Poverty*, p. 20.
33. Ibid., p. 12.
34. For more details see NAPO's submission to the Minister of Finance — 1984. (NAPO also advocates that the age exemption and the pension deduction on the personal income-tax form, both of which are regressive in impact, be eliminated, to be replaced by a universal, refundable age credit.)

Notes: The Emerging Political Activists

1. *Forum*, Vol. 2, No. 1 (Kalamazoo, Michigan: National Action Forum for Older Women, Summer, 1979): 1.

2. "A Dialogue," ed. Dieter Hessel, *Maggie Kuhn on Aging* (Philadelphia: The Westminster Press, 1977), p. 9.
3. Ibid., p. 11.
4. This information is contained in an undated pamphlet issued by the Gray Panthers.
5. Ibid.
6. Ibid.
7. Conversation with Tish Sommers in Oakland, California, February, 1980.
8. Laurie Shields, *Displaced Homemakers: Organizing for a New Life* (New York: McGraw-Hill Book Company, 1981), p. ix.
9. Ibid., p. 177.
10. The description and analysis of the Displaced Homemaker movement is derived from an interview with Tish Sommers and from Shields' book.
11. Shields, p. 125.
12. "Unfinished Business," *Ms. Magazine* (November 1980): 87.

Notes: Conclusions

1. *No Cause for Rejoicing* (Ottawa: Report of the New Democratic Party Task Force on Older Women in Canada, June 1983), p. 4.
2. Rose Dobrof, "The Family Relationships and Living Arrangements of Older Women" in *Older Women in the City* (New York: Arno Press, 1979), pp. 143 – 144.
3. Kathryn Painter, *Granny Battering* (Unpublished Dissertation, Lanchester Polytechnic, Coventry, England, 1980), pp. 12 – 18.
4. Dobrof, pp. 143 – 149.
5. Linda J. Davis and Elaine M. Brody, *Rape and Older Women: A Guide to Prevention and Protection* (Washington: U.S. Department of Health, Education, and Welfare, 1979), p. 5.
6. "Resources: Abuse of the Elderly," *Response*, Vol. 4, No. 2 (November/December 1980): 3.
7. Davis and Brody, p. 30.

8. Marjorie H. Cantor, "Health of the Inner City Elderly," a paper presented to the 27th annual meeting of the Gerontological Society of Portland, Oregon in October 1974 (New York City: Office for the Aging), p. 12.

9. Tish Sommers and Laurie Shields, "Older Women and Health Care: Strategy for Survival," *Gray Paper No. 3: Issues for Action* (Oakland: Older Women's League Educational Fund, 1980), p. 15.

10. Verna Pedrin and Sheryl Brown, "Sexism and Ageism: Obstacles to Health Care for Women," in *Second Opinion* (San Francisco: The Coalition for the Medical Rights of Women, March 1981), pp. 1 – 2.

11. Sommers and Shields, pp. 7 – 20.

Notes: Appendix

1. David P. Ross, *The Canadian Fact Book on Poverty – 1983* (Toronto: James Lorimer and Company, 1983), p. 1.

2. *A Look at Poverty Lines: Measuring Income Adequacy* (Toronto: The Social Planning Council of Metropolitan Toronto), Vol. 2, No. 3, September 1983, p. 1.

3. Ibid., p. 1.

4. Ibid., pp. 1 – 2.

5. Ross, p. 71.

6. *A Look*, p. 3.

7. Ross, p. 71.

8. *A Look*, pp. 3-4.

9. Ibid., p. 5.

10. Ross, p. 41.

11. *Survey of Old Age Security and Canada Pension Plan Retirement Benefit Recipients, July 1981* (Ottawa: Health and Welfare Canada, November 1983), summary, pp. 1–2.

Acknowledgements

There is a wide range of individuals and organizations who provided information, leads, sources, practical experience, and extremely valuable insights in the research that went into this book.

Portions of the research were done during a year spent outside Canada. I would like to thank the following: in Britain: Audrey Noble and Donald Bell of Age Concern, Cathy Hobdell, of Islington Victim Support, The National Women's Aid Federation, The London Rape Crisis Centre, June Hemer of the National Association of Widows, Ann Sedley of the National Council for Civil Liberties, Pat Goddard, Ann Stanyer, Miriam David, and Jane Lewis; in France: Karen Dezeuze; in Holland: Dr. Hedi Albarda; and in the United States: Sheryl Brown and Verna Pedrin of The Coalition of Medical Rights for Women, Tish Sommers of The Older Women's League, Pat Durham with Options for Women Over Forty, Linda Eberth of The Sexual Trauma Services, Jean Hassett with the California Victim/Witness Assistance Program, Debbie Lee with the Family Violence Project, Dee Bergman with Alternatives for Better Living for Elders, Majorie Cantor with the New York Department for the Aging, Marilyn Flood with the City of New York Commission on the Status of Women, Polly Taylor and Micky Spencer with Broomstick, Judith Layzer, Lee Lewis, and Hannah Weinberg.

In Canada, a number of organizations and individuals were extremely helpful. I would like to thank: St. Christopher's House, St. Stephen's Community House, Woodgreen Community Centre, Cecil Community Centre, Dixon Hall, Central Neighbourhood Centre, Thelma Rosner, Edith

Johnston, Shelagh Wilkinson, Marion Colby, Elspeth Latimer, Trudy Don, Sheila Neysmith, Hellie Wilson, Anne Hill, Helen Carscellen, Lee Grills, Frieda Forman, Didi Radcliffe, Judith Golden, Sister St. Michael Guinan, Mary O'Brien, Bonnie Laing, Hope Holmestead, Shirley Wheatley, Susan Sole, Lionel Orlikow, Raye Ackerman, and Ethel Cohen.

Murray Lightman, my agent and friend, contributed his considerable skills and gave excellent advice throughout. I know he really would have liked to be a hockey star, but I am glad he decided to be my agent and lawyer instead.

It was stimulating and great fun to work with my editor, Charis Wahl. While I very much appreciate her ideas and support, it is really her lovely sense of the absurd that I admire most.

I am grateful for the care with which Deborah Campbell typed the first draft of the manuscript.

I would especially like to thank my close friend Louise Ford who directed me to outstanding people and important research materials. Her support and special knowledge were invaluable to me.

Another very good friend, Tovah Rabinovitch, supplied me with a mountain of background materials in the early part of my research and so generously shared with me the findings from her doctoral dissertation.

Mary Jane Mossman, an old and dear friend, very generously shared sources and information. I thank her for her patience and support as I struggled with this book.

My friend Mary Nesbitt was always nearby through the lows as well as the highs that are an inevitable part of writing a book. I thank her for her warmth and moral support.

Barbara Earle, yet another special friend, spent many hours reading and listening to my manuscript. I am grateful for her constant encouragement and support.

Financial assistance was generously given by the Canada Council and the Ontario Arts Council. Without their support, I could not have begun or finished this book.

The person who has participated in every aspect of this book's growth, from gestation to finished product is the wonderful man with whom I share my life, Ernie Lightman.

271

He has unselfishly given of his time and his expertise as an economist and professor of social policy. He has given me marvelous ideas and has contributed fresh insights. I thank him for all these things and, most gratefully, for being my very dear friend.

I want to express my gratitude to all those women who shared their experiences with me. They have been a source of strength and courage, and they have taught me much about life.

This book is dedicated to the memory of my grandmother, Chana Glicksman. She was my dearest friend and the wisest woman I have ever known. It was she who inspired me to write this book about society's most neglected and least valued people – older women.